THE END OF SOLITUDE

THE END OF SOLITUDE

Selected Essays on Culture and Society

―――――――――

WILLIAM DERESIEWICZ

HENRY HOLT AND COMPANY

NEW YORK

Henry Holt and Company
Publishers since 1866
120 Broadway
New York, New York 10271

www.henryholt.com

Henry Holt® and ⓗ® are registered trademarks of Macmillan Publishing Group,
LLC.

Library of Congress Cataloging-in-Publication Data is available.

ISBN: 9781250858641

Our books may be purchased in bulk for promotional, educational, or busi-
ness use. Please contact your local bookseller or the Macmillan Corporate and
Premium Sales Department at (800) 221-7945, extension 5442, or by e-mail at
MacmillanSpecialMarkets@macmillan.com.

First Edition 2022

Designed by Gabriel Guma

Printed in the United States of America

10 9 8 7 6 5 4 3 2 1

To Jill

CONTENTS

Preface   xi

TECHNOLOGY CULTURE

The End of Solitude   3
Solitude and Leadership   11
Faux Friendship   25
Culture against Culture   37
The Girl with the High-Speed Connection   45
The Ghost in the Machine   47
All in a Dream   49

HIGHER EDUCATION

The Disadvantages of an Elite Education   53
The Neoliberal Arts   65
The Defunding of the American Mind   77
On Political Correctness   91
Change Your Mind First: College and the Urge to Save the World   105
Why I Left Academia (Since You're Wondering)   113
Heal for America   123
On the Beach   125
In Memoriam   129

THE SOCIAL IMAGINATION

Generation Sell   133
Heroes   139
Just Friends   143

Seeing Things   147
The True Church   149
Arms and the Man   151
Latter-Day Saint   153

ARTS

The Maker's Hand   157
Upper Middle Brow   163
Food, Food Culture, Culture   167
The Platinum Age   173
Merce Cunningham: Celestial Mechanics   185
Mark Morris: Home Coming   193
Studies Show Arts Have Value   201

LETTERS

Alfred Kazin: Fiery Particle of Spirit   205
Harold Rosenberg: The Individual Nuisance   209
Harold Bloom: The Horror, the Horror   223
Clive James: Letter to the Twenty-First Century   233
Mark Greif: Facing Reality   241
Hunting the Whale   251
How's That Again?   261

MY PEOPLE

Birthrights   265
A Jew in the Northwest   277
The Limits of Limits   293
Parade's End   295
Day of Atonement   297

Publication Notes   299

Acknowledgments   301

PREFACE

When I was twelve years old or thereabouts, I started making little speeches in my head. This wasn't something planned or purposeful; I just found myself doing it at a certain point. One such tirade, I remember—I composed it walking back from synagogue one Sabbath afternoon—was a riff on Benjamin Disraeli's famous retort to an anti-Semitic colleague, "When your ancestors were painting themselves blue" (a reference to the ancient Scots), "mine were priests in the temple of Solomon." I was a proud young Jew. And, in retrospect, I was destined to be an essayist.

This book presents a selection of the pieces I have published since that ardent afternoon—though the record is notably blank for the first many years. For a great while, my literary output was largely inflicted on friends, in the form of long (long, long, *long*, long) letters. Ten typewritten pages would not have been atypical for a lonely evening in my early twenties. So many thoughts! Sometimes, usually after a few months of stunned silence, my correspondent might even reply. But thoughts are one thing; thoughts worth publishing, in prose worth reading, are something else. The first piece included here was written when I was twenty-nine; the vast majority, when I was over forty-five. It takes a long time to have an original idea.

Which is not to say I wasn't writing in the interval. I had started taking dance in college, and around the time that I was composing those letters I began to publish dance reviews, the best of which, on Mark Morris and Merce Cunningham, the choreographers I most esteemed, are included here. In the meantime, I was also in graduate school, doing a doctorate in English lit. When a teaching job took me away from New York, I switched to writing book reviews, a form that suited me more comfortably in any case. Of the many I have written since, I have selected some that deal with the work of prominent critics and intellectuals—role models, admirations, cautionary examples—as these belong most naturally within the present volume.

It was only as I was leaving academia, at forty-four, in 2008, and for reasons explained in this book—only, in other words, when I became a full-time writer—that my work as an essayist gathered momentum. I was no longer teaching; I was no longer responsible for producing academic scholarship. My attention, which for nearly twenty years had largely been focused on the past, and the works of the past, could turn to the world I was actually living in. Obsessions old and new could get their head. Higher ed, for one: elite institutions and what the system centered on them does to those who enter it, the degradation of the college idea in the age of neoliberalism, the depredations of the academic labor market, and, most recently, the intellectual and moral malady we called, until not long ago, political correctness. Social media, for another, the inevitable subject: what the internet is doing to our inner lives and intimate relationships. The arts, as always. My Jewishness, which has traveled many miles since that day I channeled Disraeli. Each is represented here by its own section.

Essay led to essay with the glorious, perilous unpredictability of a freelance career. When, in 2011, the *New York Times* relaunched its *Week in Review* as the *Sunday Review*, and was briefly taking chances on writers and subjects, I got the opportunity to roam more freely across the culture. Some of the results are included here under the rubric of "The Social Imagination." More happily still, around the same time, Robert Wilson, the editor of the *American Scholar*, invited me to join the magazine's new online venture: five blogs by five writers, one for each weekday. Composing a tight, shapely argument in the space of a couple of pages—something I could turn out in a single gesture, a single morning—turned out to be exhilarating. A friend referred to the pieces (or, at least, some of the better ones) as idea bullets, and that's pretty much what I was going for. I held down my slot for a little more than two years, 116 weekly mini-essays, the best of which are represented here by the pieces whose titles appear in italics.

Four essays are published in this volume for the first time. "Culture against Culture" enlists on the side of the arts and humanities in their battle not with science but with scientism, the belief that science is adequate to address all problems—an older culture war, still smoldering. "The Maker's Hand" pays tribute, in the age of "content," to the artist and their magic that shapes matter into meaning. "Change Your Mind First: College and the Urge to Save the World" questions the rush to "social justice" as the defining purpose of an undergraduate career. As for "Why I Left Academia (Since You're Wondering)," let's just say that I had some things to get off my chest.

If there is a single theme that joins the essays in this book, it is my attempt to defend, and, as well as I can, to enact, a certain conception of the self. It is one that I have come to think of as the modern self, a self that emerged in the Renaissance, reached its zenith in the nineteenth and twentieth centuries, and appears now to be passing into history. In other words, the individual: developed in solitude, in fearless dialogue, by reading, through education as the nurturing of souls; embodied in original art and independent thought; beset by the online cacophony, by education as the manufacture of producers, by groupthink and the politics of groups. To be an individual, the years have taught me, takes a constant effort. These essays are an offering to those who wish to be one, too.

THE END OF SOLITUDE

Technology Culture

THE END OF SOLITUDE

What does the contemporary self want? The camera created a culture of celebrity; the computer has created a culture of connectivity. As the two technologies converge—broadband tipping the web from text to image, social networking spreading the mesh of interconnection ever wider—the two cultures betray a common impulse. Celebrity and connectivity are both ways of becoming known. This is what the contemporary self wants. It wants to be recognized, wants to be connected: it wants to be seen. If not by the millions, on *Survivor* or *Oprah*, then by the hundreds, on Twitter or Facebook. The great contemporary terror is anonymity. If Lionel Trilling was right, if the property that grounded the self, in Romanticism, was sincerity, and in modernism it was authenticity, then in postmodernism it is visibility.

So we live exclusively in relation to others, and what disappears from our lives is solitude. Technology is taking away our privacy and our concentration, but it is also taking away our ability to be by ourselves. Though I shouldn't say taking away. We are doing this to ourselves; we are discarding these riches as fast as we can. I was told that a teenager I know had sent three thousand instant messages one recent month. That's one hundred a day, or about one every ten waking minutes, morning, noon, and night, weekdays and weekends, class time, lunchtime, homework time, and tooth-brushing time. So, on average, she's never alone for more than ten minutes at once. Which means, she's never alone. I once asked my students about the place that solitude has in their lives. One of them admitted that she finds the prospect of being alone so unsettling that she will sit with a friend even when she has a paper to write. Another said, why would anybody want to be alone?

To that remarkable question, history offers a number of answers. Humans may be social animals, but solitude has traditionally been a societal value. In particular, the act of being alone has always been understood as an essential dimension of religious experience, albeit one restricted to a self-selected few.

Through the solitude of rare spirits, the community renews its relationship with God. The prophet and the hermit, the sadhu and the yogi, pursue their vision quests, invite their trances, in desert or forest or cave. Social life is a bustle of petty concerns, a jostle of quotidian interests, and the still, small voice speaks only in silence. Collective experience may be the human norm, but the solitary encounter with God is the egregious act that refreshes that norm. Religious solitude is a kind of self-correcting social mechanism, a way of burning out the underbrush of moral habit and spiritual custom. The seer returns with new tablets or new dances, their face bright with the old truth.

Like other religious values, solitude was democratized by the Reformation and secularized by Romanticism. In Marilynne Robinson's interpretation, Calvinism created the modern self by turning the soul inward, impelling it to encounter God, like the prophets of old, in "profound isolation." To her enumeration of Calvin, Marguerite de Navarre, and Milton as pioneering early modern selves, we can add Montaigne, Hamlet, and even Don Quixote. The last of these alerts us to the essential role of reading in this transformation. "[T]he soul encountered itself in response to a text," Robinson writes, "first Genesis or Matthew and then *Paradise Lost* or *Leaves of Grass*." With Protestantism and printing, the quest for the divine voice became available to, even incumbent upon, all.

But it is with Romanticism that solitude achieved its greatest cultural salience, becoming both literal and literary. Protestant solitude was still only figurative. Rousseau and Wordsworth made it physical. The self was now encountered not in God but Nature, and to encounter Nature one had to go to it. And go to it with a special sensibility: the poet displaced the saint as social seer and cultural exemplar. But since Romanticism also inherited the eighteenth-century idea of social sympathy, Romantic solitude existed in a dialectical relationship with friendship. For Emerson, "The soul environs itself with friends, that it may enter into a grander self-acquaintance or solitude; and it goes alone, for a season, that it may exalt its conversation or society." The Romantic practice of solitude is neatly captured by Trilling's "sincerity": the belief that the self is validated by a congruity of private essence and public appearance, one that stabilizes its relationship with both itself and others. Especially, as Emerson suggests, one beloved other. Hence the famous Romantic friendship pairs: Goethe and Schiller, Wordsworth and Coleridge, Hawthorne and Melville.

Modernism decoupled this dialectic. Its conception of solitude was harsher, more adversarial, more isolating. As a model of the self and its interactions, Hume's social sympathy gave way to Pater's thick wall of personality and Freud's narcissism—the sense that the soul, self-enclosed and inaccessible to others, can't choose but be alone. With exceptions, like Woolf, the modernists fought shy of friendship. Joyce and Proust disparaged it; Lawrence was wary of it; the modernist friendship pairs—Conrad and Ford, Eliot and Pound, Hemingway and Fitzgerald—were altogether cooler than their Romantic counterparts.

The world was now understood as an assault on the self, and with good reason. The Romantic ideal of solitude developed in part as a reaction to the emergence of the modern city. In modernism, the city is not only more menacing than ever; it is inescapable, a labyrinth: Eliot's London, Joyce's Dublin. The mob, the human mass, presses in. Hell is other people. The soul is forced back into itself—hence the development of a more austere, more embattled form of self-validation, Trilling's "authenticity," where one's essential relationship is with oneself. Solitude becomes the arena of heroic self-discovery, a voyage through interior realms made vast and terrifying by Nietzschean and Freudian insights. To achieve authenticity is to look upon these visions without flinching; Trilling's exemplar here is Mr. Kurtz. Protestant self-examination becomes Freudian analysis, and the culture hero, once a prophet of God, then a poet of Nature, is now a novelist of self—a Dostoyevsky, a Joyce, a Proust.

But we no longer live in the modernist city, and our great fear is not submersion by the mass but isolation from the herd. After World War II, urbanization gave way to suburbanization, and with it the universal threat of loneliness. What technologies of transportation exacerbated—we could live farther and farther apart—technologies of communication redressed—we could bring ourselves closer and closer together. Or so, at least, we imagined. The first of those technologies, the first simulacrum of proximity, was the telephone. "Reach out and touch someone," the slogan went. But through the '70s and '80s, our isolation grew. Suburbs became exurbs. Families grew smaller or splintered apart. Mothers went to work. The electronic hearth became the television in every room. Even in childhood, certainly in adolescence, we were trapped inside our own cocoons. Soaring crime rates, and even more sharply escalating rates of moral panic, pulled children off the streets. The idea that you could go outside and run around the neighborhood with your friends, once unquestionable, became unthinkable. The child who grew up between the world wars as part of an extended family within a tight-knit urban community became the kid who sat alone in front of a big television, in a big house, on a big lot. We were lost in space.

In these circumstances, the internet arrived as an incalculable blessing. We should never forget that. It has allowed isolated people to communicate with each other and marginalized people to find each other. The busy parent can stay in touch with far-flung friends. The gay adolescent no longer must feel like a freak. But as the internet's dimensionality has grown, it has quickly become too much of a good thing. Ten years ago, we were writing emails on desktop computers and transmitting them over dial-up connections. Now we are sending text messages on our BlackBerrys, posting pictures on our MySpace pages, and following complete strangers on Twitter. A constant stream of mediated contact, virtual, notional, or simulated, keeps us wired into the electronic hive—though contact, or at least two-way contact, seems increasingly beside the point. The goal now, it seems, is simply to be known, to become a sort of miniature celebrity. How many friends do I have on Facebook? How many people are following me on Twitter? How many Google hits does my name generate? Visibility secures our self-esteem, becoming a substitute, twice removed, for genuine connection. Not long ago, it was easy to feel lonely. Now it is impossible to be alone.

Which means that we are losing both halves of the Romantic dialectic. What does friendship mean when you have 532 "friends"? How does it enhance my sense of closeness when Facebook tells me that Sally McNally (whom I haven't seen since high school, and wasn't really friends with even then) "is making coffee and staring off into space"? Exchanging emails, let alone instant messaging or writing on people's "walls," is very far from having a sustained conversation. Never mind the information that facial and vocal cues convey. We respond instinctively, deep in our bodies, to faces and voices. Letters, which had their own sensuality, once sought to reproduce the contours of the voice through the medium of language, but to pull off that trick, one needs to know how to write. Emoticons won't do it. My students told me they have little time for intimacy. And, of course, they have no time whatsoever for solitude.

But at least friendship, if not intimacy, is still something they want. As jarring as the new dispensation may be for people in their thirties and forties, the real problem is that it is completely natural for people in their teens and twenties. Young people today appear to have no desire for solitude, have never heard of it, cannot imagine why it might be worth having. In fact, their use of technology—or to be fair, our use of technology—seems to involve a constant effort to stave off the possibility of solitude, a continuous attempt, as we sit alone at our computers, to maintain the imaginative presence of others. As long ago as 1952, Trilling could write of "the modern fear of being cut off from the social group even for a moment," and now we have equipped ourselves with the means to prevent that fear from ever being realized. Which does not mean that we have put it to rest. Quite the contrary. Remember my student, who couldn't even write a paper by herself. The more we keep aloneness at bay, the less are we able to deal with it and the more terrifying it grows.

The situation is analogous, it seems to me, to the previous generation's experience of boredom. The two emotions, of course, loneliness and boredom, are closely allied. They are also both characteristically modern—neither word existed, at least in our sense, before the nineteenth century. Suburbanization, by eliminating the stimulation as well as the sociability of urban or traditional village life, exacerbated the tendency to both. But the great age of boredom came in with television, and precisely because television was designed to alleviate that feeling. Boredom is not a necessary consequence of having nothing to do; it is only the negative experience of that condition. Television, by eliminating the need to learn to make use of one's lack of occupation, prevents one from discovering how to enjoy it. In fact, it renders that condition fearsome, its prospect intolerable. You are terrified of being bored—so you turn on the television.

I speak from experience. I grew up in the '60s and '70s, deep in the heart of the age of television. I was trained to be bored; boredom was cultivated within me like a precious crop. It took me years to discover that having nothing to do does not have to be a bad thing. (And my nervous system will never fully adjust to the idea. I still have to fight against boredom, am permanently damaged in this respect.) But there is an alternative to boredom, and it is what Whitman called idleness: a state of passive receptivity to the world.

So it is with the current generation's experience of being alone. Being alone does not have to make you feel lonely. That is precisely the recognition implicit in the idea of solitude, which is to loneliness what idleness is to boredom. Loneliness is not the absence of company; it is grief about that absence. The lost sheep is lonely; the shepherd is not lonely. But the internet is as powerful a machine for the production of loneliness as television is for the manufacture of boredom. If six hours of television a day creates the aptitude for boredom, the inability to sit still, a hundred instant messages a day creates the aptitude for loneliness, the inability to be by yourself. You could call your schoolmates when I was a teenager, but you couldn't call them a hundred times a day. You could get together with your friends when I was in college, but you couldn't always get together with them when you wanted to, because you couldn't always find them. If boredom is the great emotion of the TV generation, loneliness is the great emotion of the generation of the web. We lost the ability to be still, our capacity for idleness. They have lost the ability to be alone, their capacity for solitude.

And losing solitude, what else have they lost? First, the propensity for introspection, that examination of the self that the Puritans and the Romantics and the modernists (and Socrates, for that matter) placed at the center of spiritual life—of wisdom, of conduct. Thoreau called it fishing "in the Walden Pond of [our] own natures," "bait[ing our] hooks with darkness." Lost, as well, is the related propensity for sustained reading. The internet brought text back into a televisual world, but it brought it back on terms dictated by that world—that is, by its remapping of our attention spans. Reading now means skipping and skimming; five minutes on the same web page is considered an eternity. This is no longer reading as Robinson described it, the encounter with a second self in the silence of mental solitude.

But we no longer believe in the solitary mind. If the Romantics had Hume and the modernists had Freud, the current psychological model—and this should come as no surprise—is that of the networked or social mind. Evolutionary psychologists tell us that our brains developed to interpret complex social signals; cognitive scientists, according to David Brooks, that "our decision-making is powerfully influenced by social context"; neuroscientists, that we have "permeable minds" that function in part through a process of "deep imitation"; psychologists, that "we are organized by our attachments"; sociologists, that our behavior is affected by "the power of social networks." The cumulative implication is that all of mental space is social—contemporary social science dovetailing here with postmodern critical theory.

One of the most striking things about the way that young people relate to one another today is that they no longer seem to believe in the existence of Thoreau's "darkness." The MySpace page has replaced the journal and the letter as a way of creating and communicating a sense of self. The suggestion is not only that such communication is to be made to the world at large rather than to oneself or one's intimates, or graphically rather than verbally, or performatively rather than narratively or analytically, but also that it can be made completely. Today's young people seem to feel that they can make themselves fully known to one another. They seem to lack a sense of their own depths, and of the value of keeping them hidden.

If they didn't, they would understand that solitude enables us to secure the integrity of the self, as well as to explore it. Few have shown this more beautifully than Woolf. In the middle of *Mrs. Dalloway*, between her navigation of the streets and her orchestration of the party, between the urban jostle and the social bustle, Clarissa goes up, "like a nun withdrawing," to her attic room. Like a nun: she returns to a state that she herself imagines as a kind of virginity. That doesn't mean that she's a prude. Virginity is classically the outward sign of spiritual inviolability, of a self untouched by the world, a soul that has preserved its integrity by refusing to descend into the chaos and self-division of sexual and social relations. It is the mark of the saint and the monk, of Antigone and Joan of Arc. Solitude is both the social image of that state and the means by which we can approximate it. And the supreme image in *Mrs. Dalloway* of the dignity of solitude itself is the old woman whom Clarissa catches sight of through her window. "Here was one room," she thinks, "there another." We are not merely social beings. We are each also separate, each solitary, each alone in our room, each miraculously our unique selves and mysteriously enclosed within that selfhood.

To remember this, to hold oneself apart from society, is to begin to think one's way beyond it. Solitude, said Emerson, "is to genius the stern friend." The university was to be praised, he believed, if only for this, that it provided students with "a separate chamber and fire"—Woolf's room of one's own, the physical space of solitude. For no real excellence, personal or social, artistic, philosophical, scientific, or moral, can arise without solitude. "The saint and poet seek privacy," Emerson said, "to ends the most public and universal."

Solitude isn't easy, and it isn't for everyone. It has surely always been the province of the few. "I believe," said Thoreau, "that men are generally still a little afraid of the dark." Marguerite and Milton will always be the exceptions, or to speak in more relevant terms, the young man or woman—for they still exist—who prefers to loaf and invite their soul, who steps to the beat of a different drummer. But if solitude disappears as a social value and idea, will even the exceptions be possible? Still, one finally cannot worry about the drift of the culture, which one is in any case powerless to reverse. One can only save oneself—and whatever else occurs, one can still always do that.

It takes a willingness to be unpopular, however. The last thing to say about solitude is that it isn't very polite. Thoreau knew that the "doubleness" that solitude cultivates, the ability to stand back and observe life dispassionately, is apt to make us a little unpleasant to our fellows, to say nothing of the offense implicit in avoiding their company. But then, he didn't worry overmuch about being genial. He didn't even like having to talk to people three times a day, at meals; one can only imagine what he would have made of instant messaging. We, however, have made of geniality—the weak smile, the polite interest, the fake invitation—a cardinal virtue. Friendship may be slipping from our grasp, but our friendliness is universal. Not for nothing does "gregarious" mean "part of the herd." But Thoreau understood that securing one's self-possession was worth a few wounded feelings. He may have put his neighbors off, but at least he was sure of himself. Those who would find solitude must not be afraid to stand alone.

[2009]

Solitude and Leadership

An address delivered to the plebe class at West Point

My title must seem like a contradiction. What has solitude to do with leadership? Solitude means being alone, and leadership implies the presence of others—the people you are leading. When we think about leadership in American history, we are apt to think of Washington, at the head of an army, or Lincoln, at the head of a nation, or King, at the head of a movement—people who have multitudes behind them, looking for direction. And when we think of solitude, we are likely to think of Thoreau, a man alone in the woods, keeping a journal and communing with nature in silence.

Leadership is what you're here to learn—the qualities of character and mind that will make you fit to command a platoon, and beyond that, perhaps, a company, a battalion, or, if you leave the military, a corporation, a foundation, a department of government. And solitude is, of all things, what you have the least of here, especially as plebes. You don't even have privacy, the opportunity simply to be physically alone, never mind solitude, the ability to be alone with your thoughts. And yet I submit to you that solitude is one of the most important necessities of true leadership. This lecture will be an attempt to explain why.

We need to begin by talking about what leadership actually means. I just spent ten years teaching at an institution that, like West Point, liked to talk about leadership, Yale University. A school that some of you might have gone to had you not come here, that some of your friends might be going to. And if not Yale, then Harvard, Stanford, MIT, and so forth. Those institutions, like West Point, see their role as the training of leaders, constantly encourage their students, like West Point, to regard themselves as leaders among their peers and future leaders of society. And indeed, when we look around at the American elite, the people in charge of government, business, academia, and all our other key institutions—senators, judges, CEOs, college presidents, and so forth—we find that they come overwhelmingly either from the Ivy League and its peer institutions or from the service academies, especially West Point.

So I began to wonder, as I taught at Yale, what leadership really consists of. My students, like you, were smart, energetic, accomplished, and often ferociously ambitious, but did all that make them leaders? Most of them, as much as I liked and even admired them, certainly didn't seem to me like leaders. Does being a leader, I wondered, mean being accomplished, being successful? Does getting straight A's make you a "leader"? I didn't think so. A great heart surgeon or a great novelist or a great shortstop may be terrific at what they do, but that doesn't mean that they're a leader. Leadership and aptitude, leadership and achievement, leadership and even excellence must be different things, or else the concept of leadership is meaningless. And it seemed to me that that had to be especially true of the kind of excellence I saw in the students around me.

See, things have changed since I attended college in the 1980s. Everything has gotten so much more intense. You have to do a great deal more today to get into a school like Yale or West Point, and you have start doing it a great deal earlier. We didn't even begin to think about college until we were juniors, and we each maybe did two or three extracurriculars. But I know what it is like for you guys now. It is an endless series of hoops, starting from way back, as early as junior high school. Classes, standardized tests, extracurriculars in school, extracurriculars outside of school. Test prep courses, admissions coaches, private tutors. I sat on the admissions committee at Yale a couple of years ago. The first thing an admissions officer would do when presenting a file was to read out what they call the "brag," the list of a student's extracurriculars. It turned out that a student who only had six or seven extracurriculars was already in trouble, because the ones who got in—in addition to perfect grades and top scores—usually had ten or twelve.

So what I saw around me were great kids who had been trained to be world-class hoop-jumpers. Any goal you set them, they could meet. Any test you gave them, they could ace. They were, as one of them put it, "excellent sheep." And I had no doubt that they would continue to jump through hoops, and ace tests, and go on to Harvard Business School or Michigan Law School or Johns Hopkins Medical School or Goldman Sachs or McKinsey or wherever. And this approach would take them far in life. They would come back for their twenty-fifth reunion as partners at White & Case, or attending physicians at Massachusetts General, or assistant secretaries in the State Department.

And that indeed is exactly what places like Yale have in mind when they talk about leaders. People who make a big name for themselves in the world, people with impressive titles, people whom the university can brag about. People who can climb the greasy pole of whatever hierarchy they decide to attach themselves to.

But that idea is desperately wrong and even dangerous. To explain why, I'm going to talk about a novel that some of you may have read, Joseph Conrad's *Heart of Darkness*. And if you haven't read it, you've almost certainly seen a movie that is based on it, *Apocalypse Now*. Marlow, in the novel, becomes Captain Willard, played by Martin Sheen. Mr. Kurtz, in the novel, becomes Colonel Kurtz, played by Marlon Brando. But the novel is not about Vietnam; it's about colonialism in the Belgian Congo three generations before Vietnam. Marlow, not a military officer but a merchant marine, a civilian ship's captain, is sent by the company that is running the country under charter from the Belgian crown to sail upriver, deep up the Congo River, to retrieve a manager who has ensconced himself in the jungle and gone rogue, just as Colonel Kurtz does in the movie.

Now every reader recognizes that the novel is about imperialism and colonialism and race relations and the darkness that lies in the human heart, but I eventually realized, as I taught the novel over and over again, that it is also about bureaucracy. "The Company," as Conrad calls it, is, after all, just that: a company—with rules and procedures and ranks, and people in power and people scrambling for power, just like in any bureaucracy. Just like in a law firm or a government department or, for that matter, a university. Just like— and here's why I'm telling you all this—the bureaucracy that you're about to join. The US Army is not only a bureaucracy; it is one of the largest and most famously bureaucratic bureaucracies in the world. It was the army, after all, that gave us that indispensable bureaucratic acronym, "snafu": "situation normal all fucked up"—or "all fouled up," in the PG version. That came from the US Army in World War II.

The point is that you need to know that when you receive your commission, you'll be joining a bureaucracy, and that as long as you stay in the army, you will be operating within one. Which means that you need to know how bureaucracies work, what kind of behavior—what kind of character—they reward, and what kind they punish.

So back to the novel. Marlow makes his way upriver in stages, just like Captain Willard in the movie. First he gets to the Outer Station. Kurtz is at the Inner Station. In between them is the Central Station, where Marlow spends the greatest amount of his time and where we get our clearest look at bureaucracy in action and the kind of people who succeed in it. This is Marlow's description of the manager of the Central Station, the top of that particular heap.

> He was commonplace in complexion, in features, in manners, and in voice. He was of middle size and of ordinary build. His eyes, of the usual blue, were perhaps remarkably cold. Otherwise there was only an indefinable, faint expression of his lips, something stealthy—a smile—not a smile—I remember it, but I can't explain. . . . He was a common trader, from his youth up employed in these parts—nothing more. He was obeyed, yet he inspired neither love nor fear, nor even respect. He inspired uneasiness. That was it! Uneasiness. Not a definite mistrust—just uneasiness—nothing more. You have no idea how effective such a . . . a faculty can be. He had no genius for organizing, for initiative, or for order even. . . . He had no learning, and no intelligence. His position had come to him—why? . . . He originated nothing, he could keep the routine going—that's all. But he was great. He was great by this little thing that it was impossible to tell what could control such a man. He never gave that secret away. Perhaps there was nothing within him. Such a suspicion made one pause.

Note the adjectives: "commonplace," "ordinary," "usual," "common." There is nothing distinguished, almost nothing even distinguishing, about this person. Around the tenth time I read that passage, I realized that it was a perfect description of the kind of person who tends to prosper in bureaucratic environments. And the only reason I did so is that it suddenly struck me as a perfect description of the head of the bureaucratic division that I was part of, the chairman of my academic department—who had that exact same smile, like a shark, and that exact same ability to make you uneasy, like you were doing something wrong, only she wasn't ever going to tell you what. And like the manager—and like so many of the people you will meet as you negotiate the bureaucracy of the army, or for that matter, of whatever institution you give your talents to after the army, be it Microsoft or the World Bank or whatever—she had no genius for organizing or initiative or even order, no particular learning or intelligence. Just the ability to keep the routine going, and beyond that, as Marlow says, her position had come to her—why?

That is really the great mystery about bureaucracies. Why is it so often that the best people are stuck in the middle, while the people who are running things—the leaders—are the mediocrities? Because excellence is not what gets you up the greasy pole. What gets you up is a talent for maneuvering. Taking credit for things you didn't do and shifting blame for things you did. Kissing up to the people above you, kicking down to the people below you. Pleasing your teachers, pleasing your superiors, picking a powerful mentor and riding his coattails until it's time to stab him in the back. Jumping through hoops. Getting along by going along. Being whatever other people want you to be, so that it finally comes to seem that, like the manager of the Central Station, you have nothing inside you at all. Not taking stupid risks, like trying to change how things are done or questioning why they're done. Just keeping the routine going.

I tell you this to forewarn you. I tell you this so that you can choose to be a different kind of leader. And I tell you this for one other reason. As I put all these pieces together—the kind of students I had, the kind of leadership they were being trained for, the kind of leaders I saw in my own institution—I realized that this is not a local problem. This is a national problem. We have a crisis of leadership in this country, across every one of our institutions. Not just in government; look at what happened to American corporations over the last few decades, as so many of the old dinosaurs collapsed: General Motors, TWA, U.S. Steel. Look at what happened to Wall Street in just the last couple of years. Most importantly for you, look at what happened during the first four years of the war in Iraq. What happened is that we were stuck. It was not the fault of the enlisted ranks or the noncoms or the junior officers. It was the fault of the senior leadership, both military and civilian. We were not just not winning; we were not even changing direction.

We have a crisis of leadership in this country, because our overwhelming power and wealth, earned under earlier generations of leaders, has made us complacent, and for too long we have been training leaders who only know how to keep the routine going. Who can answer questions, but don't know how to ask them. Who can meet goals, but don't know how to set them. Who think about *how* to get things done, not whether they're worth doing in the first place. What we have now are the greatest technocrats the world has ever seen, people who have been trained to be incredibly good at one specific thing, but who have no interest in anything beyond their area of expertise. What we don't have are leaders.

What we don't have, in other words, are thinkers. People who can think for themselves. People who can formulate a new direction: for the country, for a corporation or a college, for the army—a new way of doing things, a new way of looking at things. People, that is to say, with vision.

Now some would say, great—tell that to the kids at Yale, but why tell it to the ones at West Point? Most people, when they think about this institution, are likely to assume that it is the last place that anyone would want to talk about thinking creatively or cultivating independence of mind. It's the army, after all. It is no accident that "regiment" is the root of "regimentation." Surely you guys who have come here must be the ultimate conformists, people who have bought into the status quo, are not the kind of young adults who think about the world, or changing the world, who ponder the issues or question authority. If you were, you would have gone to somewhere like Amherst or Pomona. You are at West Point because you want to be told what to do and how to think.

But you know that that's not true. And I know it, too, since otherwise I would have never been invited here to talk to you. To quote your course director, Colonel Krawczyk, in a lecture that he gave last year to English 102:

> From the very earliest days of this country, the model for our officers, which was built on the model of the citizenry and reflective of democratic ideals, was to be different. They were to be possessed of a democratic spirit marked by independent judgment, the freedom to measure action and to express disagreement, and the crucial responsibility never to tolerate tyranny.

All the more so now. The changing nature of warfare means that officers, including junior officers, are required, more than ever, to be able to think independently, creatively, and flexibly, to deploy a range of skills in fluid and complex situations: lieutenant colonels who are essentially functioning as provincial governors in Iraq, or captains who find themselves in charge of a remote town in the Afghan countryside. People who need to know how to do a lot more than follow orders and execute routines.

Look at the most successful, most acclaimed, and perhaps the finest sol-dier of his generation, General David Petraeus. He is one of those rare people who rises through a bureaucracy for the right reasons. He is a thinker. He is an intellectual. In fact, *Prospect* magazine named him Public Intellectual of the Year in 2008—that is, in the world. He has a PhD from Princeton, but what makes him a thinker is not that he has a PhD or that he went to Prince-ton. I can assure you from personal experience that there are a lot of highly educated people who don't know how to think at all.

No, what makes him a thinker—and a leader—is precisely his ability to think things through for himself. And because of that ability, he also has the confidence, the courage, to advocate for his ideas even when they are unpop-ular. Even when they do not please his superiors. Courage: there is physical courage, which you all possess in abundance, and then there is another kind of courage, moral courage, the courage to stand up for what you believe.

It wasn't always easy for him. His path to his present position was hardly straight. When he was running Mosul as commander of the 101st Airborne and developing the strategy that he would later formulate in the Counterin-surgency Manual, then ultimately apply throughout Iraq, he pissed a lot of people off. He was way ahead of the leadership in Baghdad and Washington, and bureaucracies don't like that sort of thing. Here he was, just another two-star, and he was saying, implicitly but loudly, that the leadership was wrong about the way it was running the war. Indeed, he wasn't rewarded at first. Quite the contrary: he was shunted to a dead-end job, put in charge of train-ing the Iraqi army, a major blow to his career. But he stuck to his beliefs, and he was ultimately vindicated. And in fact one of the central elements of his counterinsurgency strategy is precisely the idea that officers need to think flexibly, creatively, and independently.

So that's the first half of the lecture, the idea that true leadership means being able to think for yourself and act on your convictions. But how do you learn to think? Let's start with how you don't learn to think. There was a study by a team of researchers at Stanford that came out a couple of months ago. The investigators wanted to understand how today's college students are able to multitask so much more effectively than are adults. The answer, they discovered—and this is by no means what they expected to find—is that they aren't. The enhanced cognitive abilities the investigators expected to find, the mental faculties that enable individuals to multitask effectively, were simply absent. In other words, people do not multitask effectively. And here's the really surprising thing: the more people multitask, the worse they are, not just at other mental operations, but at multitasking itself.

The researchers separated their subjects into high multitaskers and low multitaskers, then tested the kinds of cognitive abilities that multitasking involves. On every test, the high multitaskers scored worse. They were worse at distinguishing between relevant and irrelevant information and ignoring the latter. In other words, they were more distractible. They were worse at "mental filing": storing information in the right conceptual boxes and retrieving it efficiently. In other words, their minds were more disorganized. They were even worse at the very thing that defines multitasking itself: switching between tasks.

Multitasking, in short, is not only not thinking; it impairs your ability to think. Thinking means concentrating on one thing long enough to develop an idea about it. Not learning other people's ideas, or memorizing information, however much those may sometimes be useful. Developing your own ideas: thinking for yourself. Which is something that you simply cannot do in bursts of twenty seconds at a time, interrupted constantly by Facebook messages or Twitter tweets or fiddling with your iPod or watching YouTube.

I find for myself that my first thought is never my best thought. My first thought is always someone else's, always what I have already heard about the subject, always the conventional wisdom. It is only by concentrating, sticking to the question, being patient, letting all the parts of my mind come into play, that I actually arrive at an original idea. By giving my brain a chance to make associations, draw connections, take me by surprise. And often that idea isn't even very good. I need time to think about *it*, too: to make mistakes and recognize them, to make false starts and correct them, to outlast my impulses, to defeat my desire to declare the job done and move on to the next thing.

Students would sometimes brag to me about how fast they wrote their papers. I would tell them that Thomas Mann, the great German novelist, remarked that a writer is someone for whom writing is more difficult than it is for other people. The best writers write more slowly, not more quickly, than everyone else, and the better they are, the slower they write. James Joyce wrote *Ulysses*, the greatest novel of the twentieth century, at the rate of about a hundred words a day, the equivalent of a short paragraph, for seven years. T. S. Eliot, one of the greatest poets our country has ever produced, wrote about 150 pages of poetry over the course of his entire career. That's less than half a page a month. And so it is with any other form of thought. You do your best thinking by slowing down and concentrating.

Now that's the third time that I used that word, "concentrating." Concentrating, focusing. Instead of solitude, you can just as easily consider this lecture to be about concentration. Think about the meaning of the word. It means gathering yourself together into a single point rather than letting yourself be dispersed into a cloud of electronic and social input. It seems to me that Facebook and Twitter and YouTube—and just so you don't think that this is a generational thing, TV and radio and magazines and even newspapers, too—are all ultimately just an elaborate excuse to run away from yourself. To avoid the difficult and troubling questions that being human throws in your way. Am I doing the right thing with my life? Do I believe the things I was taught as a child? What do the words I live by—words like "duty," "honor," "country"—really mean? Am I happy?

You and the members of the other service academies are in a unique position among college students, especially today. Not only do you know that you're going to have a job when you graduate, you know who your employer is going to be. But what will happen after you fulfill your commitment to the army? How are you going to figure out what you want to do with the rest of your life, unless you know who you are? Unless you are able to listen to yourself, to that quiet voice inside that tells you what you really care about, what you really believe in—indeed, how those values and beliefs might be evolving under the pressure of your experiences. Students everywhere agonize over these questions, and while you may not be doing so now, you are only postponing them for a few years.

And maybe some of you *are* agonizing over them now. Not everyone who starts here decides to finish here. It is no wonder and no cause for shame. You are being put through some of the most demanding training that anyone can ask of people your age, and you are committing yourself to work of awesome responsibility and mortal danger. The very rigor and regimentation to which you are quite properly subject has the natural tendency to make you lose touch with the very passion that brought you here in the first place. I saw exactly the same kind of thing among my students at Yale. It's not that they were robots. Quite the contrary. They were often intensely idealistic, but the overwhelming weight of their practical responsibilities, all of those hoops that they had to jump through, would make them lose sight of those very ideals. Of why were they doing it all in the first place.

So it's perfectly natural to have doubts, or questions, or even just difficulties. The question is, what you do with them? Do you suppress them? Do you distract yourself from them? Do you pretend they don't exist? Or do you confront them: directly, honestly, courageously. If you take the latter course, you will find that the answers to these dilemmas are not to be found on Twitter or Comedy Central or even in the *New York Times*, for that matter. They can only be found within: free from distraction, free from peer pressure, in solitude.

But solitude need not mean introspection. Let's go back to *Heart of Darkness*. It is the solitude of concentration that rescues Marlow amidst the madness of the Central Station. He discovers, when he gets there, that the steamboat he is meant to use has a giant hole in its hull, and that no one is going to help him fix it. "I let him run on," he says, "this papier-mache Mephistopheles"—he's talking not about the manager but his assistant, who is even worse, since he is still trying to climb his way up the pole, and who has been raving away at him one day. You can think of him as the internet, the ever-present social buzz, chattering away at you 24/7—

> I let him run on, this papier-mache Mephistopheles, and it seemed to me that if I tried I could poke my forefinger through him, and would find nothing inside but a little loose dirt, maybe. It was a great comfort to turn from that chap . . . to the battered, twisted, ruined, tin-pot steamboat. . . . I had expended enough hard work on her to make me love her. No influential friend would have served me better. She had given me a chance to come out a bit—to find out what I could do. No, I don't like work. I had rather laze about and think of all the fine things that can be done. I don't like work—no man does—but I like what is in the work—the chance to find yourself. Your own reality—for yourself, not for others—what no other man can ever know.

"The chance to find yourself." Now that phrase, "find yourself," has acquired a bad reputation. It suggests an aimless liberal-arts college graduate—an English major, no doubt, someone who went to a place like Amherst or Pomona—who is too spoiled to get a real job and spends their time staring off into space. But here is Marlow, a mariner, a ship's captain. A more practical, hardheaded person you could not find. And I should say that Conrad,

Marlow's creator, spent twenty years as a merchant marine, eight of them as a captain himself, before he became a novelist, so this isn't some writer's idea of a sailor. Marlow believes in the need to find yourself just as much as anybody does, and the way to do it, he says, is work, solitary work. Concentration. Climbing on that steamboat and spending a few uninterrupted hours hammering it into shape. Or building a house, or cooking a meal, or even writing a college paper, if you really put yourself into it.

"Your own reality—for yourself, not for others." Thinking for yourself means finding yourself, finding your own reality. Here's the other problem with Facebook and Twitter and even the *New York Times*. When you expose yourself to those things, especially in the constant way that people now do—older people as well as younger ones—you are continuously bombarding yourself with a stream of other people's thoughts. You are marinating yourself in the conventional wisdom. In *other* people's reality: for others, not for yourself. You are creating a cacophony in which it is impossible to hear your own voice, whether it is yourself that you are thinking about or anything else. That's what Emerson meant when he said that "He who should inspire and lead his race must be defended from travelling with the souls of other men, from living, breathing, reading, and writing in the daily, time-worn yoke of their opinions." Notice that he says "lead." Leadership means finding a new direction, not putting yourself at the front of the herd that's heading toward the cliff.

There is a third form of solitude, and that is reading—specifically, books. Why is that any better than reading tweets or Facebook posts? Well, sometimes it's not. Sometimes, you need to put down a book, as well, if only to think about what you're reading, what *you* think about what you're reading. But a book has a couple of advantages over a tweet. First, the person who wrote it thought about it a lot more carefully. The book is the result of *their* solitude, *their* attempt to think for themselves.

Second, most books are old. That is not a disadvantage: it is precisely their value. They stand against the conventional wisdom of today, simply by not being *from* today. Even if they merely reflect the conventional wisdom of their own day, they say something different than what you hear all the time. But the great books, the ones that you find on a syllabus, the ones that people have continued to read, do not reflect the conventional wisdom of their day. They say things that possess the permanent power to disrupt our habits of thought. They were revolutionary in their own day, and they are revolutionary still. And when I say "revolutionary," I am deliberately evoking the American Revolution, which resulted precisely from this kind of independent thinking. Without solitude—the solitude of Adams and Jefferson and Hamilton and Madison and Paine—there would be no United States.

So solitude can involve introspection, it can involve the concentration of focused work, and it can involve sustained reading. All of these help you to know yourself better. But there is one more form of solitude that I will list, and it will seem counterintuitive: friendship. Friendship, of course, is in an obvious respect the opposite of solitude; it means being with others. But I'm referring to one sort of friendship in particular: the deep friendship of intimate conversation. Long, uninterrupted talk with one other person. Not Skyping with three other people and texting with two more while you hang out in a friend's room studying and listening to music.

Introspection means talking to yourself, and one of the best ways of talking to yourself is by talking to someone else. Someone you can trust, someone to whom you can unfold your soul. Someone with whom you feel safe enough to acknowledge things—to acknowledge things to yourself—that you otherwise can't. Doubts you aren't supposed to have, questions that you aren't supposed to ask. Feelings or opinions that would get you laughed at by the group or reprimanded by the authorities.

But this kind of friendship takes just as much time and just as much patience as solitude in the more literal sense. And our new electronic world has disrupted it just as violently. Instead of one or two true friends with whom we can sit and talk for hours at a time, we have 968 "friends," people with whom we never actually talk, just bounce little messages off a hundred times a day. This is not friendship; this, too, is distraction.

Now I know that none of this is easy for you. Even if you threw away your cell phones and unplugged your computers, the rigors of your training keep you far too busy to make solitude, in any of these forms, anything less than very difficult to find. But the highest reason that you need to try is precisely what the job that you are training for will demand of you.

You have probably heard about the hazing scandal at the US naval base in Bahrain that was all over the news last month—abuse that involved an entire unit and that was orchestrated, allegedly, by the senior noncommissioned officer in charge. Now, what are you going to do if you are confronted with a comparable situation in your own unit? Will you have the courage to do what is right? Will you even know what is right? It is easy to learn a code of conduct, not so easy to put it into practice, especially if you risk losing the loyalty of your subordinates, or the trust of your peers, or the approval of your superiors. What if you are not the commanding officer, but you witness your superiors condoning conduct that you think is wrong?

Again, what will you do the first time that you have to write a letter to the mother of a fallen soldier? How will you find words of comfort that are more than just empty formulas? Or yet again, how will you find the strength and wisdom to challenge an unwise order, or question a wrongheaded policy?

These are truly formidable dilemmas, more so than most of us ever face, let alone when we are twenty-three. The time to start preparing for them is now. And the way to do so is by thinking through these issues for yourself—morality, mortality, honor—so that you will be equipped to deal with them when they arise. Waiting until you have to confront them in practice would be like waiting for your first firefight to learn how to shoot your weapon. Once the situation is upon you, it's too late. You need to know, already, who you are and what you believe: not what the army believes, not what your peers believe (that may be exactly the problem), but what you believe.

And how can you know that unless you have taken counsel with yourself in solitude? I started by noting that solitude and leadership would appear to be antithetical. But it seems to me in fact that solitude is the very essence of leadership. The position of leader is ultimately an intensely solitary, even an intensely lonely one. However many people you consult with, you are finally the one who has to make the hard decisions. And at such moments, all you really have is yourself.

[2009]

FAUX FRIENDSHIP

[a] numberless multitude of people, of whom no one was
close, no one was distant . . .

—*War and Peace*

We live in an age when friendship has become both all and nothing at all. Already the characteristically modern relationship, it has in recent decades become the universal one: the form of connection in terms of which all others are understood, against which all others are measured, into which all others have dissolved. Romantic partners refer to each other as boyfriend and girlfriend. Spouses boast that they are each other's best friend. Parents urge their young children and beg their teenage ones to think of them as friends. Adult siblings, released from the structural competition that in traditional society made them anything but friends (think of Jacob and Esau), now treat one another in exactly those terms. Teachers, clergymen, and even bosses seek to mitigate and legitimate their authority by asking those they oversee to regard them as friends. We're all on a first-name basis, and when we vote for president, we ask ourselves whom we'd rather have a beer with. As the anthropologist Robert Brain has put it, we're friends with everyone now.

Yet what, in our brave new mediated world, is friendship becoming? The Facebook phenomenon, so sudden and forceful a distortion of social space, needs little elaboration. Having been relegated to our screens, are our friendships now more than a form of distraction? When they've shrunk to the size of a wall post, do they retain any content? If I have 768 "friends," in what sense do I have any? Facebook is not the whole of contemporary friendship, but it sure looks a lot like its future. Yet Facebook—and MySpace, and Twitter, and whatever we're stampeding for next—are just the latest stages of a long attenuation. They've accelerated the fragmentation of consciousness, but they didn't initiate it. They have reified the idea of universal friendship, but they didn't invent it. In retrospect, it seems inevitable that once we decided to become friends with everyone, we would forget how to be friends with anyone. We may pride ourselves today on our aptitude for friendship—friends, after all, are the only people we have left—but it's not clear that we still even know what it means.

How did we come to this pass? The idea of friendship in ancient times could not have been more different. David and Jonathan, Achilles and Patroclus: far from being ordinary and universal, friendship, for the ancients, was rare, precious, and hard-won. In a world ordered by relations of kin and kingdom, its elective affinities were exceptional, even subversive, cutting across established lines of allegiance. David loves Jonathan despite the enmity of Saul; Achilles's bond with Patroclus outweighs his loyalty to the Greeks. Friendship was a high calling, demanding extraordinary qualities of character—rooted in virtue, for Aristotle and Cicero, and dedicated to the pursuit of goodness and truth. And because it was seen as superior to marriage and at least equal in value to sexual love, its expression often reached an erotic intensity. Jonathan's love, David sings, "was more wondrous to me than the love of women." Achilles and Patroclus are not lovers—the men share a tent, but they share their beds with concubines—they are something greater. Achilles refuses to live without his friend, just as Nisus dies to avenge Euryalus, and Damon offers himself in place of Pythias.

The rise of Christianity put the classical ideal in eclipse. Christian thought discouraged intense interpersonal bonds, for the heart should be directed to God. Within monastic communities, particular attachments were seen as threats to group cohesion. In medieval society, friendship entailed specific expectations and obligations, often formalized in oaths. "Standing surety"—guaranteeing a loan, as in *The Merchant of Venice*—was a chief institution of early modern friendship. Godparenthood functioned in Catholic society (and in many places, still functions) as a form of alliance between families, a relationship not between godparent and godchild, but godparent and parent. In medieval England, godparents were "godsibs"; in Latin America, god-fathers are "compadres," co-fathers, a word we have taken as synonymous with friendship itself.

The classical notion of friendship was revived, along with other ancient modes of feeling, by the Renaissance. Truth and virtue, again, above all. "Those who venture to criticize us perform a remarkable act of friendship," wrote Montaigne, "for to undertake to wound and offend a man for his own good is to have a healthy love for him." His bond with Etienne, he avowed, stood higher not only than marriage and erotic attachment, but also than filial, fraternal, and homosexual love. "So many coincidences are needed to build up such a friendship that it is a lot if fortune can do it once in three centuries." The highly structured and, as it were, economic nature of medieval friendship explains why true friendship was held to be so rare in classical and neoclassical thought: precisely because relations in traditional societies were dominated by interest. Thus the "true friend" stood against the self-interested "flatterer" or "false friend," as Shakespeare sets Horatio—"more an antique Roman than a Dane"—against Rosencrantz and Guildenstern. Sancho Panza begins as Don Quixote's dependent and ends as his friend; by the close of their journey, he has come to understand that friendship itself has become the reward he was seeking.

Classical friendship, now called romantic friendship, persisted through the eighteenth and nineteenth centuries, giving us the great friendships of Goethe and Schiller, Byron and Shelley, Emerson and Thoreau. Wordsworth addressed his magnum opus to his "dear Friend" Coleridge. Tennyson lamented Hallam—"My friend . . . My Arthur . . . Dear as the mother to the son"—in the poem that became his masterpiece. Speaking of his first encounter with Hawthorne, Melville was unashamed to write that "a man of deep and noble nature has seized me." But, meanwhile, the growth of commercial society was shifting the very grounds of personal life toward the conditions essential for the emergence of modern friendship. Capitalism, said Hume and Smith, by making economic relations impersonal, allowed for private relationships based on nothing other than affection and affinity. We don't know the people who make the things we buy and do not need to know the people who sell them. The ones we do know—neighbors, fellow parishioners, people from high school or college, parents of our children's friends—have no bearing on our economic lives. One teaches at a school in the suburbs; another works for a business across town; a third lives on the opposite side of the country. We are nothing to one another but what we choose to become, and we can unbecome it whenever we want.

Add to this the growth of democracy, an ideology of universal equality and inter-involvement. We are citizens now, not subjects, bound together directly rather than through allegiance to a monarch. But what is to bind us emotionally, make us something more than an aggregate of political monads? One answer was nationalism, but another grew out of the eighteenth-century notion of social sympathy: friendship, or at least, friendliness, as the affective substructure of modern society. It is no accident that fraternity made a third with liberty and equality as the watchwords of the French Revolution at the dawn of the modern age. Wordsworth in Britain and Whitman in America made visions of universal friendship central to their democratic vistas. For

Mary Wollstonecraft, a leading early feminist, friendship was to be the key term of a renegotiated sexual contract, a new domestic democracy.

Now we can understand why friendship has become the characteristically modern relationship. Modernity believes in equality. Friendships, unlike traditional relationships, are egalitarian. Modernity believes in individualism. Friendships serve no public purpose and exist independent of all other bonds. Modernity believes in choice. Friendships, unlike blood ties, are elective; indeed, the rise of friendship coincided with the shift away from arranged marriage. Modernity believes in self-expression. Friends, because we choose them, give us back an image of ourselves. Modernity believes in freedom. Even modern marriage entails contractual obligations, but friendship involves no fixed commitments. The modern temper runs toward unrestricted fluidity and flexibility, the endless play of possibility, and so is perfectly suited to the informal, improvisational nature of friendship. We can be friends with whomever we want, however we want, for as long as we want.

Social changes have played their role, as well. As industrialization uprooted people from extended families and traditional communities and packed them into urban centers, friendship emerged to salve the anonymity and rootlessness of modern life. The process is virtually instinctive now: you graduate from college, move to New York or LA, and assemble the gang that takes you through your twenties. Only it's not just your twenties anymore. The transformations of family life over the last few decades have made friendship even more important still. Between the rise of divorce and the growth of single parenthood, adults in contemporary households often no longer have spouses, let alone traditional extended families, to turn to for support. Children, let loose by the weakening of parental authority and supervision, spin out of orbit at ever-earlier ages. Both look to friends to replace the older structures. Friends may be "the family we choose," as the modern proverb has it, but for many of us there is no choice but to make our friends our family, since our other families—the ones we come from or the ones we try to start—have fallen asunder. And even those who grow up in a stable family and end up creating another one pass more and more time between the two. We have yet to find a satisfactory name for that period of life, now typically a decade but often a great deal longer, between the end of adolescence and the making of definitive life choices, but the one thing we know is that friendship is absolutely central to it.

Inevitably, the classical ideal has faded. The image of the one true friend, a soul mate rare to find but dearly beloved, has completely disappeared from our culture. We have our better or lesser friends, even our best friends, but no one in a very long time has talked about friendship the way that Montaigne and Tennyson did. That glib neologism "bff," which plays at a lifelong avowal, bespeaks an ironic awareness of the mobility of our connections: best friends forever may not be on speaking terms by this time next month. We save our fiercest energies for sex. Indeed, between the rise of Freudianism and the contemporaneous emergence of homosexuality to social visibility, we've taught ourselves to shun expressions of intense affection between friends—male friends in particular, though even Oprah was forced to defend her relationship with Gayle King—and have rewritten historical friendships, like Achilles's with Patroclus, as sexual. For all the talk of "bromance" lately (or "man dates"), the term is yet another device to manage the sexual anxiety aroused by straight male friendships—whether in the friends themselves or the people around them—and the typical bromance plot instructs the callow bonds of youth to give way to mature heterosexual relationships. At best, intense friendships are something we're expected to grow out of.

As for the moral content of classical friendship, its commitment to virtue and mutual improvement, that, too, has been lost. We have ceased to believe that a friend's highest purpose is to summon us to the good by offering moral advice and correction. We practice, instead, the nonjudgmental friendship of unconditional acceptance and support—"therapeutic" friendship, in the sociologist Robert Bellah's scornful term. We seem to be terribly fragile today. A friend fulfills her duty, we suppose, by taking our side—validating our feelings, supporting our decisions, helping us feel good about ourselves. We tell white lies, make excuses when a friend does something wrong, do what we can to keep the boat steady. We're busy people; we want our friendships fun and friction-free.

Yet even as friendship became universal and the classical ideal lost its force, a new kind of idealism arose, a new repository for some of friendship's deepest needs: the group friendship or friendship circle. Companies of superior spirits go back at least as far as Pythagoras and Plato, and they achieved renewed importance in the salons and coffeehouses of the seventeenth and eighteenth centuries, but the Romantic age gave them a fresh impetus and emphasis. The idea of friendship became explicitly central to their self-conception, whether in Wordsworth's circle or the "small band of true friends" who witness Emma's marriage in Austen. At the same time, the notion of superiority acquired a utopian cast, so that the circle was seen—not least for its emphasis on friendship—as the harbinger of a better age.

The same would be true, a century later, of the Bloomsbury Group, two of whose members, Forster and Woolf, wrote novel after novel about friendship. It was the former who famously enunciated the group's political creed. "If I had to choose between betraying my country and betraying my friend," he wrote, "I hope I should have the guts to betray my country." Modernism was the great age of the coterie, and like the legendary friendships of antiquity, modernist friendship circles—bohemian, artistic, transgressive—set their face against existing structures and norms. Friendship became, on this account, a kind of alternate society, a refuge from the values of the larger, fallen world.

In the second half of the twentieth century, the idea that the most significant part of one's emotional life properly takes place, not within one's family but within one's group of friends, became general. The Romantic-Bloomsburyan prophecy of society as a set of friendship circles was, to a great extent, realized. Mary McCarthy offered an early and tart view of the desirability of such a dispensation in her novel *The Group*; Barry Levinson, a later, kinder one in his movie *Diner*. Both works remind us that the ubiquity of group friendship owes a great deal to the rise of youth culture. Indeed, modernity associates friendship itself with youth, a time of life it likewise regards as standing apart from false adult values. "The dear peculiar bond of youth," Byron called friendship, inverting the classical belief that its true practice demands maturity and wisdom. With modernity's elevation of youth to supreme status as the most vital and authentic period of life, friendship became the object of intense emotion in two contradictory but often simultaneous directions. We have sought to prolong youth indefinitely by holding fast to our youthful friendships, and we have mourned the loss of youth through an unremitting nostalgia for those friendships. One of the most striking things about the way the twentieth century understood friendship was its tendency to view it through the filter of memory, as if it could only be recognized after its loss, and as if that loss were inevitable.

The culture of group friendship reached its apogee in the 1960s. Two of the counterculture's most salient and ideologically charged social forms were the commune—a community of friends in self-imagined retreat from a heartlessly corporatized society—and the rock-and-roll "band" (not "group" or "combo"), its name evoking Shakespeare's "band of brothers" and Robin Hood's band of Merry Men, its great exemplar the Beatles. Communes, bands, and other '60s friendship groups (including Woodstock, the apotheosis of both the commune and the rock concert) were celebrated as joyous, creative places of eternal youth—havens from the adult world. To go through life within one was the era's utopian dream; it is no wonder that the Beatles' breakup was received as a generational tragedy.

It is also no wonder that 1960s group friendship began to generate its own nostalgia as the baby boom began to hit its thirties. *The Big Chill*, in 1983, depicted boomers attempting to recapture the magic of a late-'60s friendship circle ("In a cold world," the movie's tagline read, "you need your friends to keep you warm"). *Thirtysomething*, which debuted in 1987, certified group friendship as the new adult norm. Most of the characters in those productions, however, were married. It was only in the 1990s that a new generation, remaining single well past thirty, found its images of group friendship in *Seinfeld*, *Sex and the City*, and, of course, *Friends*. By that point, though, the notion of friendship as a redoubt of moral resistance, a shelter from normative pressures and incubator of social ideals, had evaporated. Your friends didn't shield you from the mainstream; they were the mainstream.

And so we return to Facebook. With the social networking sites of the new century—Friendster and MySpace were launched in 2003, Facebook in 2004—the friendship circle has expanded to engulf the whole of social space, and, in so doing, destroyed both its own nature and that of the individual friendship itself. Facebook's very premise—and promise—is that it makes our friendship circles visible. There they are, my friends, all in the same place. Except, of course, they are not in the same place—or rather, they are not my friends. They are simulacra of my friends, little dehydrated packets of images and information, no more my friends than a set of baseball cards is the New York Mets.

I remember realizing a few years ago that most of the members of what I thought of as my "circle" didn't actually know one another. One I'd met in graduate school, another at a job, one in Boston, another in Brooklyn, one lived in Minneapolis, another in Israel, so that I was ultimately able to enumerate some fourteen people, none of whom had met any of the others. To imagine that they constituted a circle, an embracing and encircling structure, was a belief, I realized, that violated the laws of feeling as well as geometry. They were no more than a set of points, and I was wandering somewhere among them.

Facebook seduces us, however, into exactly that illusion, inviting us to believe that by assembling a list, we have conjured a group. Visual juxtaposition creates the mirage of emotional proximity. "It's like they're all having a conversation," a friend once said about her Facebook page, full of posts and comments from friends and friends of friends. "Except they're not."

Friendship is devolving, in other words, from a relationship to a feeling—from something people share to something each of us hugs privately to ourselves in the loneliness of our electronic caves, rearranging the tokens of connection like a lonely child playing with dolls. There is an analogy here to community, which long ago trod the same path. As the traditional community disappeared, the face-to-face community, we held on to what we had lost—the closeness, the rootedness—by clinging to the word, no matter how much that required us to water down its meaning. So we speak of the Jewish "community" and the medical "community" and the "community" of readers, even though none of them actually is one. Instead of community, what we have now, if we're lucky, is a "sense of community"—the feeling, without the structure; a private emotion, not a collective experience. And now friendship, which arose to its present importance as a replacement for community, is going the same way. We have "friends," just as we belong to "communities." Scanning my Facebook page, I give myself, precisely, a "sense of connection." Not an actual connection, just a sense.

What purpose do all those wall posts and status updates serve? On the first beautiful weekend of spring this year, a friend posted this update from Central Park: "[So-and-so] is in the Park with the rest of the City." The first question that comes to mind is, if you're enjoying a beautiful day in the park, why don't you give your iPhone a rest? But the more important one is, why did you need to tell us that? We have always shared our little private observations and moments of feeling—they are part of what friendship is about, part of the way we remain present in one another's lives—but things are different now. Until a few years ago, you could only share your thoughts with one friend at a time (on the phone, say), or maybe with a small group, later, in person. And when you did, you were talking to specific people, and you tailored what you said, and how you said it, to them—to their interests, to their personalities, most of all, to your degree of mutual intimacy. "Reach out and touch someone," the telephone company slogan, meant someone in particular, someone you were actually thinking about. It meant having a conversation. But now we are broadcasting our stream of consciousness, live from Central Park, to all five hundred of our friends at once, hoping that someone, anyone, will confirm our existence by answering back. Not only, at such moments, have we stopped talking to our friends as individuals; we have stopped thinking of them as individuals. We have turned them into an undifferentiated mass, a kind of audience or faceless public. We address ourselves not to a circle but to a cloud.

It's amazing how fast things have changed. Not only don't we have Words-worth and Coleridge anymore; we don't even have Jerry and George. Today, Ross and Chandler would be writing on each other's walls. Carrie and the girls would be posting status updates, and if they did manage to find the time for lunch, they'd be too busy checking their BlackBerrys to have a real con-versation. *Sex* and *Friends* went off the air just five years ago, and already we inhabit a different world. Friendship has been smoothly integrated into our new electronic lifestyles. We are too busy to spare our friends more time than it takes to send a text. We are too busy sending texts.

The new group friendship, already vitiated itself, is cannibalizing our indi-vidual friendships as the boundaries blur between the two. The most dis-turbing thing about Facebook is the extent to which people are willing—are eager—to conduct their private lives in public. "hola cutie-pie! i'm in town on wednesday. lunch?" "Julie, I'm so glad we're back in touch. xoxox." "Sorry for not calling, I'm going through a tough time." Have these people forgotten how to use email, or do they actually prefer to stage the emotional equivalent of a public grope? I can understand "[So-and-so] is in the Park with the rest of the City," but I am incapable of comprehending this kind of exhibition-ism. Perhaps I need to surrender the idea that the value of friendship lies precisely in the space of privacy it creates: not the secrets that two people exchange so much as the unique and inviolate world they build up between them, the spiderweb of shared discovery they spin out, slowly and carefully, together. There is something faintly obscene about performing that intimacy in front of everyone you know, as if its real purpose were to show how deep you are. Are we really so hungry for validation? So desperate to prove we have friends?

But surely Facebook has its benefits. Long-lost friends can reconnect; far-flung ones can stay in touch. I wonder, though. Having recently moved across the country, I thought that Facebook would help me feel connected to the friends I'd left behind. But now I find the opposite is true. Reading about the mundane details of their lives, a steady stream of trivia and ephemera, leaves me feeling both empty and unpleasantly full, as if I had just binged on junk food, and precisely because it reminds me of the real sustenance, the real knowledge, we exchange by email or phone or face-to-face. And the whole theatrical quality of the business, the sense that my friends are doing their best to impersonate themselves, only makes it worse. The person I read about, I cannot help but feel, is not quite the person I know.

As for getting back in touch with old friends—yes, when they're people you really love, it's a miracle. But most of the time, they're not. They are someone that you knew for a summer in camp, or a mid-level friend from high school. They do not matter to you as individuals anymore, certainly not the individuals that they've become; they matter because they made up the texture of your experience at a certain moment in your life, in conjunction with all the other people you knew. Tear them out of that texture—read about their brats, look at their vacation photos—and they mean nothing. Tear out enough of them, and you ruin the texture itself, replace a matrix of feeling and memory, the deep subsoil of experience, with a spurious sense of familiarity. Your eighteen-year-old self knows them. Your forty-year-old self should not know them. Facebook holds out a utopian possibility: what once was lost will now be found. But the heaven of the past is a promised land destroyed in the reaching. Facebook here becomes the anti-madeleine, an eraser of memory. Proust understood that memory is a skittish creature that peeks from its hole only when it isn't being sought. Mementos, souvenirs, snapshots, reunions, and now, this: all of them modes of amnesia, foes of true remembering. The past should remain in the heart, where it belongs.

Finally, the new social networking sites have falsified our understanding of intimacy itself, and with it, our understanding of ourselves. The absurd idea, bruited about in the media, that a MySpace profile or "25 Random Things About Me" can tell us more about a person than even a good friend might be aware of is based on a desiccated set of notions about what knowing someone means. First, that intimacy is confessional, an idea both peculiarly American and peculiarly young, perhaps because both types of individuals tend to travel among strangers and so believe that the instant disgorging of the self is the quickest route to familiarity. Second, that identity is reducible to information: the name of your cat, your favorite song, the stupid thing you did in seventh grade. Third, that it is reducible, in particular, to the kind of information that social networking sites are most interested in eliciting, consumer preferences. Forget that we are all conducting market research on ourselves. Far worse is that Facebook amplifies our long-standing tendency to see ourselves ("I'm a Skin Bracer man!") in just those terms. We put on T-shirts that proclaim our brand loyalties, pique ourselves on owning a Mac, and now put up lists of our favorite songs. "15 movies in 15 minutes. Rule: Don't take too long to think about it."

So information replaces experience, as it has throughout the culture. Yet when I think about my friends, what makes them who they are and why I love them, it is not the names of their siblings that come to mind, or their fear of spiders. It is their qualities of soul. This one's emotional generosity, that one's moral seriousness, the dark humor of a third. Yet even these are just descriptions, and no more specify them uniquely than to say that one has red hair, another is tall. To understand what they really look like, you would need to see a picture. And to understand who they really are, you would have to hear about the things they've done. Character, revealed through action: the two eternal elements of narrative. In order to know someone, you have to listen to their stories.

But that is precisely what the Facebook page does not leave room for, or five hundred friends, time for. Literally does not leave room for. Email, with its scrolling format and etiquette of quick response, already trimmed the letter down to a certain acceptable maximum, perhaps a thousand words. Now, with Facebook, the box is shrinking even more, leaving perhaps a third of that length as the conventional limit for a message, far less for a comment. (And we all know the deal on Twitter.) The ten-page missive has gone the way of the buggy whip, soon to be followed, it seems, by the three-hour conversation.

They call it social networking for a reason. Networking once meant something specific: climbing the jungle gym of professional contacts in order to advance your career. The truth is that Hume and Smith were not completely right. Commercial society did not eliminate the self-interested aspects of making friends and influencing people; it just changed the way we went about it. Now, in the age of the entrepreneurial self, even our closest relationships are being fitted onto this template. A recent book on the sociology of modern science describes a networking event at a West Coast university. "There do not seem to be any singletons—disconsolately lurking at the margins—nor do dyads appear, except fleetingly." No solitude, no friendship, no space for refusal—the exact contemporary paradigm. At the same time, the author assures us, "face-time" is valued in this "community" as a "high-bandwidth interaction," offering "unusual capacity for interruption, repair, feedback and learning." Actual human contact, rendered "unusual" and weighed by the values of a systems engineer. We have given our hearts to machines, and now we're becoming machines. The face of friendship in the new century.

[2009]

Culture against Culture

When we speak about culture, we need to start by recognizing that we use the word in two quite different senses. There is the older, Matthew Arnold sense of culture as high culture: "the best," as Arnold put it, "that has been thought and said." And there is the newer, anthropological sense of culture as the total pattern of habits, beliefs, and practices that belongs to a particular group of people. So we speak, in the second sense, of American culture or youth culture, or we isolate a particular strain in such a culture, as we often do with respect to contemporary culture, and speak about a culture of narcissism or a culture of disbelief.

Culture in the first sense is conscious. In fact, it involves the very highest development of consciousness and self-consciousness: in art, in literature, in philosophy, in criticism, in religion. Culture in the second sense is largely unconscious. It involves the things we do and believe without being aware that we are doing and believing them. The ways we think and feel without our knowing why. The myths, the metaphors, the sacred terms, the unspoken assumptions that govern our individual and collective lives. The words we use, and the words we don't use. Culture, in that sense, thinks us.

But the two senses are not just distinct. The first understands itself, or ought to understand itself, in relation to the second. And that relation is not comfortable but adversarial. That is Arnold's meaning in the passage that includes his famous formulation. For him, as it should be for us, culture is neither ornament nor entertainment. It is, he says, a "criticism of life," "a pursuit of our total perfection by means of getting to know, on all the matters which most concern us, the best which has been thought and said in the world; and, through this knowledge, turning a stream of fresh and free thought upon our stock notions and habits."

Culture is not a diversion at the end of the day. It should be the inner substance of every day, the means by which we question, continually, our stock notions and habits. If culture in the other sense thinks us, culture in this sense is our opportunity to think it back, to think it through.

That is the first meaning that I have in mind for my titular phrase. But I mean something else, as well, something that has to do with the particular culture in which we find ourselves today. One of the most conspicuous things about that culture is its veneration of science and technology. Our culture is scientistic: it believes that science is the only form of truth, that there is only one way of knowing: objective, empirical, quantitative. But our culture also displays—this is the technology part—what I have come to think of as the engineering mentality. You pick up whiffs of this on the discussion threads, in the blog posts and TED talks, in the pronouncements of the potentates of Silicon Valley. The engineering mentality is the attitude that social problems are susceptible to technological procedures and solutions, that society is nothing other than a big machine, a set of systems that are capable of being optimized if only ordinary people, with their fuzzy notions and foolish opinions, would get out of the way. It expresses itself, with the weary arrogance of the guy who fixes your computer, as a disdain for politics: for its messiness, its muddle, its constipation and corruption. Just let the guys who know how to get things done, the attitude goes, get them done.

Another thing that is conspicuous about contemporary culture, at least if you have anything to do with education, is its contempt for the humanities. I needn't belabor the point, except to note that much of that contempt appears to derive from the fact that the humanities don't seem to *produce* anything. Science forms the basis of technology, and the social sciences give rise to their own kinds of technology in the form, for example, of public policy. But with the humanities, there just does not seem anything that you can *do*. So, in our utilitarian culture, what value could they have?

As the reader may have figured out, I am sneaking up on the famous dichotomy of "the two cultures." The two cultures, as the argument was first expounded by C. P. Snow in 1959 and has been variously taken up from time to time since then, are, precisely, the scientific and the literary or humanistic. From the beginning, however, the notion didn't merely involve an even-handed description of two different intellectual traditions or milieus. It was also a highly invidious distinction. It was already an effort to elevate one at the cost of the other. Scientists, said Snow, "have the future in their bones," whereas literary intellectuals are "natural Luddites." Scientists are, morally speaking, "the soundest group of intellectuals we have," whereas the vast majority of literary intellectuals are "not only politically silly, but politically wicked."

Science good, humanities bad: just like today. And just like today, as Lionel Trilling pointed out in his response to Snow, the argument for the superior wisdom and virtue of scientists and technologists is ultimately an argument not for a better politics, but for no politics, for a transcendence of politics. It expresses a desire to have done with politics. "The Two Cultures" was written at the height of the Cold War. Snow believed that our only hope of staving off the threat of nuclear annihilation, and of solving the world's other ills, lay in a union of scientists—those most moral and most forward-looking of men—across the geopolitical divide. Like later exponents of the two-cultures argument, and like so many in Silicon Valley today, he comes to us from a point of view of technological salvationism. Of the belief that society can be engineered to an optimal state, if only the right people were put in charge.

I am arguing, in other words, that my first two cultures and my second two cultures are the same. Our total culture, our unconscious culture, is a culture of science and technology. Our culture of art and thought, our conscious culture, far from being superfluous, needs to stand and criticize the first. And what it needs to criticize most of all is the notion that we can ever be done with politics, or that we should ever want to be. And what it can *do* most of all is to prepare us for political life—that life, as Aristotle tells us, that is proper to us as human beings.

In order to explain what I mean, I'd like to start with the familiar observation that science is cumulative while the arts and humanities aren't. Scientific knowledge progresses. Physicists today know more than physicists did a hundred years ago. Which also means that science can forget its past. But culture is not cumulative or progressive. Woolf does not supersede Shakespeare. Nor, I would add, does one interpretation of Shakespeare supersede another. Which also means that culture always remains available to us. Homer and Plato are still valuable, still relevant, in a way that Archimedes and Galen are not, and so are different readings of Homer and Plato.

To put that in a different way, all that science can be said to know is what we know, or think we know, today: our best current picture of reality. Transpose that notion to the arts and humanities—replace "science" with "the arts and humanities"—and the new formulation is meaningless. It isn't wrong; it is, as the mathematicians say, not even wrong. Art does not represent our best current picture of reality, because there is no single definitive picture of reality that art proposes—and no single definitive picture of the arts that the humanities (by which I mean, in particular, the disciplined study of the arts) proposes. There are no definitive representations and no definitive interpretations.

The circumstance will be familiar to anyone who has taught the humanities. In the humanities classroom, there is no one right answer—a fact that sometimes drives the scientists crazy or adds to their disdain for the humanities. It is important to recognize—as many students and even teachers do not—that there *are* wrong answers, answers that do not take sufficiently rigorous account of the evidence of the text. But there is no one right answer; there is only an open-ended multiplicity of right answers—of truthful representations in art and valid interpretations in the study of art.

Now why should all this be? If you believe, as I do, that the arts and humanities are not an inferior form of knowledge to science (or indeed something other than knowledge entirely, like distraction or social capital), but rather a different form, then what do these circumstances tell us about what kind of form it is and what it is the knowledge of?

This is not an easy question to answer. I approach it like this. What else does humanistic inquiry resemble? In plainer terms, what else is the experience of reading and trying to say something sensible about a novel or a drama, for example, like? Where else do we encounter a welter of miscellaneous circumstances, a jumble of characters, scenes, ideas, and feelings, organized within a loose, complex, and hidden structure, through which we must navigate some kind of cognitive path, out of which we must make some kind of sense, one that we know will only be a partial and indeed a temporary sense, one possible sense out of an endless array of others, a sense that we ourselves will probably repudiate tomorrow or a year from now in favor of a different one?

The answer is: everywhere. Every time we get up in the morning. What I just described, in that convoluted sentence whose structure was meant to mimic the convolutions of the thing it describes, is the experience of being in the world—that is, the human world, the world of human relationships. Such is the function of art, especially of literary art. Art reproduces, albeit in an artificial and selective way, the experience of being in the world. It is, as George Eliot said, "the nearest thing to life." It is always partial in both senses, just as our experience is always partial: always subjective and personal, and always just a little fragment of the whole. And with art, so with criti-cism. If art gives voice to our experience of life, then criticism gives voice to our experience of art.

Art enables us to ask, in an organized way, and criticism helps us start to answer, in a necessarily provisional way, the questions that are asked of us by life itself, by the fact of living with other people, and indeed, of living with ourselves. Questions that don't have answers, or at least, not single or final or even stable answers. Questions that we each answer differently and, with the passage of time, in different ways. Science speaks to our relationship with the material world, which can be known and mastered. That is what tech-nology is. Culture speaks to our relationship with one another, who cannot be mastered and cannot be known—not, at least, in any stable or final way. That is what society is.

As everybody recognizes, if only from their experience of living in a fam-ily—of dealing with parents, siblings, partners, and children—relationships are never finalized, never stable, always in the process of renegotiation and reappraisal, even, or especially, with respect to the most foundational things. And our understanding of other people, and indeed, of ourselves, is likewise never final, and may not even be cumulative or progressive.

In culture as in life, we are always starting from the beginning. In science, you almost never reappraise foundational truths, and certainly not until you've mastered the existing state of knowledge. Nor do undergraduates, except in rare cases, contribute new insights to a discipline. But in the humanities class-room, foundational issues are always on the table, and, as every teacher of the humanities knows—and this is one of the great things about being a teacher of the humanities, as well as another remarkable fact about the humanities—even the lowliest freshman, even a student in high school, is capable of new and striking insights.

There is one more arena in which we are always asking foundational ques-tions—in fact, those same foundational questions, questions of value and virtue—and that is politics. Politics, whatever it may look like on the nightly news, is at bottom an effort to construct a collective life by compounding our individual answers to foundational moral and philosophical questions. Aristotle, after all, does not say that man is a *social* animal. There are many social animals. Bees are social animals, but they do not have parliaments. Ants are social animals, but they do not hold elections. To be a *political* animal is to possess the freedom to determine what society should look like.

In politics, too, we are always starting from the beginning. The fact that political questions are never finally resolved is not a flaw of politics; it is the essence and the point of politics. As long as there are people—especially new people, who have a right to decide for themselves how society ought to be organized—there will never be an end to politics.

That is why the engineering mentality tends to envision futures that are inhabited by individuals who behave like robots (the paradigm being the hyperrational Mr. Spock) or who are robots. Technological salvationism is naïve because all salvationism is naïve. Trilling, in his response to Snow, acknowledges that, as he puts it, "The world will not be saved by teaching English at universities." But, he adds, "It is very hard to say what will save the world." I understand this to mean not that the world is doomed to immi-nent apocalyptic destruction—another crypto-religious illusion—but that salvation, like damnation, is simply the wrong way to think about our pre-dicament. Humanity will muddle on more or less well, traveling the endless round of our imperfectible nature, necessarily debating our irresolvable, unavoidable moral and political conundra.

Which doesn't mean we don't face urgent problems. Today, even more than in the days of Snow, the world indeed appears to be in need of saving. But the specter of climate change demonstrates why technology is not ade-quate to address, let alone to solve, our collective problems. We already have the technology to check the threat of climate change, and if we don't have it now, we will have it tomorrow. The problem, precisely, is political. And the problem of politics is not to get "them" to see that "we" are right. The problem is not to get Congress to pass a carbon tax. It is increasingly evident that the self-inflicted threats we face—not only climate change but resource depletion, the disappearance of work in the face of automation, the helplessly widening gap between wealthy and poor—will require fundamental social change, which will in turn require that we ask foundational questions. We will need to reexamine and, if need be, discard the values and virtues that we most take for granted, like growth and ambition and economic freedom.

We rarely any longer speak of "culture" in the Matthew Arnold sense. The word embarrasses us. Still less do we speak of being or becoming "cultured," or, as we also used to say, "cultivated." What strikes me now about these words is that they all bespeak a process in which we are the receivers of an action. Becoming cultured is something that happens *to* us; we are cultivated in the way a field is cultivated, and culture is the plow. In the words of David Neidorf, the former president of Deep Springs College, to read a book truly is to cooperate with its effort to teach you something.

The truth is that there is a technology that corresponds to the humanities; there are powers to which the humanities give rise. But they are invisible, because they are internal. The humanities cultivate, culture cultivates, our powers of sympathy and understanding. They do not give us mastery; they give us, or they ought to give us, receptivity, humility, the recognition that our individual comprehension is only ever very partial, and that the experiences of others are equally valid. The humanities, in these dreary days of death by a thousand budget cuts, often seek to justify themselves in terms of the rhetorical abilities they instill. They teach you, their proponents insist to those who'd do away with them, to speak well and write well. But the most important thing they do is to teach you to listen well.

The technologies the humanities underwrite, in other words, are those capacities that we require for collective life, for political life. We used to speak of education, particularly higher education, as a preparation for citizenship. Now we speak of it as a preparation for "global citizenship." But a global citizen is very different from an actual citizen. The "citizen" in "global citizen" is really just a metaphor. Strictly speaking, you can't be a citizen of something unless that thing is a political community. "Global citizen" is an oxymoron; "global citizen" is just another one of the euphemisms of education in the age of neoliberalism. It means a person who is fit for competition in the globalized economy. And the globalized economy, especially under the neoliberal assault on the state and its regulatory power, is more or less the negation of citizenship.

The liberal arts are called the liberal arts because they are understood to constitute the kind of education that is proper to free people. But freedom doesn't mean the absence of government. It does not denote the kind of libertarianism that is now so fashionable in Silicon Valley, with its call for radical autonomy. The word "autonomous," in fact, appears for the first time in Homer, but it describes the Cyclopes. "Autonomous" means that you're a law unto yourself, *auto-nomos*. It is the antithesis of civilization, of culture, and it was the worst thing that Homer could imagine. The Cyclopes are free, all right. "They have no laws nor assemblies of the people, but live in caves on the tops of high mountains; each is lord and master in his family, and they take no account of their neighbours." They sound a lot like libertarians. And when one of them gets his eye poked out, the others shrug and say, "Tough luck."

Freedom, for us as for the Greeks, means the privilege of participating in collective self-government, the collective constitution of a political community. Our dominant culture, our technological culture, often claims that it wants to save humanity—in fact, it often justifies itself in precisely those terms—but only, it seems, at the cost of abolishing it, or at least, of abolishing what makes it human. Against it, we need to oppose that which is most intensely human. Culture, against culture.

[2017]

THE GIRL WITH THE
HIGH-SPEED CONNECTION

In some ways she seems like a throwback: black-clad, hard-eyed, spiky-haired; sullen, violent, antisocial—more punk than hipster, more '70s than now. But she is confident, and competent, in a way that the punks never were. She hacks computers at will, rides a mean motorcycle, kicks ass, and rescues her lover from a serial killer. She is Lisbeth Salander, needless to say, heroine of Stieg Larsson's blockbuster *Millennium* trilogy (The Girl With This, The Girl Who That), played in the English adaptation by Rooney Mara, in the Swedish by Noomi Rapace.

She is not the first of the new breed of girl heroes, though she is maybe the biggest. There was Jennifer Garner's character in *Alias*, Hanna in the 2011 movie of the same name, and Katniss Everdeen, of course, in *The Hunger Games*, to name just a few. But there seems to be something uniquely compelling about her. It is, I think, her self-enclosure. She works for herself and, for the most part, on her own. She repels intimacy and punishes anyone who invades her privacy. She is sexually assertive, sexually omnivorous, sexually detached. She's never bewildered, never at a loss, always supremely oriented within her environment. She does what she pleases and gets what she wants.

The secret of her self-sufficiency is simple: it is her computer. Which makes her a symbol not only of her generation but also of her time. The punks were powerless, in the wreck of the '70s urban decay, and everything about them—their rage, their disaffection, their secession from social norms—originated in that. About the only tools they had were bricks and guitars. But now the means of agency are in everybody's reach, the young even more than the old (or so, at least, we like to imagine). The hipster, you might say, is a punk with a computer, and Lisbeth, with her iconic tattoo, is a hipster superhero. Self-sufficient, self-pleasing, self-employed: she lives the contemporary dream.

The generational aspect is quite to the point. Lisbeth's heroics consist of doing battle with evil adults, including her own father. She is a sort of one-girl WikiLeaks, exposing the existing order with the self-righteous fury of a wounded child. At the same time, she joins with, beds, and rescues another father figure, the series' hero Mikael Blomkvist. Lisbeth's creator, Stieg Larsson, was born in 1954. She personifies our romance with technology, but she also embodies an older generation's dread of and desire for the digital strangers in their midst.

[2012]

The Ghost in the Machine

Once, we dreamed of gods and angels. The beasts were below us—that we knew. But we feared becoming beasts ourselves, told tales of metamorphosis, the blurry line between us: Circe's wand and pen; Ovid's spiders, birds, and bears. We were made of clay and spirit, half-nature, half-something else. If there were animals beneath us, there must be gods above. Might we rise to join them, just as we could sink to the others? Those myths we also told: Hercules, Castor, Aeneas. Christianity made the prospect universal. The gods became angels, and Heaven was open to all. We would be purged of mortal dross and sprout celestial wings.

Now we have other dreams. Not beasts and angels, but machines. For Marinetti and the Futurists a century ago, the machine was the new deity. Bright, powerful, glorious, swift: the airplane, the steamship, the automobile—pure reason, the mind made metal. For Kurt Vonnegut during the postwar boom—he had worked for General Electric—Marinetti's vision of a posthuman future was all too imminent. In *Player Piano*, machines have made the human all but obsolete.

Machines above us, equivocal gods, but also machines below, regarded with the same anxiety of kinship that the Greeks felt about the animals. The word "robot" was invented by the Czech science fiction writer Karel Čapek in 1920, and the concept has haunted our imagination ever since. *Blade Runner*, *A.I.*: Where do we stop and the machines start? How can we tell the difference between us? What does it mean to be human anyway? Do we really have souls, or is it all just fancy wiring?

But lately, something new. We don't just worship our machines; we enter them. I mean the ones with screens, of course, and the virtual worlds they contain. Think of *Avatar*. Ostensibly a Rousseauistic fable of return to nature, the movie is really a fantasy about disappearing into an alternative reality accessed technologically. Jake, the hero, lies in a pod in a lab, but his spirit gallops free on Pandora. The planet is supposed to be a real place, but it feels computer generated (in part because we know it is). The avatars are blue, not green: not nature's color but the computer's. Jake is paraplegic, but his avatar—lithe, comely, ten feet tall—restores his powers and then some. As for the Na'vi, Pandora's indigenes, they are already living in an internet—connected, USB-style, with animals, the planet, one another. At the end, Jake unites completely with his icon, shedding his human body and entering the other world for good.

The kick is the same in *The Matrix*, even if the premise is different. The Matrix is supposed to be an evil place, but it sure seems a heck of a lot more fun than that cruddy ship they fly around in. Like Jake in his pod, Neo and friends close their eyes, plug themselves in, and descend into infantile dreams of omnipotence, flying like angels or gods.

"Avatar" is the word for a user's graphical representation in a video game. That is what these movies are, of course: very expensive, collective video games. And that is our latest dream: to become pure spirit by becoming pure energy, pure pixels, pure information. To shed our pimply bodies and be free.

[2012]

ALL IN A DREAM

Space colonies. That's the latest thing you hear from the heralds of the future. President Gingrich is going to set up a state on the moon. We're heading toward a "multiplanetary civilization," says Elon Musk. Our future lies in the stars, we're told.

As a species of megalomania, this is hard to beat. As a plan for technological salvation, it is more plausible than the one where we upload our brains into our computers, surviving forever in a paradise of circuitry. But not a lot more plausible. The resources required to maintain a colony in space would be, well, astronomical. We would have to keep people alive, indefinitely, in inconceivably inhospitable conditions. The nearest known planets with even potentially earthlike climates are twenty light-years away. That means that a round-trip at 10 percent the speed of light, several hundred times faster than anything we've yet achieved, would take four hundred years.

But forget the logistical problems. If we live long enough as a species, we might overcome them—energy from fusion (which always seems to be about fifty years away), and so forth. No, think about what life in a space colony would actually be *like*. It would be like living in an airport. In Antarctica. Only much worse. Forever. When I hear someone talk about space colonies, I think, that's a person who has never studied the humanities. That's a person who has never stopped to think about what it feels like to go through an average day—what life is about, what makes it worth living, what makes it endurable. A person who is blessed with a technological imagination but no other kind.

The only way we are going to end up living in space is if we are forced to. "In the long run," said the head of NASA in 2005, "a single-planet species will not survive." His agency conducts research into climate change, so he ought to know. This is not exactly a self-fulfilling prophecy, but it's certainly one we're doing everything we can to realize. It is not hard to foresee a time when living in a giant refrigerator on Mars is better than the alternative, and we abandon the Earth altogether.

Except that "we" won't abandon the Earth. Who do you think will get to go, when the time comes? The ones who can pay their way. Elon Musk will get to go, and former president Romney, and a bunch of their friends. It's going to be like the last helicopter out of Saigon. The rest of us will get to stay behind and watch each other slowly die. Our future lies in the stars? Their future, buddy. Not yours or mine.

[2012]

Higher Education

The Disadvantages of
an Elite Education

It didn't dawn on me that there might be a few holes in my education until I was thirty-five. I'd just bought a house, the pipes needed fixing, and the plumber was standing in my kitchen. There he was, a short, beefy guy with a goatee and a Red Sox cap and a thick Boston accent, and I suddenly learned that I didn't have the slightest idea what to say to him. So alien was his experience to me, so unguessable his values, so mysterious his very language, that I couldn't succeed in engaging him in a few minutes of small talk before he got down to work. Fourteen years of higher education and a handful of Ivy League degrees, and there I was, stiff and stupid, struck dumb by my own dumbness. I could carry on conversations with people from other countries, in other languages, but I couldn't talk to the man who was standing in my own house.

It's not surprising that it took me so long to discover the extent of my mis-education, because the last thing that an elite education will teach you is its own inadequacy. As two dozen years at Yale and Columbia have shown me, elite colleges relentlessly encourage their students to flatter themselves for being there, and for what being there can do for them. And the advantages of an elite education are indeed undeniable. You learn to think, at least in certain ways, and you make the contacts needed to launch yourself into a life that is rich in all of society's most cherished rewards. The idea that, while some opportunities are being created, others are being canceled, and while some abilities are being developed, others are being crippled, is, within this context, not only outrageous; it is literally inconceivable.

I'm not talking about curricula or the culture wars, the closing or opening of the American mind, political correctness, canon formation, or what have you. I'm talking about the whole system in which these skirmishes play out. Not just the Ivy League and its peer institutions, but also the mechanisms that get you there in the first place: the private and affluent public "feeder" schools, the ever-growing parastructure of tutors and test-prep courses and enrichment programs, the whole admissions frenzy and everything that leads up to and away from it. The medium, as always, is the message. Before, after, and around the elite college classroom, a constellation of values is ceaselessly inculcated. As globalization sharpens economic insecurity, we are increasingly committing ourselves—as students, as parents, as a society—to a vast apparatus of educational advantage. With so many resources devoted to the business of elite academics and so many people scrambling for the limited space at the top of the ladder, it is worth asking what exactly it is you get in the end. What it is we all get, for the elite students of today, as their institutions never tire of reminding them, will be the leaders of society tomorrow.

The first disadvantage of an elite education, as I learned in my kitchen that day, is that it makes you incapable of talking to people who aren't exactly like you, for the simple reason that you never meet any of them. Elite schools pride themselves on their "diversity," but that diversity is almost entirely a matter of race. With respect to class, these schools are largely—indeed increasingly— homogeneous. Visit any elite campus in our great nation, and you can thrill to the heartwarming spectacle of the children of white businesspeople and professionals studying and playing alongside the children of black, Asian, and Latino businesspeople and professionals. At the same time, because these schools tend to cultivate liberal attitudes, they leave their students in the paradoxical position of wanting to advocate on behalf of the working class while being unable to hold a simple conversation with anyone in it. Witness the last two Democratic presidential nominees, Al Gore and John Kerry: one each from Harvard and Yale, both earnest, decent, intelligent men, both utterly incapable of communicating with the larger electorate.

But it's not just a matter of class. My education taught me to believe that people who didn't go to an Ivy League or equivalent school were not worth talking to, regardless of their class. I was given the unmistakable message that such people were beneath me. We were "the best and the brightest," as these places love to say, and everyone else was, well, something else: less good, less bright. I learned to give that understanding little nod, that slightly sympathetic "oh," when someone told me that they went to a less prestigious college. (If I had gone to Harvard, I would have learned to say "near

Boston" when I was asked where I went to school—the Cambridge version of noblesse oblige.) I never learned that there are smart people who don't go to elite colleges, often precisely for reasons of class. I never learned that there are smart people who don't go to college at all.

I also never learned that there are smart people who aren't "smart." The existence of multiple forms of intelligence has become a commonplace, but however much they like to sprinkle their incoming classes with a few actors or violinists, elite universities select for and develop one form of intelligence only: analytic. While this is broadly true of all universities, elite schools, precisely because their students (and faculty and administrators) possess this one form of intelligence to such a high degree, are more apt to ignore the value of others. One naturally prizes what one most possesses and most makes for one's advantages. But social intelligence and emotional intelligence and creative ability, to name just three, are not distributed preferentially among the educational elite. The "best" are the brightest only in one narrow sense. But one needs to wander away from that elite to begin to discover this.

What about people who aren't bright in any sense? I have a friend who went to Yale, but before that to a typically mediocre public high school. One of the values of going to such a school, she once remarked, is that it teaches you to relate to stupid people. Some people are smart in the elite-college way, some are smart in other ways, and some aren't smart at all. It should be an embarrassment not to know how to talk to any of them, if only because talking to people is the only real way of knowing them. Elite institutions are supposed to provide a humanistic education, but the first principle of humanism is Terence's: "nothing human is alien to me." The first disadvantage of an elite education is how very much of the human it alienates you from.

The second disadvantage, implicit in what I've been saying, is that an elite education inculcates a false sense of self-worth. Getting to an elite college, being at an elite college, and going on from an elite college all involve numerical rankings: SAT, GPA, GRE. You learn to think of yourself in terms of those numbers. They come to signify not only your fate, but your identity; not only your identity, but your value. It's been said that what those tests really measure is your ability to take tests, but even if they measure something real, it is only a small slice of the real. The problem begins when students are encouraged to forget that, when academic excellence becomes excellence in some absolute sense, when "better at X" becomes simply "better."

There is nothing wrong with taking pride in one's intellect or knowledge. There is something wrong with the smugness and self-congratulation that elite schools connive at from the moment the fat envelopes arrive in the mail. From orientation to graduation, the message is implicit in every tone of voice and tilt of the head, every old-school tradition, every speech from the dean. The message is, you have arrived. Welcome to the club. And the corollary is equally clear: you deserve everything your presence here is going to enable you to get. When people say that students at elite schools have a strong sense of entitlement, that is what they mean: the belief that you deserve more than other people because your SAT scores are higher.

At Yale, and no doubt elsewhere, the message is reinforced in embarrassingly literal terms. The physical form of the university—its quads and residential colleges, with their Gothic stone facades and wrought-iron portals—is constituted by the locked gate set into the encircling wall. Everyone carries around ID cards that determine which gates they can enter and which ones they can't. The gate, in other words, is a kind of governing metaphor, because the social form of the university, as is true of every elite school, is constituted the same way. Elite colleges are walled domains guarded by locked gates, with admission granted only to the elect. The aptitude with which students absorb this lesson is demonstrated by the avidity with which they erect still more gates within those gates, special realms of ever-greater exclusivity—at Yale, most obviously, the famous secret societies, or, as they should probably be called, the open-secret societies, since true secrecy would defeat their purpose. There is no point in excluding people if they don't know that they've been excluded.

One of the great errors of an elite education, then, is that it teaches you to think that measures of intelligence and academic achievement are measures of value in some moral or metaphysical sense. But they're not. Graduates of elite schools are not more valuable than stupid people, or talentless people, or even lazy people. Their pain does not hurt more. Their souls do not weigh more. If I were religious, I would say, God does not love them more. The political implications should be clear. As John Ruskin told an older elite, grabbing everything you can is not less wicked when you grab it with the power of your brains than it is when you grab it with the power of your fists. "Work must always be," he wrote, "and captains of work must always be," but "there is a wide difference between being captains . . . of work, and taking the profits of it."

Nor do the political implications stop there. An elite education not only ushers you into the upper classes; it trains you for the life that you will lead once you get there. I didn't understand this until I began to compare my experience, and even more, my students' experience, with the experience of a friend who went to Cleveland State. There are due dates and attendance requirements at places like Yale, but no one takes them very seriously. Extensions are available for the asking; threats to deduct credit for missed classes are rarely, if ever, carried out. In other words, students at places like Yale get an endless string of second chances. Not so at places like Cleveland State. My friend got a D in a class in which she'd been running an A because she was coming off a waitressing shift and had to hand in her term paper an hour late.

That may be an extreme example, but it is unthinkable at an elite school. Just as unthinkably, she had no one to appeal to. Students at places like Cleveland State, unlike those at places like Yale, don't have platoons of advisers and tutors and deans to write out excuses for late work, give them extra help when they need it, pick them up when they fall down. They get their education wholesale, from an indifferent bureaucracy, not handed to them in individually wrapped packages by smiling clerks. There are few, if any, opportunities for the kinds of contacts I saw my students get routinely—classes with visiting power brokers, dinners with foreign dignitaries. There are also few, if any, of the kinds of special funds that, at places like Yale, are available in profusion: travel stipends, research fellowships, performance grants. Each year, my department awards dozens of cash prizes for everything from freshman essays to senior projects. This year, those awards came to over $80,000—in just one department.

Students at places like Cleveland State also don't get A minuses just for doing the work. There has been a lot of hand-wringing lately over grade inflation, and it is a scandal, but the most scandalous thing about it is how uneven it has been. Forty years ago, the average GPA at both public and private universities was about 2.6. Since then, it's gone up everywhere, but not by anything like the same amount. The average GPA at public universities is now about 3.0, a B; at private universities, it's about 3.3, just short of a B+. And at most of the Ivies, it's closer to 3.4. But there are always students who do not do the work, or who are taking a class outside their field (for fun, or to fulfill a requirement), or who aren't up to standard to start with (athletes, legacies). At a school like Yale, the typical student who comes to class and works hard expects nothing less than an A–. And most of the time, they get it.

In short, the way that students are treated in college prepares them for the social position they will occupy once they get out. At schools like Cleveland State, they're being prepared for positions somewhere in the middle of the class system, in the depths of one bureaucracy or another. They're being conditioned for lives with few second chances, no extensions, little support, narrow opportunity—lives of subordination, supervision, and control, lives of deadlines, not guidelines. At places like Yale, of course, it is the reverse. The elite likes to think of itself as a meritocracy, but that is true only up to a point. Getting through the gate is very difficult, but once you're in, there's almost nothing you can do to get kicked out. Not the most abject academic failure, not the most heinous act of plagiarism, not even threatening a fellow student with bodily harm—I've witnessed or heard of all three—will get you expelled. The feeling is that, by gosh, it just wouldn't be fair—in other words, the self-protectiveness of the old boys' club, even if it now includes girls. Elite schools certainly nurture excellence, but they also nurture what a former Yale instructor I know referred to as "entitled mediocrity." A is the mark of excellence; A– is the mark of entitled mediocrity. It's another one of those metaphors, not so much a grade as a promise. It means, don't worry, we'll take care of you.

Here, too, college reflects the way things work in the adult world (unless it is the other way around). For the elite, there is always another chance (a bailout, a pardon, a stint in rehab), always plenty of contacts and special stipends (the country club, the conference, the year-end bonus, the dividend). If Al Gore and John Kerry represent one of the characteristic products of an elite education, George W. Bush represents another. It is no coincidence that our current president, the apotheosis of entitled mediocrity, went to Yale. Entitled mediocrity is indeed the operating principle of his administration, but as Enron and WorldCom and the other scandals of the dot-com meltdown demonstrated, it is also the operating principle of corporate America. The fat salaries paid to underperforming CEOs are an adult version of the A–. Anyone who remembers the injured sanctimony with which Ken Lay, the CEO of Enron, greeted the notion that he should be held accountable for his actions will understand the mentality in question—the belief that once you're in the club, you've got a God-given right to stay in the club. But you don't need to remember Ken Lay, because the whole dynamic played out again last year in the case of Scooter Libby, another Yale man.

If one of the disadvantages of an elite education is the temptation it offers to mediocrity, another is the temptation it offers to security. When parents explain why they work so hard to give their children the best possible education, they invariably say, because of the opportunities it opens up. But what of the opportunities it shuts down? An elite education gives you the opportunity to be rich—which is, after all, what we're talking about—but it takes away the opportunity not to be. Yet the opportunity not to be rich is one of the greatest opportunities with which young Americans have been blessed. We live in a society that is itself so wealthy that it can afford to provide a decent living to whole classes of people who in other countries exist (or in earlier times existed) on the brink of poverty, or at least, of indignity. You can live decently in the United States as a teacher, or a community organizer, or a civil rights lawyer—that is, by any reasonable definition of decency. You have to live in an ordinary house instead of an apartment in Manhattan or a mansion in LA; you have to drive a Honda instead of a BMW or a Hummer; you have to vacation in Florida instead of Barbados or Paris, but what are such losses when set against the opportunity to do work you believe in, work you are suited for, work you love, every day of your life?

Yet it is precisely that opportunity that an elite education takes away. How can I be a teacher—wouldn't that be a waste of my expensive education? Wouldn't I be squandering the opportunities my parents worked so hard to provide? What will my friends think? How will I face my classmates at our twentieth reunion, when they're all rich lawyers or important people in New York? And the question that lies behind all these: Isn't it beneath me? So a whole universe of possibility closes, and you miss your true calling.

This is not to say that students from elite colleges never pursue a riskier or less lucrative course after graduation, but even when they do, they are apt to give up more quickly than others. This would not seem to make sense, especially since such students tend to graduate with less debt and are more likely to be able to float by on family money for a while. I wasn't aware of the phenomenon myself until I heard about it from a couple of graduate students in my department, one from Yale College, one from Harvard. They were talking about trying to write poetry, how college friends had called it quits within a year or two while people they knew from less prestigious schools were still at it. So why should this be? Because students from elite schools expect success, and they expect it now. They have, by definition, never experienced anything else; their whole identities have been constituted around their ability to succeed. The idea of not being successful terrifies them, disorients them, defeats them. They've been driven their whole lives by a fear of failure— often, in the first instance, by their parents' fear of failure. The first time that I blew a test, I walked out of the room feeling like I no longer knew who I was. The second time, it was easier; I had started to learn that failure isn't the end of the world.

But if you're afraid to fail, you're afraid to take risks, which begins to explain the final and most damning disadvantage of an elite education: that it is profoundly anti-intellectual. This will seem counterintuitive. Aren't kids at elite schools the smartest ones around, at least in the narrow academic sense? Don't they work harder than anyone else—indeed, than any previous generation? They are. They do. But being an intellectual is not the same as being smart. Being an intellectual means more than doing your homework. If so few kids come to college understanding this, it is no wonder. They are products of a system that rarely asked them to think about anything bigger than the next assignment, that forgot to teach them, along the way to the prestige admissions and the lucrative jobs, that the most important achievements can't be measured by a letter or a number or a name. That forgot that the true purpose of education is to make minds, not careers.

Being an intellectual means, first of all, being passionate about ideas— and not just for the duration of a semester, for the sake of pleasing the teacher or getting an A. A friend who teaches at a branch campus of the University of Connecticut once complained to me that his students don't think for themselves. Well, I said, Yale students think for themselves, but only because they know we want them to. I've had many wonderful students at Yale and Columbia, bright, thoughtful, creative kids whom it's been a pleasure to talk with and learn from. But most of them have seemed content to color within the lines their education had marked out for them. Only a small minority have seen their education as part of a larger intellectual journey, have approached the work of the mind with a pilgrim soul. And they've tended to feel like freaks, not least because they have gotten so little support from the university itself. Places like Yale, as one of them put it to me, are not conducive to searchers.

Places like Yale, in other words, are simply not set up to help students ask the big questions. I don't believe there ever was a golden age of intellectualism in the American university, but in the nineteenth century, students might at least have had a chance of hearing such questions raised in chapel or in the literary societies and debating clubs that flourished on campus. Throughout much of the twentieth century, with the growth of the ideal of liberal education in American colleges, they might have encountered them in the classrooms of professors possessed of a strong sense of pedagogic mission. Instructors like that still exist in this country, but the increasingly dire exigencies of academic professionalization have made them all but extinct at elite universities. Professors at top research institutions are valued exclusively for the quality of their scholarly work; time spent on teaching is time lost. If students want a conversion experience, they're better off at a liberal arts college.

No, when elite universities boast that they teach their students how to think, they mean that they teach them the analytic and rhetorical skills necessary for success in law or medicine or science or business. But a liberal arts education is supposed to mean something more than that, as universities still dimly feel. So when students get to college, they hear a couple of speeches urging them to ask the big questions, and when they graduate, they hear a couple of more speeches urging them to ask the big questions. And in between, they spend four years taking courses that train them to ask the little questions—specialized courses, taught by specialized professors, aimed at specialized students. For although the notion of breadth is implicit in the very idea of a liberal arts education, the admissions process increasingly selects for kids who have already begun to think of themselves in specialized terms—the junior journalist, the budding astronomer, the language prodigy. We are slouching, even at elite schools, toward a glorified form of vocational training.

Indeed, that seems to be exactly what those schools desire. There's a reason that elite schools speak of training "leaders" rather than thinkers. An independent mind is independent of all allegiances, and elite schools, which receive a large percentage of their funds in the form of alumni donations, are strongly invested in fostering institutional loyalty. As another friend, a third-generation Yalie, once remarked, the purpose of Yale College is to manufacture Yale alumni. But for the system to work, those alumni need money. At Yale, the long-term drift of students away from majors in the humanities and basic sciences toward more practical ones like computer science and economics has been abetted by administrative indifference. The college career office has little to say to students not interested in law, medicine, or business, and elite universities are certainly not going to do anything to discourage the large percentage of their graduates who take their degrees to Wall Street.

Being an intellectual begins with thinking your way outside of your assumptions and the system that enforces them. But since students who win admission to elite schools are precisely the ones who have best learned to work within the system, it is very difficult for them to see outside it, to see that it is even there. Long before they got to college, they transformed themselves into world-class hoop-jumpers and teacher-pleasers, getting A's in every class no matter how boring they found the teacher or how pointless the subject, racking up ten or twelve extracurricular activities no matter what else they wanted to do with their time. Paradoxically, the situation may be better at second-tier schools, and in particular, again, at liberal arts colleges, than at the most prestigious universities. Some students end up at second-tier schools because they're exactly like students at Harvard or Yale, only less gifted or driven. But others end up there because they are more independent of spirit. They didn't get straight A's because they couldn't be bothered to give everything in every class (or they did, but decided to pass on the Ivies anyway). They concentrated on the ones that meant the most to them, or a single strong extracurricular passion, or projects that had nothing to do with school or even looking good on a college application. Maybe they just sat in their room, reading a lot. These are the kinds of kids who are likely, once they get to college, to be more interested in the human spirit than in school spirit, and to think about leaving college bearing questions, not résumés.

I've been struck, during my time at Yale, by how similar all the students look. You hardly see any hippies or punks or art-school types, and at a college that was known in the '80s as the "Gay Ivy," few out lesbians and no gender queers. The geeks don't look that geeky; the fashionable kids go in for understated elegance. Thirty-two flavors, all of them vanilla. Elite schools have become places of a narrow and suffocating conformity. Everyone feels pressure to maintain the kind of appearance—and affect—that go with achievement. (Dress for success, medicate for success.) I know from long experience as an adviser that not every Yale student is perfectly well-adjusted, which is exactly why it worries me that so many of them act as if they were. The tyranny of normalcy must be very heavy in their lives. One consequence is that those who can't get with the program (and they tend to be students from poorer backgrounds) often polarize in the opposite direction, flying off into extremes of disaffection and self-destruction. But another has to do with the large majority who can.

I taught a class several years ago in the literature of friendship. One day, we were discussing Virginia Woolf's *The Waves*, which follows a group of friends from childhood to middle age. In high school, one of them falls in love with another boy. He thinks, "To whom can I expose the urgency of my own passion? . . . There is nobody—here among these grey arches, and moaning pigeons, and cheerful games and tradition and emulation, all so skillfully organized to prevent feeling alone." A pretty good description of an elite college campus, including the part about never being allowed to feel alone. What did my students think of this, I wanted to know. What does it mean to go to school at a place where you're never alone? Well, one of them said, I do feel uncomfortable sitting in my room by myself. Even when I have to write a paper, I'll do it at a friend's. Another asked, why would anybody want to be alone? What can you do by yourself that you can't do with someone else?

So there they were: one young person who had lost the capacity for solitude and another who couldn't see the point of it. The ability to engage in introspection, I put it to my students that day, is the essential precondition for living the life of the mind, and the essential precondition for introspection is solitude. They took this in for a second, then one of them said, with a dawning sense of self-awareness, "So are you saying that we're all just, like, really excellent sheep?" Well, I don't know. But I do know that the life of the mind is lived one mind at a time: one solitary, skeptical, resistant mind at a time, and the best place to cultivate it is not within an educational system whose real purpose is to reproduce the class system.

The schools that produced the likes of John Kerry and George Bush are indeed giving us our next generation of leaders. The kid who's loading up on AP courses junior year, the kid who's double majoring while editing three campus publications, the kid whom everybody wants at their school but nobody wants in their classroom, the kid who doesn't have a minute to breathe, let alone think, will eventually be running a corporation or an institution or a government. She will have many achievements but little experience, great success but no vision. The disadvantage of an elite education is that it's given us the elite we have, and the elite we're going to have.

[2008]

THE NEOLIBERAL ARTS

I recently spent a semester at an elite liberal arts college. At prominent points around the campus, in hopeful shades of yellow and green, banners displayed the following pair of texts. The first was attributed to the institution's founder, which dates it to the 1920s. The second was said to have been extracted from the latest version of its mission statement:

> The paramount obligation of a college is to develop in its students the ability to think clearly and independently, and the ability to live confidently, courageously, and hopefully.

> leadership
> service
> integrity
> creativity

Let us take a moment to compare the two. The first thing to observe about the older one is that it is a sentence. It expresses an idea by placing concepts in relation to one another within the structure of a syntax. It is, moreover, a carefully crafted sentence: a parallel structure underscored by repetition, five adverbs balanced two against three.

A spatial arrangement, the sentence also implies a temporal sequence. Thinking clearly, it wants us to recognize, leads to thinking independently. Thinking independently leads to living confidently. Living confidently leads to living courageously. Living courageously leads to living hopefully. And the sequence begins with a college that recognizes that it has an obligation to its students, an obligation to develop their abilities to think and live.

Lastly, the sentence is attributed to an individual. It expresses her convictions and ideals. It announces that she is prepared to hold herself accountable for certain responsibilities.

The second text is not a sentence. It is four words floating in space, unconnected to each other or to any other concept. Four words—four slogans, really—whose meaning and function are left undefined, available for whatever interpretation the reader cares to project onto them.

Four slogans, three of which—"leadership," "service," and "creativity"—are the loudest buzzwords in contemporary higher education. ("Integrity" is presumably intended as a synonym for the more familiar "character," which for colleges at this point means nothing more than not cheating.) The text is not the statement of an individual; it is the emanation of a bureaucracy. In this case, a literally anonymous bureaucracy, for no one (including the president and the dean of faculty) could tell me when this version of the institution's mission statement was formulated or by whom. No one could even tell me who had decided to hang those banners up around the campus. The words had just appeared, as if enunciated by the zeitgeist.

But the most important thing to note about the second text is what it doesn't talk about: thinking or learning. Both in what it does and doesn't say, it therefore constitutes an apt reflection of the current state of higher education. College is seldom about thinking or learning anymore. Everyone is running around trying to figure out what it is about. So far, they have come up with buzzwords, mainly those three.

This is education in the age of neoliberalism. Call it Reaganism or Thatcherism, economism or market fundamentalism, neoliberalism is an ideology that reduces all values to money values. The worth of a thing is the price of the thing. The worth of a person is the wealth of the person. Neoliberalism tells you that you are valuable exclusively in terms of your activity in the marketplace—in Wordsworth's phrase, your getting and spending.

The purpose of education in a neoliberal age is to produce producers. I wrote a book last year that said that elite American universities no longer provide their students, by and large, with what I called a real education, one that addresses them as complete human beings rather than as future specialists—that enables them, as I put it, to build a self or (following John Keats) become a soul. Of all the responses the book elicited, the most dismaying was this: that so many individuals associated with those institutions said not, "Of course we provide our students with a real education," but rather, "What is this 'real education' nonsense, anyway?"

A representative example came from Steven Pinker, the Harvard psychologist:

> Perhaps I am emblematic of everything that is wrong with elite American education, but I have no idea how to get my students to build a self or become a soul. It isn't taught in graduate school, and in the hundreds of faculty appointments and promotions I have participated in, we've never evaluated a candidate on how well he or she could accomplish it.

Pinker is correct. He *is* emblematic of everything that is wrong with elite American education. David Brooks, responding both to Pinker and myself, laid out the matter very clearly. College, he noted, has three potential purposes: the commercial (preparing to start a career), the cognitive (learning stuff, or better, learning how to think), and the moral (the purpose that Pinker and his ilk find so mysterious). "Moral," here, does not mean learning right from wrong. It means developing the ability to make autonomous choices—to determine your own beliefs, independent of parents, peers, and society. To live confidently, courageously, and hopefully.

Only the commercial purpose now survives as a recognized value. Even the cognitive purpose, which one would think should be the center of a college education, is tolerated only in so far as it contributes to the first. Everybody knows that the percentage of students majoring in English has plummeted since the 1960s. But the percentage majoring in the physical sciences—physics, chemistry, geology, astronomy, and so forth—has fallen even farther, some 60 percent. As of 2012, only 1.5 percent of students graduated with a degree in one of those subjects, and only 1.1 percent in math. At most colleges, the lion's share of students major in vocational fields: business, communications, education, health. But even at elite institutions, the most popular majors are the practical, or as Brooks might say, the commercial ones: economics, biology, engineering, and computer science.

It is not the humanities per se that are under attack. It is learning as such: learning for its own sake, curiosity for its own sake, ideas for their own sake. It is the liberal arts, but understood in their true meaning, as all of those fields in which knowledge is pursued as an end in itself, the sciences and social sciences as well. History majors endure the same kind of ritual hazing ("Oh, so you decided to go for the big bucks") as do people who major in French or philosophy, and so do sociology and political science majors. Everybody talks about STEM—science, technology, engineering, and math—but no one's really interested in science, and no one's really interested math: interested in funding them, interested in having their kids or their constituents pursue a career in them. So that leaves technology and engineering, which means (since the second is a subset of the first) it leaves technology.

As for the moral purpose, the notion that college might prepare you for the whole of life by inciting you to contemplation and reflection, it is typically dismissed with one of two historical arguments. The first attributes the idea to the 1960s. The hippies may have been into that sort of navel-gazing, but kids today are too wised-up to fall for it. The second relegates it to the nineteenth century. Liberal education was a luxury of the leisured class, the WASP aristocracy. When people from the lower reaches of society began to go to college in the twentieth century, they went so they could climb the economic ladder.

Needless to say, these criticisms cannot both be true, because they contradict each other. In fact, neither is, though each contains a piece of truth. The moral purpose was important in the '60s, and it was important in the nineteenth century. But it was also important between and before. It was important from the beginning of higher education in America. Most early American colleges were founded as church-affiliated institutions; molding students' character was their primary aim. The mission was largely secularized across the late nineteenth and early twentieth centuries, but it was not abandoned. That is why we have, or had, Great Books courses and other humanities and "general education" sequences and requirements. That is why colleges established English departments, began to teach Shakespeare and Hawthorne: precisely to create a liberal curriculum for students who did not come from the WASP aristocracy and had not studied Latin and Greek.

As the country moved to mass higher education—through the Land Grant Acts of 1862 and 1890, through the G.I. Bill, through the postwar explosion of public colleges and universities—the idea of a liberal education was carried right along. The heyday of public higher ed, the 1960s, *was* the heyday of the liberal arts. If those middle- and working-class kids were going to college just to get a better job, why were so many of them majoring in English? Because they also wanted to learn, think, reflect, and grow. They wanted what the WASP aristocrats had gotten, and the country was wise enough, or generous enough, or egalitarian enough, to let them have it.

A different version of the "nineteenth century" argument was made by Joshua Rothman in the *New Yorker*. When I complain about the admissions process at elite colleges, which turns the whole of childhood and adolescence into a high-stakes, twelve-year sprint, what I'm really complaining about, he said, is modernity. We're all going faster and faster, and have been for two hundred years. Students are no exception.

Rothman is wrong, but he is wrong in an illuminating way. Modernity *is* an age of ever-increasing acceleration, but only, until lately, for adults. For the young, modernity means—or rather, meant—something different. The modern age, in fact, invented the notion of youth as an interval between childhood and adulthood, and it invented it as a time of unique privileges and obligations. From the Romantics, at the dawn of modernity, all the way through the counterculture of the 1960s and '70s, the young were understood to have a special role: to step outside the world and question it. To change it, with whatever opposition from adults. (Hence the association of youth and revolution, another modern institution.) As college became common as a stage of life—one that coincided, not coincidentally, with the beginning of youth—it naturally incorporated that idea. It was the time to think about the world as it existed, and the world that you wanted to make.

But we no longer have the youth of modernity. Now we have the youth of postmodernity. The youth, in other words, of neoliberalism. Students rarely any longer get the chance to question and reflect—not about their lives, and certainly not about the world. Modernity understood itself as a condition of constant flux, which is precisely why the historical mission of youth in every generation was to imagine a way forward to a different state. But moving forward to a different state is a possibility that neoliberalism excludes. Neoliberalism believes that we have reached "the end of history," a steady-state condition of free-market capitalism that will go on replicating itself forever. The historical mission of youth is no longer desirable or even conceivable. The world is not going to change, so we don't need young people to imagine how it might.

All we need them to do, as Rothman rightly says, is to start running faster and faster, so that by the time they finish college, they can make the leap into the rat race. Youth, now, is nothing more than a preliminary form of adulthood, and the quiet desperation of middle age has been imported backward into adolescence. (If Arthur Miller had been at work today, it would have been *Death of a Senior*.) And as everybody knows by now, it isn't just postmodern youth; it is also postmodern childhood—for children, too, increasingly are miniature adults, chasing endlessly for rank and status.

This is not inevitable. This is the result of choices we have made, driven by an ideology that we have allowed to impose itself upon us. And we are all complicit. "So you decided to go for the big bucks," "What are you going to do with that?": the thing I find so striking about those kinds of comments is not that people make them, but that they seem to feel compelled to make them. It's as if we'd all decided, by unspoken consent, to police our children's aspirations. When an adult asks a college student what they're going to do with that, the question that we ought to ask is what's at stake for the *adult*.

I wrote a book about elite higher education in America, but if I could summarize the correspondence I've received in response, I would do so like this: it's not just *elite* higher education; it's not just *higher* education; and it's not just America. I still believe that the selective admissions process is a uniquely baleful institution with uniquely baleful consequences, that liberal arts colleges are apt to do a better job of providing a real education than research universities, and that there is no necessary correlation between institutional prestige and educational quality. But the most important problems that I talk about are everywhere, at every level: at small regional colleges and large state universities, at prep schools and public high schools, at grade schools and community colleges, in Canada, Britain, Korea, Brazil. They are everywhere, because neoliberalism is everywhere.

We see its shadow in the relentless focus on "basic skills" in K–12, as if knowledge were simply an assemblage of methods and facts. In the move to "informational" texts in high school English classes, as if the purpose of learning to read were to understand a memo. In our various testing regimes, as if all learning could be quantified. In the frenzy of the MOOCs, as if education were nothing more than information transfer. In the tables that rank colleges and majors by average starting salary, as if earning power were the only thing you got from school.

We see it in the rhetoric of politicians, who have lately adopted a kind of fill-in-the-blank formulation when it comes to the purpose of public universities. Marco Rubio has said that we need welders, not philosophy majors.

Matt Bevin, the governor of Kentucky, that we need engineers, not French majors. Rick Scott, the governor of Florida, that we don't need anthropology majors. Pat McCrory, the former governor of North Carolina, that we don't need gender studies majors. Nor is this kind of talk confined to conservatives; Barack Obama has essentially said that we don't need art history majors. But the prize goes to Scott Walker, who attempted to rewrite the mission statement of the University of Wisconsin, one of the country's greatest public systems, to strike language about public service and improving the human condition and to delete the phrase, "Basic to every purpose of the system is the search for truth." Instead, the university's exclusive mission would henceforth be to "meet the state's workforce needs."

A couple of years ago, I sat down with the newly appointed president of a top-ten liberal arts college. He had come from a professional school (law, in his case), as so many college deans and presidents now seem to do.

I started by telling him that I had just visited an upper-level class, and that no one there had been able to give me a decent definition of "leadership," even though the college trumpeted the term at every opportunity. He declined to offer one himself. Instead he said, a bit belligerently, "I've been here five months, and no one has been able to give me a satisfactory definition of the liberal arts."

I offered the one I supplied above: the liberal arts are those fields in which knowledge is pursued for its own sake. When you study the liberal arts, I added, what you are principally learning to do is make arguments.

"Scientists don't make arguments," he said (a statement that would've come as a surprise to the scientists on the faculty). "And what about painters? *They* don't make arguments."

I tried to explain the difference between the fine and liberal arts (the latter are "arts" only by an accident of derivation), but with little success. "So what do *you* think the college should be about?" I finally asked him.

"Leadership," he said.

If college is seldom about thinking and learning anymore, that's because very few people are interested in thinking and learning, least of all students. As Richard Arum and Josipa Roksa report in *Academically Adrift: Limited Learning on College Campuses*, the number of hours per week that students spend studying for their classes has been falling steadily for decades and is now about half of what it was in 1961. And as anyone associated with a college can tell you, ambitious undergraduates devote the bulk of their time and energy, and certainly of their passion, to extracurriculars. Pinker, in the response I mentioned, wonders why he finds himself addressing half-empty lecture halls. I can tell him why: because his students don't much care about the things he's trying to teach them.

Why should they, given the messages that they've received about their education? The college classroom does or ought to do one thing particularly well, which is to teach you to think analytically. That is why a rigorous college education requires you to be as smart as possible and think as hard as possible, and why it's good at training you for those professions that demand the same: law, medicine, finance, consulting, science, and academia itself. Nor is it an accident that the first four of those (the four that also happen to be lucrative) are the top choices among graduates of the most selective schools.

But business, broadly speaking, does not require you to be as smart as possible or think as hard as possible. It's good to be smart, and it's good to think hard, but you needn't be extremely smart or think extremely hard. Instead, you need a different set of skills: organizational skills, people skills—things that professors and their classes aren't particularly good at teaching.

So as college is increasingly understood in terms of job and career, and job and career increasingly mean business, especially entrepreneurship (in this age that idealizes the entrepreneur), students have developed a parallel curriculum for themselves, a parallel college, where they can get the skills they think they really need. Those extracurriculars that students are deserting the classroom for are less and less what Pinker denigrates as "recreational" and more and more oriented toward future employment: entrepreneurial endeavors, nonprofit ventures, various forms of volunteerism and employment. The big thing now on campuses—or rather, off them—is internships.

All of which explains a new kind of unhappiness I sense among professors. There are a lot of things about being an academic that basically suck: the committee work, the petty politics, the endless slog for tenure and promotion, the relentless status competition. What makes it all worthwhile, for many people, is the vigorous intellectual dialogue you get to have with vibrant young minds. But now that kind of contact is increasingly unusual. Not because students are dumber than they used to be, but because so few of them approach their studies with a sense of intellectual mission. College is a way, learning is a way, of getting somewhere else. Students will come to your office—rushing from one activity, rushing off to the next—to find out what they need to do to get a better grade. Very few will seek you out to talk about ideas in an open-ended way. Professors, many of them, do still deeply care about thinking and learning. But they often find that they're the only ones.

They certainly cannot count on much support from their administrations. In this age of the customer-service mentality in academia, colleges are falling all over themselves to give their students what they think they think they want. Which means that they are trying to retrofit an institution that was designed to teach analytic skills—and, not incidentally, provide young people with an opportunity to reflect upon the big questions—for an age that wants a very different set of things. That is how the president of a top liberal arts college can end up telling me that he's not interested in the liberal arts but is interested in leadership. That is why, around the country, even as they cut departments, starve the liberal arts, freeze professorial salaries, and turn their classrooms over to adjuncts, colleges and universities are establishing centers and offices and institutes, and hiring coordinators and deanlets, and launching initiatives, and creating courses and programs, for the inculcation of leadership, the promotion of service, and the fostering of creativity. They, like their students, are busy constructing a parallel college. What will happen to the old one now is anybody's guess.

So what's so bad about leadership, service, and creativity? What's bad about them is that, as they're understood on campus and beyond, they are all encased in neoliberal assumptions. Neoliberalism, which dovetails perfectly with meritocracy, is ultimately a caste system: "winners and losers," "makers and takers," "the best and the brightest," the whole gospel of Ayn Rand and her Übermenschen. That's what "leadership" is finally about. There are leaders, and then there is everyone else: the led, presumably—the followers, the little people. Leaders get things done; leaders take command. When colleges promise to make their students leaders, they're telling them they're going to be in charge.

"Service" is what the winners engage in when they find themselves in a benevolent mood. Call it Clintonism, by analogy with Reaganism. Bill Clinton not only ratified the neoliberal consensus as president; he has extended its logic as a former president. Reaganism means the rich have all the money, as well as all the power. Clintonism means they use their money and power, or a bit of it, to help the less fortunate—because the less fortunate (i.e., the losers) can't help themselves. Hence the Clinton Foundation, hence every philanthropic or altruistic endeavor on the part of highly privileged, highly credentialed, highly resourced elites, including all those nonprofits or socially conscious for-profits that college students start or dream of starting.

"Creativity," meanwhile, is basically a business concept, one that is aligned with the other clichés that have come to us from the management schools by way of Silicon Valley: "disruption," "innovation," "transformation." "Creativity" is not about becoming an artist. No one wants you to become an artist. It's about devising "innovative" products, services, and techniques—"solutions," which imply that you already know the problem. "Creativity" means design thinking, as the writer Amy Whitaker has put it, not art thinking: getting from A to a predetermined B, not engaging in an open-ended exploratory process, in the course of which you discover the B.

Students often say they want to change the world, but what kind of change are they talking about? What kind of change are their colleges preparing them to make? Leadership, service, and creativity do not mean fundamental change—remember, fundamental change is out in neoliberalism—they mean technological or technocratic change within a static social framework, within a market framework. Which is really too bad, because the biggest challenges we face, including climate change, will require nothing less than fundamental change, a new organization of society. If we have ever needed young people to imagine a different world, it is now.

We have always been, in the United States, what Lionel Trilling called a business civilization. But we have also always had a range of counterbalancing institutions, countercultural institutions, to advance a different set of values: the churches, the arts, the democratic tradition itself. When the pendulum has swung too far in one direction (and it is always the same direction), new institutions or movements arise, or old ones renew their mission. Education in general, and higher education in particular, has always been one of those institutions. But now the market has become so powerful that it is swallowing the very things that are supposed to restrain it. Artists are becoming "creatives." Journalism has become "the media." Government is bought and paid for. The prosperity gospel has arisen as one of the most prominent movements in American Christianity. And colleges and universities are acting like businesses, and in the service of businesses.

What is to be done? Those very same WASP aristocrats—enough of them, at least, including several presidents of Harvard and Yale—when facing the failure of their own class in the form of the Great Depression, succeeded in superseding themselves and creating a new system, the meritocracy we live with now. But I'm not sure we possess the moral resources to do something comparable. The WASPs had been taught that leadership meant putting the collective good ahead of your own. But meritocracy means looking out for number one, and neoliberalism does not believe in the collective. As Margaret Thatcher famously put it, "there's no such thing" as society. "There are individual men and women, and there are families." As for elite university presidents, they are little more these days than lackeys of the plutocracy, with all the moral stature of the butler in a country house.

Neoliberalism disarms us in another sense, as well. For all its talk of freedom and individual initiative, it is remarkably good at inculcating a sense of helplessness. So much of the rhetoric around college today, and so much of the negative response to my suggestion that students worry less about pursuing wealth and more about constructing a sense of purpose for themselves, bespeak the idea that young people, that all people, are the passive objects of economic forces. That they have no agency, no options. That they have to do what the market tells them. A Princeton student literally made this argument to me. If the market is incentivizing me to go to Wall Street, he said, then who am I to argue?

I have also had the pleasure, since my book came out, of hearing from a lot of people who are pushing back against the dictates of neoliberal education: starting high schools, starting colleges, creating alternatives to high school and college, making documentaries, launching nonprofits, parenting in different ways, conducting their lives in different ways. I welcome these efforts, but if these are all we do, then we are ultimately perpetuating the fundamental problem, which is that we no longer believe in public solutions. We only believe in market solutions, or at least, private-sector solutions: one-at-a-time solutions, individual solutions.

The worst thing about "leadership," the notion that society should be run by highly trained elites, is that it has usurped the place of "citizenship," the notion that it should be run by everyone together. Citizenship, not coincidentally—the creation of an informed populace for the sake of maintaining a free society, a self-governing society—was long the guiding principle of education in the United States. To escape from neoliberal education, we must escape from neoliberalism. Instead of treating higher education as a commodity, we need to treat it as a right. Instead of seeing it in terms of market purposes, we need to see it once again in terms of public purposes. That means resurrecting one of the great achievements of postwar society: free, high-quality mass public higher education. An end to the artificial scarcity of educational resources. An end to the idea that students must compete for the privilege of going to a decent college, and that they then must pay for it.

The liberal arts—specifically, who gets to study them—are a political issue, not merely a cultural one. To deprive individuals of a liberal education, of the chance to learn about and reflect upon the most important questions of personal and public value in a rigorous and systematic way, is to effectively exclude them from the fields of consciousness: the professions that shape the way we think and therefore the way that society looks—journalism, publishing, the media, law, public policy, the arts, entertainment, and education itself, particularly higher education. It is to exclude them from the possibility of full political participation. Marco Rubio himself was a political science major, and so was Barack Obama. Matt Bevin was an East Asian studies major. Monopolizing access to liberal education is one of the ways that privileged groups defend their privilege. Or as Woodrow Wilson put it: "We want one class of persons to have a liberal education, and we want another class . . . very much larger . . . to forgo the privilege of a liberal education and fit themselves to perform specific difficult manual tasks." Substitute "technical" for "manual," and the sentiment is precisely the same today. It is not the advocates of a liberal education who are the elitists; it is those who would reserve it for the lucky few.

Earl Shorris was an American writer and social critic who founded the Clemente Course in the Humanities, a yearlong program in Western literature and philosophy, since widely emulated, for poor adults in New York City. He did not do it for cultural reasons. "The way out of poverty was politics," he later wrote, "[b]ut to enter the public world, to practice the political life, the poor had first to learn to reflect." It is no coincidence, Shorris noted, that politics (or, as we might call it, democracy) and reflection (or, as we might call it, philosophy) began in Athens at the same time. But, he added, "to open this avenue to reflection and politics a major distinction between the preparation for the life of the rich and the life of the poor had to be eliminated." Or as the matter was put by Robert Maynard Hutchins, longtime president of the University of Chicago, founder of the organization that would later become the Public Broadcasting System, and a great believer in mass democratic education, "The best education for the best is the best education for all."

[2015]

The Defunding of the American Mind

One day some years ago when I was still at Yale, I was approached by a student who was interested in going to graduate school. She had her eye on Columbia, where I had gone myself. Did I know someone there she could talk to? I did indeed, an old professor of mine. When I wrote to make the introduction, however, he refused to even meet with her. "I won't talk to students about graduate school anymore," he explained. "Grad school is a suicide mission."

While my old professor's policy may be extreme, his feeling is universal. Most faculty members I know are willing to talk to students about pursuing a PhD, but their advice comes down to three words: don't do it. My own was never that absolute. Go if you feel that your happiness depends on it, I'd say—it can be a great experience—but be aware of what you're signing up for. You're going to be in school for at least seven years, probably more like nine, and there's a very good chance that you won't get a job at the end of it.

At Yale, in an English department that was perennially ranked in the top ten, we were overjoyed if half our graduating students found positions. That's right—half. Imagine running a medical school on that basis. As Christopher Newfield points out in *Unmaking the Public University*, that's the kind of unemployment rate you'd expect to find among inner-city high school dropouts. And this was before the financial collapse. Since then, the market's been a bloodbath—often only a handful of jobs in a given field, sometimes fewer, and, as always, hundreds of people competing for each.

It wasn't supposed to be like this. When I started graduate school in 1989, we were assured that the disastrous job market of the previous two decades would be coming to an end, because the large cohort of professors who had started their careers in the 1960s, when the postwar boom and the baby boom combined to more than double college enrollments, was going to start retiring. Well, it did, but things kept getting worse. Instead of replacing those retirees with new tenure-track hires, departments shifted the teaching load to part-time instructors: adjuncts, postdocs, graduate students. From 1991 to 2003, the number of full-time faculty members increased by 18 percent, but the number of part-timers increased by 87 percent, to almost half of the entire faculty.

But as Jack Schuster and Martin Finkelstein point out in *The American Faculty*, the move to part-time labor is already an old story. Less visible but equally important has been the advent and rapid expansion of full-time positions that are *not* tenure-track. No one talks about this transformation—the creation of yet another academic underclass—yet as far back as 1993, such positions already constituted the majority of new hires. As of 2003, more than a third of *full*-time faculty were working off the tenure track. By then, tenure-track professors—the "normal" kind of academic appointment—represented no more than 35 percent of the American faculty.

The reasons for these trends can be expressed in a single word, or buzz-word: efficiency. Contingent academic labor, as non-tenure-track faculty, part-time and full-time, are formally known, is cheaper to hire and easier to fire. It saves departments money and gives them greater flexibility in staffing courses. Over the last twenty years, in other words—or really, over the last forty—what's happened in academia is what's happened throughout the American economy. Good, secure, well-paying positions—tenured appointments in the academy, union jobs on the factory floor—are being replaced by temporary, low-wage employment.

You would think that departments would respond to the Somme-like conditions that they are sending out their newly minted PhDs to face by cutting down the size of their graduate programs. If demand drops, supply should drop to meet it. In fact, many departments are doing the opposite. The job market be damned—more important is maintaining the flow of labor to their own domestic sweatshops, the pipeline of graduate students who staff discussion sections and teach introductory and service courses like freshman composition and first-year calculus. (Professors also need dissertations to direct, or how to justify their own existence?) From 1991 to 2011, for example, the number of bachelor's degrees conferred in English increased by only 3 percent, but the number of PhDs increased by 27 percent. As Louis Menand puts it in *The Marketplace of Ideas*, the system is now designed to produce not PhDs so much as ABDs: students who, having finished their other degree requirements, are "all but dissertation" (or "already been dicked," as we used to say in graduate school)—i.e., people who have entered the long limbo of low-wage research and teaching that chews up four, five, six years of a young scholar's life.

If anything, as Menand notes, the glut of PhDs works well for departments at both ends, since it also gives them the whip hand when it comes to making new hires. Graduate programs occupy a highly unusual and advantageous market position: they are both the producers and the consumers of academic labor. Yet as producers, they have no financial stake in whether their product actually "sells"—that is, whether their graduates get jobs. So they have every incentive to keep prices low by maintaining the oversupply.

Still, there's a difference between a Roger Smith, firing workers at General Motors, and the faculty of an academic department, treating its students like surplus goods. For the CEO of a large corporation, workers are essentially entries on a balance sheet, separated from the boardroom by a great gulf of culture and physical distance. If they are treated without mercy, that is not entirely surprising. But the relationship between professors and graduate students could hardly be more intimate. Professors used to *be* graduate students. They belong to the same culture, and the same community. Your dissertation director is your mentor, your role model, the person who spends all those years overseeing your research and often the one you came to your program to study under in the first place. You, in turn, are their intellectual progeny; if you make good, their professional pride. The economic violence of the academic system is inflicted at very close quarters.

How professors square their Jekyll and Hyde roles in the process—teachers of individual students, co-managers of a system that exploits them as a group—I do not know. Denial, no doubt, along with the rationale that this is just the way it is, so what can you do? Teaching lower-level classes is part of the training, you hear a lot, especially when supposedly progressive academics explain why graduate-student unions are such a bad idea. They're students, not workers! But graduate students do not teach because they need to learn how, even if the experience is indeed very valuable; they teach because departments need "bodies in the classroom," as one of my professors at Columbia once delicately put it.

I always found it beautifully apt that my old department occupies the same space where the infamous Milgram obedience experiments were conducted at Yale in the early 1960s. (Yes, really.) Pay no attention to those screams that are coming from the other room, the subjects were told as they administered the (supposed) electric shocks; it's for their own good. A perfect allegory of the relationship between tenured professors and graduate students (and tenured professors and untenured ones, for that matter).

Well, so what? So a bunch of spoiled kids are having trouble finding jobs—so is everybody else. Here's so what. First of all, they're not spoiled. They're doing exactly what we always complain our brightest students do not do: eschewing the big bucks of Wall Street, consulting, or corporate law to pursue their ideals and be of service. Academia may once have been a cushy gig, but now we are talking about highly talented young people who are willing to spend their twenties living on subsistence wages when they could be getting rich, and their friends *are* getting rich, simply because they believe in knowledge, ideas, inquiry, teaching, following their passion. To leave more than half of them holding the bag at the end of it all, over thirty and left to scrounge for a new career, is a human tragedy.

Sure, lots of people have it worse. But here's another reason we should care: it's also a social tragedy, and not just because it represents a colossal waste of human capital. If we don't improve conditions for people going into academia, no one's going to want to do it anymore. And then it won't be just the students who are suffering. Scholarship itself will suffer, which means the country will. Knowledge is a nation's most important resource, and the vast majority of knowledge is created in the academy.

It isn't just the sciences that matter; it is also the humanities and social sciences. On the work that is done in the academy depends the strength of our economy, our public policy, and our culture. We need our best young minds pursuing atmospheric research and international affairs and religious studies, chemistry and ethnography and art history. By pursuing their individual interests, narrowly understood, departments are betraying both the values they are pledged to uphold—the pursuit of knowledge, the spirit of critical inquiry, the extension of the humanistic tradition—and the nation they exist to serve.

We've been here before. Pay was so low in the nineteenth century, when academia was still a gentleman's profession, that in 1902 Andrew Carnegie founded the pension program that would evolve into TIAA-CREF, the massive retirement fund. After World War II, when higher education was regarded as an urgent national priority, a consensus emerged that salaries were too low to attract the best people. Compensation soared through the 1950s and

'60s, then hit the skids around 1970 and didn't recover for almost thirty years. It's no surprise that the percentage of college freshmen expressing an interest in academia was more than three times higher in 1966 than it was in 2004. Next time you are wondering why there are so few people of color on university faculties, ask yourself why anyone from a lower-income background, even a middle-class background—anyone without a trust fund or at least a safety net—would enter a field that offers such desperate prospects. If you care about diversity, you need to care about economics.

Still, the answer now is not to raise professors' salaries. The answer is to hire more professors: real ones, not academic lettuce-pickers. Yet that's the last thing schools are apt to do. What we have seen instead over the last forty years, in addition to the raising of a reserve army of contingent labor, is a kind of administrative elephantiasis—an explosion in the number of people working at colleges and universities who aren't faculty, full-time or part-time, of any kind. From 1976 to 2001, the number of nonfaculty professionals ballooned by nearly 240 percent, growing more than three times as fast as the faculty itself. Coaching staffs and salaries have grown without limit; athletic departments are virtually separate colleges within universities now, competing (successfully) with academics. The size of presidential salaries—over $1 million in several dozen cases—has become notorious. Nor is it only the presidents; at Yale in 2007, compensation for the next six most highly paid officers averaged over $430,000.

As Gaye Tuchman explains in *Wannabe U*, a case study in the sorrows of academic corporatization, deans, provosts, and presidents are no longer professors who cycle through administrative duties and then return to teaching and research. Instead, they have evolved to become a separate stratum of managerial careerists, jumping, like any other executive, from job to job and school to school: isolated from the faculty and its values, loyal to an ethos of short-term expansion, and trading in the business blather of measurability, revenue streams, mission statements, and the like. They do not have the long-term health of their institutions at heart. They want to pump up the stock price (i.e., *U.S. News* ranking), then move on to the next fat post.

If you're tenured, of course, life is still good (at least until the new provost decides to shut down your entire department). In fact, the revolution in the structure of the academic labor force has come about in good measure to protect the senior professoriate. The faculty has steadily grayed in recent decades, a process exacerbated by the abolition of mandatory retirement in 1986. By 1998, over half were fifty or older. Departments found themselves "tenured in," with a large bolus of highly compensated senior faculty and room, often increasingly squeezed, for just a few juniors (another reason jobs have been so hard to find). Contingent labor is desirable above all because it saves money for senior salaries (as well as relieving the tenure track of the disagreeable business of low-level courses). By 2004, while pay for assistant and associate professors still stood more or less where it had in 1970, that for full professors had increased about 10 percent.

Academia, in other words, has become a microcosm of the American economy as a whole: a self-enriching aristocracy, a swelling and increasingly immiserated proletariat, and a shrinking middle class. The same devil's bargain stabilizes the system: the middle, or at least the upper middle, the tenured professoriate, is allowed to retain its prerogatives—its comfortable compensation packages, its workplace autonomy, and, of course, its job security—in return for acquiescing to the exploitation of the bottom by the top and, indirectly, the betrayal of the future of the entire enterprise.

But now those prerogatives are also under threat. I am not joining the call for the abolition of tenure. Tenure certainly has its problems. It crowds out opportunities for young scholars and allows academic deadwood to accumulate on faculty rolls. But eliminating it would be like curing diabetes by shooting the patient. For one thing, it would remove the last incentive for any sane person to enter the profession. People still put up with everything they have to endure as graduate students and untenured professors for the sake of a shot at that golden prize, and now you're going to take away the prize? No, it isn't good that so many of academia's rewards are backloaded into a single moment of occupational transfiguration, one that sits like a mirage at the end of twelve or fifteen years of Sinaitic wandering. Yes, the job market would eventually rebalance itself if the profession moved to a system, say, of seven-year contracts. But long before it did, we would lose a generation of talent.

Besides, *how* would the job market rebalance itself? If the people who now have tenure continued to serve under some other contractual system, the same surplus of labor would be chasing the same scarcity of employment. Things would get better for new PhDs only if institutions started getting rid of senior people. Which, as the way things work in other industries reminds us, they would probably be glad to do. Why retain a fifty-five-year-old, when you can replace them with a twenty-nine-year-old at half the price? Now that's a thought to swell a provost's revenue stream. Talk about efficiency.

And what exactly are you supposed to do at that point, if you've spent your career becoming an expert, for example, in Etruscan history? Academia exists in part to support research the private sector won't pay for, knowledge that can't be converted into a quick buck or even a slow one, but that adds value to society in other ways. Who's going to pursue that kind of inquiry if they know there's a good chance they're going to get thrown out in the snow when they're fifty (having only started to earn a real salary when they were thirty, to boot)? Doctors and lawyers can set up their own practices, but a professor can't start his own university. This kind of thing is appalling enough when it happens to blue-collar workers. In an industry that requires a dozen years of postsecondary education just to gain an entry-level position, it is unthinkable.

Nor should we pooh-pooh the threat that the abolition of tenure would pose to academic freedom, as Andrew Hacker and Claudia Dreifus do in *Higher Education?* "We have scoured all the sources we could find," they write, "yet we could not find any academic research whose findings ended up threatening the jobs of tenured faculty members." Of course not: because they had tenure. If deans and trustees (and alumni and politicians) rarely even try to have professors fired, that's because they know they stand so little chance of success. Before tenure existed, arbitrary and politically motivated dismissals were common—the reason that the American Association of University Professors, under the leadership of John Dewey and others, insisted on establishing the tenure system in the first place in the early twentieth century. They are still common, for those who don't have tenure. Imagine what the current gang of red-state legislators would do if they could get their hands on public-university professors? Hacker and Dreifus, who recognize the importance of academic freedom, call instead of tenure for "presidents and trustees with backbone" (a species as wonderful as the unicorn, and almost as numerous). Sure, and as long as the king is a good man, we don't need laws. Academics play a special role in society. They tell us things that we don't want to hear: about global warming, or the historical Jesus, or the way we raise our children. That is why they need to have protection.

But tenure isn't the only the thing that is under assault in the top-down, corporatized academy. As Cary Nelson explains in *No University Is an Island*, so is shared governance—the principle that universities should be controlled by their faculty. Shared governance, which protects academic values against the encroachments of the spreadsheet brigade, is itself threatened by the changing structure of academic work. The growth of contingent labor undermines it both directly—no one asks an adjunct what they think of how things run—and indirectly. More people chasing fewer jobs means that everyone is squeezed for extra productivity, just like at Walmart. As of 1998, faculty worked about seven hours more, on average, per week than they had in 1972, to a total of almost fifty (the stereotype of the lazy academic is, like that of the welfare queen, a politically expedient myth). Not surprisingly, they also reported a shrinking sense of influence over campus-wide affairs. Who's got the time? Academic labor is becoming like every other part of the American workforce: cowed, harried, docile, disempowered.

In macropolitical terms, the erosion of tenure and shared governance undermines the power of a large body of liberal professionals. In this it resembles the campaign against the teachers' unions. Tenure, in fact, is a lot like unionization: imperfect, open to corruption and abuse, but incomparably better than the alternative. Indeed, tenure is what professors have instead of unions (at least at private universities, where they're banned by law from organizing). As for shared governance, it is nothing other than one of the left's long-standing goals: employee control of the workplace. Yes, professors have it better than a lot of other workers, including a lot of others in the academy. But the answer is to level up, not down.

Of course, some sectors of the academy—the ones that educate the children of the wealthy and the upper middle class—continue to maintain their privilege. The class gradient is getting steeper not only between contingent labor and the tenure track, and junior and senior faculty within the latter, but between institutions, as well. Professors at doctoral-granting universities not only get paid a lot more than their colleagues at other four-year schools; the difference is growing—from 17 percent in 1984 to 28 percent in 2003. (During the same period, their advantage over professors at community colleges increased from 33 percent to 49 percent.) The rich, in other words—or rather, those who serve the rich—are getting richer. In 1970, in what now seems like an alternate universe, faculty at public institutions actually made about 10 percent *more* than those at private ones. By 1999, the lines had crossed, and public salaries stood 5 percent lower. Nor is money the only difference. The average student-faculty ratio at private colleges and universities is 10.8:1; at public institutions, it is 15.9:1.

And here we come to the most important issue facing American higher education. Public institutions enroll about three-quarters of the nation's college students, and public institutions are everywhere under financial attack. As Nancy Folbre explains in *Saving State U*, spending on higher education, as a percentage of state budgets, has been plummeting for over twenty years, and now stands at about two-thirds of what it was in 1980. The six-year graduation rate at public universities is now a dismal 60 percent, a function of class size and availability, faculty accessibility, the use of contingent instructors, and, of course, tuition. Private universities, whose tax-exempt status is predicated on the notion that they serve the public good, actually lobby their state legislatures, in some cases, against public funding for state schools, which they see as competitors. In any case, a large portion of state scholarship aid goes to students at private colleges (in some states, more than half)—a kind of voucher system for higher ed.

Meanwhile, public universities have been shifting their financial-aid criteria from need to merit to attract students with higher scores (good old *U.S. News* again), who tend to come from richer families. For this and many other reasons, state universities are getting harder and harder for the average family to afford. In 1999, the average cost of sending a child to a public university came to 18 percent of median family income; by 2007, it was 25 percent. It's no surprise that during the 2000s, between 1.4 million and 2.4 million students were prevented from going to college for financial reasons—about 50 percent more than during the 1990s. And, of course, in the present climate of universal fiscal crisis, it's all about to get much worse.

Our system of public higher education is one of the great achievements of American civilization. In its breadth and excellence, it has no peer. It embodies some of our nation's highest ideals: democracy, equality, opportunity, self-improvement, useful knowledge, and collective public purpose. The same Congress that funded the transcontinental railroad—in the middle of a civil war, no less—also passed the Morrill Land Grant Act of 1862, which set the system on its feet. Public higher education is a bulwark against hereditary privilege and an engine of social mobility. It is altogether to the point that the strongest state systems are not to be found in the Northeast, the domain of the old WASP aristocracy and its elite private colleges and universities, but in places like Michigan, Wisconsin, Illinois, Virginia, North Carolina, and, above all, California.

Now the system is in danger of falling into ruin. Public higher education was essential to creating the mass middle class of the postwar decades—and, with it, a new birth of political empowerment and human flourishing—and the defunding of public higher education has been essential to its slow destruction. But it was not only the postwar middle class that public higher education helped create; it was the postwar prosperity altogether. Knowledge, again, is our most important resource. States that balance their budgets on the backs of their public universities are eating their seed corn. As for private colleges and universities, they are also in trouble, for reasons that will sound familiar: too much spending during the boom years—much of it on construction, much of it driven by the desire to improve "market position" relative to competitors by offering amenities like new dorms and student centers that have nothing to do with teaching or research—supported by too much borrowing, has led to a debt crisis.

Among the class of academic managers responsible for creating the trouble in the first place, an industry of reform has sprung up, along with a literature of reform to go with it. Books like Mark C. Taylor's *Crisis on Campus*, James Garland's *Saving Alma Mater*, and Robert Zemsky's *Making Reform Work* propose their variously visionary schemes. Nearly all involve technology to drive efficiency. Online courses, distance learning, do-it-yourself instruction: this is the future that we're being offered. Why teach a required art history course to twenty students at a time when you can march them through a self-guided online textbook followed by a multiple-choice exam? Why have professors or even graduate students grade papers when you can outsource them to BAs around the country, even around the world? Why waste time with office hours when students can interact with their professors via email?

The other great hope—I know you'll never see this coming—is the market. After all, it works so well in healthcare, and we're already trying it in K–12. Garland, a former president of Miami of Ohio (a public institution), argues for a voucher system. Instead of giving money to schools, the state would give it to students, with the credit good at any college in the state—in other words, at private ones, as well. Now the student would run the show (as the customer should, of course), scouring the market like a savvy consumer. Universities, in turn, "would compete with one another by tailoring their course offerings, degree programs, student services, and extracurricular activities" to the needs of our newly empowered eighteen-year-olds, and the invisible hand would rain down its blessings.

But do we really want our higher education system redesigned by the self-identified needs of high school seniors? This is what the British are about to try, and in a country with one of Europe's most distinguished intellectual traditions, they seem poised to destroy the liberal arts altogether. How much do eighteen-year-olds even know about what they want out of college? About not only what it can get them, but what it can give them? These are young people who don't know what college is, who they are, whom they might want to be—things you need a college education, and specifically a liberal arts education, to help you figure out.

Yet the liberal arts, we know, are dying. All the political and parental pressure is pushing in the other direction, toward the "practical," narrowly conceived: the instrumental, the utilitarian, the immediately negotiable. Last year, SUNY Albany announced plans to close its departments of French, Italian, Russian, classics, and theater—a wholesale slaughter of the humanities. Garland enumerates the fields that a state legislature might want to encourage its young people to enter, listing "engineering, agriculture, nursing, math and science education, or any other area of state importance." Apparently, political science, philosophy, history, and sociology, among others, are not areas of state importance. Zemsky wants to consider reducing college to three years—meaning less time for young people to figure out what to study, to take courses in a range of disciplines, to explore, to mature, to think.

When politicians talk about higher education, from Barack Obama all the way down, they talk almost exclusively about math and science. And technology indeed creates the future. But it is not enough to create the future. We also need to organize it, as the social sciences enable us to do. We need to make sense of it, as the humanities enable us to do. A system of higher education that ignores the liberal arts, as Jonathan Cole points out in *The Great American University*, is what they have in China, where they don't want people to think about other ways to organize society, or other meanings than the authorized ones. A scientific education creates technologists. A liberal arts education creates citizens: people who can think broadly and critically about themselves and the world.

Yet of course it is precisely China (and Singapore, that other great democracy) that Obama holds up as the model to emulate in our new Sputnik moment. It's funny—after the original Sputnik, we didn't decide to become more like the Soviet Union; we decided to become a better version of ourselves. But apparently we don't possess that kind of confidence anymore.

There is a large, public debate in this country about primary and secondary education. There is a smaller, less public debate about higher education. What I fail to understand is why they aren't the same debate. We all know that students in elementary and high school learn best in small classrooms with the individualized attention of motivated teachers. It is the same in college. Education, as the saying goes, is lighting a fire, not filling a bucket. The word comes from the Latin for "educe," lead forth. Learning is not about downloading a certain quantity of information into your brain, as the proponents of online instruction believe. It is about the kind of interchange and incitement—the leading forth of new ideas and powers—that can only happen in a seminar ("seminar" being a fancy name for what every class already is in K–12). It is labor-intensive; it is face-to-face; it is one at a time.

The recent study showing that a lot of kids aren't learning much in college comes as no surprise to me. The system is no longer set up to challenge them. If we're going to make college an intellectually rigorous experience for the students who already go—still more, for all the ones who want to go—we're going to need a lot more teachers: well-paid, institutionally supported, socially valued. As of 2003, there were about four hundred thousand tenure-track professors in the United States (as compared to about four million primary- and secondary-school teachers). Between reducing class sizes, reversing the shift to contingent labor, and beefing up our college-completion rates, we're going to need several times that number.

So where is the money supposed to come from? It is the same question we ask about the federal budget, and the answer is the same. We're still a very wealthy country. There's plenty of money, if we tax ourselves appropriately and spend our resources on the right things. Just as we need to wrestle with the $700 billion gorilla of defense, so do universities need to take on administrative edema and extracurricular spending. We can start with presidential salaries. Universities, like corporations, claim they need to pay the going rate for top talent. The argument is not only dubious—whom exactly are they competing with for the services of these managerial titans, aside from one another?—it is beside the point. Academia is not supposed to be a place to get rich. If your ego can't survive on $200,000 a year, on top of the prestige of a university presidency, you need to find another line of work. Once, there were academic leaders who put themselves forward as champions of social progress: people like James B. Conant at Harvard, Kingman Brewster at Yale, Clark Kerr at the University of California, and Theodore Hesburgh at Notre Dame. What a statement it would make if the Ivy League presidents got together and announced that they were going to give themselves an immediate pay cut of 75 percent. What a way to restore academia's moral prestige and demonstrate some leadership again.

But leadership will have to come from somewhere else, as well. Just as in society at large, the academic upper middle class will need to rethink its alliances. Its dignity will not survive forever if it doesn't fight for that of everyone below them in the academic hierarchy. (First, they came for the graduate students, but I didn't speak out because I wasn't a graduate student. . . .) For all of its pretensions to public importance (every academic secretly believes that they're a public intellectual), the professoriate is awfully quiet, essentially nonexistent as a collective voice. If the academy is going to once again become a decent place to work, if our best young minds are going to be attracted back to the profession, if higher education is going to be reclaimed as part of the American promise, if teaching and research are going to make the country strong again, then professors need to get off their asses and organize: department by department, institution by institution, state by state, across the nation as a whole. Tenured professors enjoy the strongest speech protections in society. It's time they started using them.

[2011]

On Political Correctness

Let us eschew the familiar examples: the disinvited speakers, the Title IX tribunals, the safe zones stocked with Play-Doh, the crusades against banh mi. The flesh-eating bacterium of political correctness, which feeds preferentially on brain tissue, and which has long been endemic on elite college campuses, reveals its true virulence not in the high-profile outbreaks that reach the national awareness, but in the myriad of ordinary cases—the everyday business as usual at institutions around the country—that are rarely even talked about.

Before I continue, a clarification (since deliberate misconstrual is itself an element of the phenomenon in question). By political correctness, I do not mean the term as it has been appropriated by the right—that is, the expectation of adherence to the norms of basic decency, like refraining from derogatory racial epithets. I mean its older, intramural denotation: the persistent attempt to suppress the expression of unwelcome beliefs and ideas.

To wit. I recently spent a semester at Scripps, a selective women's college near Los Angeles. One of my students, from a Chinese American family, explained that the first thing she learned when she arrived on campus was to keep quiet about her Christian faith and her nonfeminist views about marriage. A second student, a self-described "strong feminist," explained that she tends to keep quiet about everything because she never knows when she might say something that you're not supposed to. A third student, a junior, wrote about a friend whom she had known since the beginning of college and who, she had just discovered, went to church every Sunday. My student hadn't even been aware that her friend was religious. When she asked her why she had concealed this, her friend said, because I don't feel comfortable being out as a religious person here.

The director of the writing center, I learned, a specialist in disability studies, was instructing people that they weren't allowed to use expressions like "that's a crazy idea" because they stigmatize the mentally ill. A student explained that she had been criticized by a peer for wearing moccasins—an act, she was informed, of cultural appropriation. An adjunct instructor described what should have been a routine pedagogical conflict over something he had said in class that had turned, when a student claimed to have felt "triggered," into, in his words, a bureaucratic "dumpster fire." He was careful now, he added, to avoid saying anything, or teaching anything, that might conceivably lead to trouble.

Students explained—young women, again, who considered themselves strong feminists—that they were afraid to speak freely among their peers, and that despite its notoriety as a platform for cyberbullying, they were grateful for Yik Yak, the social media app, because it allowed them to say anonymously what they couldn't say in their own name. Above all, my students told me that while they generally identified with the sentiments and norms that travel under the name of political correctness, they thought that it had simply gone too far—way too far. Everybody felt oppressed, as they put it, by the "PC police"—everybody, that is, except for those whom everybody else regarded as members of the PC police.

I saw all this, and a good bit more, while teaching one class, for twelve students, during one semester, at one college. And I have no reason to believe that things are substantially different at other elite private institutions, and plenty of reasons not to believe it: from conversations with individuals at many schools, from my broader experience in higher education, from what I've read not only in the mainstream media but also in the higher education press. Undoubtedly better at some places than others, undoubtedly worse at the liberal arts colleges in general than at the universities in general, but broadly similar across the board.

This is how I've come to understand the situation: selective private colleges are now religious institutions. The religion in question is not Methodism or Catholicism but an extreme version of the belief system of the liberal elite: the liberal professional, managerial, and creative classes, which produce a large majority of students enrolled at such institutions and an even larger majority of faculty and administrators who work at them. To attend those schools is to be socialized, and, not infrequently, indoctrinated, into that religion.

When I spoke about these issues with a group of students recently at Whitman College, a selective school in Washington State, that idea—that elite private colleges are religious institutions—resonated with them instantly.

I also recently received an email from a student who had transferred from Oral Roberts, the evangelical Christian university in Tulsa, Oklahoma, to Columbia, my alma mater. The latter, he found to his surprise, is *also* a religious school, only there the faith, he said, is the religion of success. The religion of success is not the same as political correctness, but, as I'll presently explain, the two go hand in hand.

What does it mean to say that these institutions are religious schools? First, that they possess a dogma, unwritten but understood by all: a set of "correct" opinions and beliefs, or at best, a narrow range within which disagreement is permitted. There is a right way to think and a right way to talk, and also a right set of things to think and talk about. Secularism is taken for granted. "Social justice" is a sacred cause. Issues of identity—principally the holy trinity of race, gender, and sexuality—occupy the center of the conversation. The presiding presence is Foucault, with his theories of power, discourse, and the social construction of the self, who holds the same position on the left as Marx once did. The fundamental questions that a college education ought to raise, in other words—questions of individual and collective virtue, of what it means to be a good person and a good society—are understood to have been settled. The assumption, on elite college campuses, is that we are already in full possession of the moral truth. This is a religious attitude. It is certainly not a scholarly or intellectual attitude.

Dogma, and the enforcement of dogma, make for ideological consensus. Students seldom disagree with one another anymore in class, I've been told about school after school. The reason, said one of the students I talked to at Whitman, is mainly that they really don't have any disagreements. When they take up an issue in class, another added, it isn't, let's talk about X, but rather, let's talk about why such-and-such position is the correct one to have on X. When my student wrote about her friend, she said she couldn't understand why anyone would feel uncomfortable being out as a religious person at a place as diverse as Scripps. But, of course, Scripps and its ilk are only diverse in terms of identity. In terms of ideology, they are all but homogenous. You don't have "different voices," as these institutions like to boast; you have different bodies, speaking with the same voice.

That lack of disagreement, by the way, is the reason that liberal students (and liberals in general) are so bad at defending their own positions. They never have to, so they never learn to. It is also why it tends to be so easy for conservatives to goad them into incoherent anger. Nothing's more enraging than an argument you cannot answer. But the reason to listen to people who disagree with you is not so you can learn to refute them. The reason is you may be wrong. In fact, you *are* wrong: about some things and probably about a lot of things. There is zero percent chance that any one of us is a hundred percent correct. That is why freedom of expression includes the right to hear as well as speak, and why disinviting campus speakers abridges the speech rights of students as well as of the speakers themselves.

Elite private colleges are ideologically homogenous because they are socially homogenous, or close to it. Their student populations largely come from the liberal upper and upper middle classes, multiracial but predominantly white and Asian, with an admixture of students from poor communities of color—two demographics with broadly similar political beliefs, as evidenced by the fact that they together constitute a large percentage of the Democratic Party base. As for faculty and managerial staff, they are even more homogenous than are their students, both in their social origins and their present milieu, which tends to be composed exclusively of other liberal professionals—if not, indeed, of other liberal academics. Unlike the campus protesters of the 1960s, today's student activists are not expressing countercultural views. They are expressing the exact views of the culture in which they find themselves (a reason that administrators tend to be so ready to accede to their demands). If you want to find the counterculture on today's elite college campuses, you need to look for the conservative students.

Which brings us to another correlate of dogma: heresy. Heresy means those beliefs that undermine the orthodox consensus, so heresy must be eradicated: by education, by reeducation—if necessary, by censorship. It makes a perfect, dreary sense that there are speech codes, or the desire for speech codes, at selective private colleges. The irony is that conservatives don't actually care if progressives disapprove of them, with the result that political correctness generally amounts to internecine warfare on the left: radical feminists excoriating other radical feminists for saying "vagina" instead of "front hole," students denouncing the director of *Boys Don't Cry* (a breakthrough, in its day, for transgender visibility and legitimacy) as a transphobic "cis white bitch," as recently happened at Reed, and so forth.

But the most effective form of censorship is self-censorship—which, in the intimate environment of a residential college, young adults are very quick to learn. A Whitman student mentioned that he's careful, when questioning consensus beliefs, to phrase his opinion in terms of "explain to me why I'm wrong." Other students—at the Claremont Colleges, at Bard—have said that any challenge to the hegemony of identity politics will get you branded as a racist (as in, "Don't talk to that guy; he's a racist"). Campus protesters, their rhetoric to the contrary notwithstanding, are not the ones being silenced: they are, after all, *not* being silent. They are in the middle of the quad, speaking their minds. The ones being silenced are the ones like my students at Scripps, like the students at Whitman, like many students, no doubt, at many places, who are keeping their mouths shut. "The religion of humanity," as David Bromwich recently remarked, "may turn out to be as dangerous as all the other religions."

The assumption on elite college campuses is not only that we are in full possession of the moral truth, but that we are in full possession of moral virtue. We don't just know the good with perfect wisdom; we embody it with perfect innocence. But regimes of virtue tend to eat their children (you can think of Salem). They tend to turn upon themselves, since everybody wants to prove that they're the holiest (you can think of the French Revolution). The ante is forever being upped. The PC commissariat reminds me of the NRA. Everyone is terrified of challenging the NRA (everyone in a position to stop them, at least), so they get whatever they demand. And then, they think up new demands. Guns in playgrounds, guns in bars.

Thus it is with political correctness. There is always something new, as my students understood, that you aren't supposed to say. Even worse, you often don't find out about a new proscription until after you have violated it. The term "political correctness," which originated in the 1970s as a form of self-mockery among progressive college students, was a deliberately ironic invocation of Stalinism. We've lost the irony, but we've kept the Stalinism. And it was a feature of Stalinism that you could be convicted for an act that wasn't a crime at the time you committed it. So you were always already guilty, or could be made to be guilty, and therefore always controllable.

You were also always under surveillance by a cadre of what Jane Austen called, in a very different context, "voluntary spies," and what my students called the PC police. Regimes of virtue generate informants (which really does wonders for social cohesion). They also generate authorities, often self-appointed authorities, like that writing director at Scripps who decreed that you aren't supposed to say "crazy." Whenever I hear that you aren't "supposed" to say something, I want to know, where did this "supposed" descend from? Who decided, and who gave them the right to decide? And whenever I hear that a given group of students says this or demands that, I want to ask, whom exactly are we talking about: all of them, or just a few of them? Did the group choose its leaders, or did the leaders choose themselves?

Let me be clear. I recognize that both the culture of political correctness and the recent forms of campus agitation are responding to enormous, intractable national problems. There *is* systemic racism, and individual bigotry, in the United States. There *is* systemic sexism, and sexual assault, in society at large. The call for safe spaces and trigger warnings, the desire to eliminate microaggressions, the demand for the removal of offensive symbols and the suppression of offensive language: however foolish most of these might be as policy prescriptions, however absurd as they work themselves out on the ground, all originate in deeply legitimate concerns.

But so much of political correctness is not about justice or creating a safe environment; it is about power. And so much of what is taking place at colleges today reflects the way that power has been reconfigured in contemporary higher education. Campus activists are taking advantage of the fact (and I suspect that a lot of them understand this, intuitively if not consciously) that students have a lot more power than they used to. The change is the result not only of the rise of the customer-service mentality in academia, but also of the proletarianization of the faculty. Students have risen; instructors have fallen. Where once administrations worked in alliance with faculty, were indeed largely composed of faculty, now they work against the faculty in alliance with students, a separate managerial stratum more interested in the satisfaction of its customers than the well-being of its employees.

In the inevitable power struggle between students and teachers, the former have gained the whip hand. The large majority of instructors today are adjuncts working term to term for a few thousand dollars a course, or contract employees with no long-term job security, or untenured professors whose careers can still be derailed. With the expansion of Title IX in 2011—the law is now being used to police classroom content—even tenured faculty are sitting with a sword above their heads. Thanks not only to the shift to contingent employment but also to the chronic glut of PhDs (the academic reserve army, to adapt a phrase from Marx), academic labor is cheap, and academic workers are vulnerable and frightened. In a conflict between a student and a teacher, almost nothing is at stake for the student beyond the possibility of receiving a low grade (which, in the current environment, means something like a B+). But the teacher could lose their job. That is the reason that so many faculty, like that adjunct instructor at Scripps, are teaching with their tails between their legs. They, too, are being silenced. Whether they know it or not, student activists (and students in general) are exploiting the precarity of an increasingly immiserated workforce. So much for social justice.

The power of political correctness is wielded not only against the faculty, however, but also against other groups within the student body, ones that don't belong to the ideologically privileged demographics or espouse the approved points of view: conservative students; religious students, particularly Christians; students who identify as Zionists, which means a lot of Jewish students; "athletes," meaning white male athletes; white students from red states; heterosexual cisgendered white men from anywhere at all, who represent, depending on the school, between a fifth and a third of all students. (I say this, by the way, as an atheist, a social democrat, a native Northeasterner, a person who believes that colleges should not have sports teams in the first place, and, in case it isn't obvious by now, a card-carrying member of the liberal elite.) I haven't heard too many people talk about creating safe spaces for Christians, or preventing microaggressions against conservatives, or banning hate speech against athletes, or disinviting socialists.

What I *have* heard, frequently, for as long as I have been involved in academia, are open expressions of contempt for, prejudice against, or hostility toward those groups or members of those groups. If you are a white man, you are routinely regarded as guilty until proven innocent, the worst possible construction is put upon your words, and anything you say on a sensitive issue is received with suspicion at best. I attended a workshop on microaggressions at the University of Missouri last year. The problem with microaggressions, the leader said, is that they "create a space of hostility," that they say, "you don't belong; you are different in a way that's not okay." Those formulations precisely describe the environment that the groups I just enumerated often encounter at elite colleges and universities, except that unlike the typical microaggression, the offense is not inadvertent. It is quite deliberate. Racism may well be a system, but bigotry and prejudice are personal attitudes, and they are freely distributed ("cis white bitch") across the political spectrum.

I am perfectly aware that men, whites, heterosexuals, and cisgendered people remain the dominant groups in society as a whole, as well as the predominant presence on college faculty. But equality is not revenge. Racism, sexism, homophobia, and transphobia are far more powerful, and far more entrenched, than their "reverse" counterparts, but that doesn't make the latter less than reprehensible, especially when practiced against college students:

individuals, in other words, who are scarcely more than adolescents and who deserve the benefit of the doubt.

I was talking about trigger warnings with that writing director at Scripps. I told her that the only student I had ever had who was so uncomfortable with course material that they had had to leave a class was a Christian young man who excused himself before the discussion of a story by Jeanette Winterson, the sexually explicit lesbian novelist. I was naïve enough to think that the director would be sympathetic to him. Instead, she snorted with contempt. (For the record, I myself was none too happy that he did that. But then, I don't believe in trigger warnings in the first place.) Progressive faculty and students often say that they want to dismantle hierarchies of power. Their actions suggest that in fact they would like to invert them. All groups are equal, but some are more equal than others.

Political correctness inculcates a mindset of us versus them. "Them" is white men, or straight cisgendered white men—aka "the patriarchy." (The phrase "dead white men," so beloved on the left, would carry little force were its last two words not already felt to constitute a pejorative.) "Us" is everybody else, the coalition of virtue (virtuous, of course, by virtue of an accident of birth). Which means that political correctness not only treats "them" as a monolith—erasing the differences among white people, like those between Jews and Mormons or Irish and English, thus effacing the specificity of their historical and sometimes also their present experience—it effaces the specificity of *everyone's* experience.

Political correctness expects us to plot our experience on the grid of identity, to interpret it in terms of our location at the intersection of a limited number of recognized categories. You are a lesbian Latina, so you must feel X. You are a white transman, so you must think Y. But identity should not precede experience; it should proceed from it. And experience is much more granular, and composed of a vastly greater number of variables, than is dreamt of in the PC philosophy. I myself am a youngest child; I was raised in the suburbs; I grew up in an Orthodox Jewish family. All those circumstances helped to make me who I am. But more to the point, my consciousness and way of being in the world have been shaped by a limitless set of experiential particulars, most of which are not reducible to *any* category. That, by the way, is one of the reasons to read literature (and to place it at the center of a college education): because it captures the complexity of lived experience, and of enacted identity, in a way that the categories of a politicized social science can never hope to match.

There is one category that the religion of the liberal elite does not recognize, that its purpose, one might almost think, is to conceal: class. Class at fancy colleges, as throughout American society, is the unspeakable word, the great forbidden truth. And the exclusion of class on selective college campuses enables the exclusion of *a* class. I have long been struck, in leftist or PC rhetoric, with how often "white" is conflated with "wealthy," as if all white people were wealthy and all wealthy people were white. In fact, almost half of poor Americans are white. Roughly 60 percent of working-class Americans are white. About two-thirds of white Americans are poor or working class. Altogether, lower-income whites make up about 40 percent of the country, yet they are almost entirely absent on elite college campuses, where they amount, at most, to a few percent and constitute, by a wide margin, the single most underrepresented group.

Not coincidentally, lower-income whites belong disproportionately to precisely those groups whom it is acceptable and even desirable, in the religion of the colleges, to demonize: conservatives, Christians, people from red states. Selective private colleges are creations of the liberal elite, and they create it in turn. If it took an electoral catastrophe to remind that elite of the existence (and ultimately, one hopes, the humanity) of the white working class, the fact should come as no surprise. They've never met them, so they neither know nor care about them. In the psychic economy of the liberal elite, the white working class plays the role of the repressed. The recent presidential campaign may be understood as the return of that repressed—and the repressed, when it returns, is always monstrous.

The exclusion of class also enables the concealment of the role that elite colleges play in reproducing class. In theory, the system is a meritocracy, which means it's meant to do the opposite, to mitigate inequality and promote social mobility. In practice, students have as much merit, to a first approximation, as their parents can purchase (the reason, for example, that SAT scores correlate with family income and, even more, with family wealth). The college admissions process, as it has been said, is a way of laundering privilege.

But the rights of ablution do not stop with the admissions process. The culture of political correctness, the religion of the private colleges, provides the affluent white and Asian students who make up the preponderant majority of their student bodies, and the affluent white and Asian professionals who make up the preponderant majority of their tenured faculty and managerial staffs, with the ideological resources to alibi or erase their privilege.

It tells them, or enables them to tell themselves, that they are children of the light—part of the solution to our social ills, not an integral component of the problem. It may speak about dismantling the elite, but its real purpose is to flatter it.

And here we come to the connection between the religion of success and the religion of political correctness. Political correctness is a fig leaf for the competitive individualism of meritocratic neoliberalism, with its worship of success above all. It provides a moral cover underneath which undergraduates can prosecute their careerist projects undisturbed. Student existence may be understood as partitioned into noncommunicating realms: campus social life (including the classroom understood as a collective space), where the enforcement of political correctness is undertaken in the name of social justice, and the individual pursuit of personal advancement, the real business going forward. The moral commitments of the first (which are often transient in any case) are safely isolated from the second.

What falls between the two is nothing less than the core purpose of a liberal arts education: inquiry into the fundamental human questions, undertaken through rational discourse. Rational discourse or, in other words, rational argument: not the us-talk of PC consensus, which isn't argument, or the them-talk of vituperation (as practiced ubiquitously on social media), which isn't rational. But inquiry into the fundamental human questions—in the words of Tolstoy, "What shall we do and how shall we live?"—threatens both the current campus creeds: political correctness, by calling its certainties into question, and the religion of success, by calling its values into question. It raises the possibility that there are different ways to think and different things to live for.

Political correctness and rational discourse are incompatible ideals. Forget "civility," the thing that college deans and presidents inevitably put forth as that which needs to "balance" free expression. The call for civility is nothing more than a management tool for nervous bureaucrats, a way of splitting every difference and puréeing them into a pablum of deanly mush. Free expression is an absolute; to balance it is to destroy it.

Fortunately, we already have a tried-and-tested rule for free expression, one specifically designed to foster rational discourse. It's called the First Amendment. First Amendment jurisprudence doesn't recognize "offensive" speech or even hate speech as categories subject to legitimate restriction. For one thing, hate is not illegal, and neither is giving offense. For another, what's hate to me may not be hate to you; what's offensive to you may be my deeply held belief. The concepts are relative and subjective. When I gave a version of this essay as a talk at Bard, the first comment from the panel of student respondents came from a young Palestinian woman, who argued that "conservative narratives" like Zionism *should* be censored because "they require the otherization, if not the dehumanization, of another group of people." She didn't seem to recognize that many Zionists would characterize the Palestinian position the same way. Once you start to ban offensive speech, there is no place to stop—or rather, where you stop will be determined by the relative positions of competing groups within the community.

In other words, again, by power. To take the most conspicuous issue around which questions of free expression are currently being disputed on campus, the disinvitation of outside speakers always reflects the power of one group over another. When a speaker is invited to campus, it means that some set of people within the institution—some department, center, committee, or student organization—wants to hear what they have to say. When they are disinvited, shouted down, or otherwise prevented from speaking, it means that another set has proved to be more powerful. And when the latter are accused of opposing free speech, they often respond, "How can we be against free speech? We are exercising it right now!" But everyone is in favor of their *own* free speech (including, for instance, Vladimir Putin). The test of your commitment to free speech as a general principle is whether you are willing to tolerate the speech of others, especially those with whom you most disagree. If you are using your speech to try to silence speech, you are not in favor of free speech. You are only in favor of yourself.

I see no reason that the First Amendment shouldn't be the guiding principle at private colleges and universities (at least the ones that profess to be secular), just as it is, perforce, at public ones. But public universities are very different places than selective private schools. Their student bodies, for the most part, are far more diverse, economically and every other way, which means you do not have a large bolus of affluent, sheltered white and Asian kids who don't know how to talk to black and brown people and need to be "educated" into "awareness" by the presence of African American and Latino students (who are expected, in turn, to "represent" their communities). When different kinds of people grow up together, rather than being introduced to one another under artificial conditions in young adulthood, they learn to talk and play and study together honestly and unselfconsciously—which means, for adolescents, often frankly and roughly—without feeling like they have to tip-toe around sensitivities that are often created by the situation itself. In today's idiom, they can be real with each other. The one thing students at elite private colleges very rarely are is "real."

True diversity means true disagreement. Political correctness can be found at public institutions, too, but it does not usually dominate them. A friend of mine who passed her education at Columbia and Yale now teaches at Hunter, part of the City University of New York. "When you meet someone at Hunter," she told me, "you can't assume they see the world the same way you do." That's about as pithy an expression of the problem at selective private schools as one can ask for. When you meet someone at Columbia or Yale or Scripps or Whitman or any of scores of other institutions, you absolutely *can* assume they see the world the same way you do. And anyone who threatens to disrupt that cozy situation must be disinvited, reeducated, or silenced. It's no surprise that the overwhelming majority of high-profile PC absurdities take place at fancy private schools like Emory or Oberlin or Harvard.

That same reassuring assumption, about the points of view of everyone around you, does not pervade selective private campuses alone, of course. It is equally the case among the liberal elite writ large: at the Manhattan dinner party, the Silicon Valley start-up, the Seattle coffee shop, the Brookline PTA. (That it is also the case in other realms of society, non-liberal and/or non-elite, is true. It is also no excuse, especially not for people who consider themselves enlightened.) This is not an accident. Selective private colleges are the training grounds of the liberal elite, and the training in question involves not only formal education for professional success, but initiation into the folkways of the tribe.

Which means that fancy private colleges have a mission that public institutions don't. People arrive at the latter from a wide range of social locations, and they return to a range that is nearly as wide. The mission is to get them through and into the job market, not to turn them into any particular kind of person. But selective private colleges (which also tend to be a lot smaller than public institutions) are in the business of creating a community, and beyond that a class. "However much diversity Yale's freshman classes may have," as one of my students once put it, "its senior classes have far less."

Selective private colleges need to decide what kind of places they want to be. Do they want to be socialization machines for the upper middle class, ideological enforcers of progressive dogma? Or do they want to be educational institutions in the only sense that really matters: places of free, frank, and fearless inquiry? When we talk about political correctness and its many florid manifestations, so much in the news of late, we are talking not only about racial injustice and other forms of systemic oppression, nor only about the coddling of privileged youth, though both are certainly in play. We are also talking—or rather not talking—about the pathologies, and the psychopathologies, of the American class system. And those are also what we need to deal with.

[2017]

CHANGE YOUR MIND FIRST: COLLEGE AND THE URGE TO SAVE THE WORLD

A new spirit, it is clear, is abroad among America's youth. Beginning with the Occupy movement in 2011, gathering additional force with the emergence of Black Lives Matter in 2014, and redoubling itself again and yet again with the election of Donald Trump, a zeal for activism and social justice unseen since the early 1970s has taken hold on campus and beyond. Ask a college student what they hope to do with their lives, and the answer is apt to be some version of "have an impact," "change things for the better," or "make the world a better place."

All this certainly marks a radical improvement over where things stood when I was young. In the early 1980s, during the first flush of the Reagan revolution, liberals were actually outnumbered by conservatives on campus. More to the point, both together were far outnumbered by moderates, who accounted, according to surveys, for well over 50 percent. My years in college also witnessed the beginning of the rush, on elite private campuses, to Wall Street and consulting. In 1983, for example, 40 percent of Princeton seniors applied for jobs at one bank, First Boston, alone. Greed was good, idealism was for suckers, and the '60s were dead and buried. It was the beginning of a great depoliticization of American youth, one that would last for thirty years.

So good for this new generation, and more power to them. But there is one important thing that seems to me to be conspicuously missing from today's impulse to socially meaningful action. We can begin to understand what it is and why it matters by considering the following passage from an essay by the educator David Neidorf, the former president of Deep Springs College. Neidorf is reporting on an exchange that he had with an eight-year-old boy:

NEIDORF: Now here's a "philosophy" question for you. What makes a person good?

Boy: Oh, that's an easy one! A good person is somebody who helps other people.

Neidorf: Really? So what does a good person help others to do?

Boy: Whatever they are trying to do.

Neidorf: Does a good person help others to do anything they might be trying to do, no matter what it is?

Boy: Well . . . no, I guess not.

Neidorf: OK, then out of all the things people try to do, which ones does a good person help them to do?

Boy: Oh, that's easy! He helps them do things that are good.

The child, Neidorf notes, spotted right away the circularity of their exchange (which reproduces, he adds, the opening argument in Plato's *Republic*). Good people are people who help other people do good. The good has been defined in terms of itself, which means it hasn't been defined at all.

The relevance of this dialogue to the generational project of today's youth, and to many of their personal projects, as well, becomes apparent when you notice that the concept of the good is embedded in the word that lies at the heart of their collective and individual self-definition, "better": to change things for the better, to make the world a better place. Better means more good, which raises the question, what is good? But the answer, as our eight-year-old discovered, is not as easy as it seems. The nature of the good is one of those questions that is likely to make you realize, once you start to think about it, that you've never really thought about it at all, that you've simply taken the answer for granted. It might even make you realize that you don't know how to think about it.

One of the problems with the concept of the good, one of the dilemmas it forces upon us, as Neidorf notes, is that it points to "real and competing ends." As the philosopher Isaiah Berlin has argued, the characteristic ideals of liberal society—freedom, equality, justice—are to some degree irreconcilably in conflict. Freedom often leads to inequality; equality often demands the diminishment of freedom. As it happens, that conflict is vividly apparent in perhaps the most important debate taking place on campuses today, the struggle over restrictions on offensive speech. On one side, freedom of expression; on the other, the desire to create an environment in which all are able to participate as equals.

And the same kinds of dilemmas arise in society as a whole, the same kinds of difficult, ongoing, sometimes irreducible conflicts between competing ends. Yet even to say that is already to assume that we have satisfying definitions for each of those ends in themselves, that we know what we mean when we speak about freedom, equality, and justice—the last of which is indeed the subject of Plato's *Republic*, a book that runs to some four hundred pages in English translation (and by the end of which, many readers down the centuries have felt, an adequate definition has still not been arrived at). Or of beauty, or truth, or happiness, or prosperity, or success.

It is easy to know what you're against, a lot harder to come up with any kind of specific idea as to what you want to put in its place—with, that is, a coherent vision of the social good. Or maybe it isn't that easy to know what you're against. Many people on the left today are eager to declare their opposition to capitalism, but the way they use the term suggests that they don't really know what it means. They appear to equate it with greed, or inequality, or markets, or money, all of which predate the emergence of capitalism by thousands of years. Nor do I hear any clear ideas—or really, any ideas at all—as to what we should put in its place. If you don't want capitalism—which means, to put it briefly, the private ownership of production, the free market distribution of goods, and the cycle of investment and profit—then what *do* you want? Centralized planning? Small-scale collectivism? Workers' control of the means of production? These are not rhetorical questions; they are genuine questions, the kinds that need to be addressed if you really do want to bring about the end of capitalism.

But that is just an example. The larger point is this: when you commit yourself to the good, to making the world a better place, you need to commit yourself, first, not to action at all, but to something that has to precede it—to reflection, contemplation, analysis, study, in a word, to thought. Yet that is what I find to be so lacking now, in progressive circles no less than anywhere else, not just on campuses but everywhere. Nobody wants to think. Certainly, nobody wants to think about their own beliefs, values, and assumptions.

Now, this is always a problem, everywhere. No one ever wants to think about their beliefs, values, and assumptions. It's too much trouble, and it's much too troubling. Asking people to think about their beliefs, values, and assumptions is exactly what Socrates, Plato's teacher, went around doing, and eventually his fellow citizens invited him to drink some hemlock. But that resistance, I believe, is especially stubborn today, particularly for young people, more particularly for college students, and most particularly for students at elite private colleges. Selective campuses today are places of consensus, and so are the communities from which their students come. The assumption, on the left, is that we are already in full possession of the truth. We already know what's good, what's bad, what's right, what's wrong. There's really nothing to discuss, except how to put our beliefs into practice.

It wasn't always like this. In fact, it is one of the ways that the '80s were actually better. Communities were not as ideologically homogenous back then, and neither were young people, not even those who went to fancy private colleges. Half of my friend group in high school were conservatives. There was no consensus, no groupthink, no getting away from radically different positions, no avoiding the need to mount a cogent response. Even within the left, at a time when Marxist ideas and ideologies were still important elements of the intellectual climate, a wide range of disagreement prevailed, as I discovered when I got to college. Trotskyites argued with social democrats, Maoists with Leninists, trade union liberals with anarcho-syndicalists, reformists with revolutionaries. Which meant that students couldn't just believe: they had to debate; they had to think things through; they had to know what they were talking about. Debate and contention, in fact, were pretty much what it meant to *be* a college student, at least at the schools and in the circles that took themselves seriously.

None of this is to idealize or even to praise the students of my generation. We really were a bunch of little stinkers, and the Marxists in particular were totally obnoxious. And the truth is we arrived on campus just as certain of ourselves as any bunch of eighteen-year-olds ever does. But something else was different then, as well. There was a different idea about what college was for.

Today, the idea is that the purpose of college is to equip you with the tools to go out and pursue your goals. Mainly this has nothing to do with ideology one way or the other. Mainly the idea is that the exclusive purpose of college is to equip you for success in the labor market. But even when it's understood in higher terms—often couched in words like "leadership" or "service" or phrases like "giving back" or "making a contribution" or, indeed, like "building a better world"—the same approach applies. College is the place where you study, say, environmental engineering or global public health or gender theory, where you develop practical skills like communication and problem-solving. But not where you question those goals, the ends to which those tools and skills are to be put. Not where you take the risk of coming out a radically different person from the one who went in, with very different beliefs, values, and assumptions.

Because that is my conception of college, an older conception of college: as a place that teaches you, precisely, how to think: that teaches you *to* think. That forces you to approach, and shows you how to approach, those fundamental questions that I touched upon before: What is the good? What are freedom, equality, and justice; beauty, truth, happiness, prosperity, and success? What do I care about, and what do I want? And a student's fundamental duty, I believe, is to take those questions on.

Now every college will tell you that it teaches you how to think: how to engage, in the campus cliché, in "critical thinking." But we need to understand—as colleges themselves in general do not—that there are two kinds of thinking that college should ask you to do, corresponding to the two conceptions of what college should be for.

The first is the instrumental kind, the kind through which you develop the tools and skills that enable you to operate in the world and on the world—to solve problems, to get things done, to become an expert, a specialist, a professional, a technocrat. Instrumental thinking involves addressing specific, technical questions, in whatever discipline, that have specific answers, ones that can be worked out through formalized, iterable methods—equations, experiments, studies, statistical models. The knowledge so acquired is also sequential and cumulative. You learn in a particular order, and you learn more and more. And just as there is nothing wrong with the instrumental purpose of college (so long as it is not the only purpose), with acquiring the ability to do things in the world, whether that means making a living or making a contribution, so is there nothing wrong with this kind of learning. It enables you to achieve what the educational bureaucrats like to call "mastery": mastery of a subject, which in turn confers mastery over the world.

But this kind of learning does not work for the other kind of thinking, the kind that's needed to address those fundamental and in some sense fundamentally irresolvable questions of value and purpose and meaning that should lie at the heart of a college education, because they lie at the heart of life itself: the questions raised by experience, the questions that have to be faced in order to navigate experience—in order to go through the world, in order to conduct your life. Such thinking can and must be rigorous and precise, but it cannot be sequential or cumulative or formalized or iterable. It also can't be captured or measured with the kinds of assessment regimes that students now are typically subjected to: multiple-choice questions, skills-based exams, memorization and regurgitation. It does not involve the same capacities as instrumental thinking, which is why we often reach for other words to name it—words like "reflection" or "contemplation," which gesture toward the soul or spirit, not just toward the intellect or mind.

To bring this distinction into sharper focus, let me offer a few points of orientation. The first one comes from Eva Brann, a longtime tutor at St. John's College in Annapolis. In *Paradoxes of Education in a Republic*, Brann contrasts instrumental reason with what she calls "the question-asking intellect." The latter functions, she says, by being receptive to the world. "A genuine question," she writes, "is an expectant vacancy, a receptive openness, a defined ignorance, and, above all, a directed desire."

The second comes from Hannah Arendt, the political philosopher, in an essay on the Pentagon Papers, or rather, on their subjects, the so-called whiz kids who ran the war in Vietnam—the gang of experts David Halberstam would later call, in a rancidly sarcastic phrase that has since lost its irony and become the standard compliment we pay our high achievers, "the best and the brightest." Arendt refers to them as "the problem-solvers," because they conducted the war by reducing it to a set of metrics: of inputs, algorithms, procedures, and finally predictions, which, "unaccountably," she says, "never came true." "The problem-solvers," Arendt writes, "did not *judge*; they calculated . . . they trusted the calculating powers of their brains at the expense of the mind's capacity for experience and its ability to learn from it." Needless to say, Arendt's calculating power corresponds to Brann's instrumental reason, and what she calls the ability to learn from experience depends on Brann's receptive openness and defined (which means, first of all, acknowledged) ignorance.

My third point of reference comes from Diana Senechal, a contemporary educator and author. In *Republic of Noise*, Senechal interrogates the assumption that students ought to achieve "mastery" over all of the material that's put in front of them: that they need to learn it completely and demonstrate that competence through certain kinds of assessment, ideally, quantifiable ones. That word "mastery," again. And mastery is a perfectly reasonable standard when you're learning calculus or chemistry or Spanish. But when you study Plato, Senechal says—or Shakespeare, I would add, or anything else in the humanities—there is no such thing as mastery. No one ever masters those works, which is precisely why they are worth coming back to again and again. And no one ever masters the questions that those works impose on us, which is why those, too, are worth coming back to, are essential to come back to, again and again. They are the questions, in the words of Geoff Dyer, that stay put—the questions, I would add, that the world asks of you, rather than the other way around. And the chief question that the world asks of you is "who are you?"

The only appropriate relationship in which to stand to those works and those questions is receptive openness, defined ignorance, and directed desire. You don't read *King Lear* so that you can master *King Lear*. You read it for what it does to you, for the way it changes you, and you take that into the next thing you read, and, indeed, into the rest of your life. And hopefully that experience—and it is an experience, not a lesson or "message"—enhances your capacity *for* experience, and your ability to learn from it.

But, says Brann, question-asking, or, as she also calls it, inquiry, "is the most difficult of activities to direct, because it demands that the teacher provide discipline while forgoing dogma." By dogma I believe Brann means not only ideological certainty, but certainty of any kind, including that which properly derives from disciplinary study. When you train students in the other, instrumental kind of thinking, you possess the answers. In the context of inquiry, you don't. The big questions are persistent questions because no one has the answers. Which means that when you operate as a teacher in the mode of inquiry, you are entitled to do so not by virtue of your expertise, because there is no expertise, but by virtue of your experience, your experience *with* experience: that is, your own history of reflection *upon* experience. By virtue, in other words, of your wisdom, which is to say, your humanity—understanding humanity as something that is not given, but achieved.

If I had to pick a single word to sum up what reflection can help you achieve, what Arendt found so missing in the problem-solvers, in the technocrats, it would indeed be "wisdom." It is no coincidence that "philosophy," a practice that was founded, in the West, by Socrates himself, means "love of wisdom." And if I had to define wisdom, I would say that it's a kind of deftness, a sort of tact or touch, in the application of knowledge, specifically such knowledge as derives from experience. A wise person is the kind of person you go to not for information, but for counsel; not for good answers, but for better questions.

Wisdom, of course, is associated with age, and for good reason. Most of us do not achieve it until relatively late in life (if then). So just as college is only the start of what will presumably be a long professional career, so should it also be the start of a long road to wisdom. Which is fine, because for all that any given college student wants to change the world, it's likely to be quite a while before they have any real power to do so. They might as well acquire some wisdom to go along with that power by the time they achieve it. If you want to see what happens when power is exercised in the absence of wisdom, you can look at today's whiz kids, the ones who run Silicon Valley and therefore determine so much of our world. As Ta-Nehisi Coates remarked in a different context, very young and very smart is always a dangerous combination. And as the musician Zoë Keating has put it, one of the problems with Silicon Valley is that tech people can't imagine that everything they make isn't totally awesome for everyone else, because they can't imagine scenarios outside their own reality.

I said that the chief question that the world imposes on you, and that college ought to help you begin to work out, is "who are you?" The heart of reflection is self-reflection; the essence of knowledge is self-knowledge. If you don't know yourself—if you haven't become visible to yourself—you don't know the biases with which you know everything else, and you also don't know the motives that move you to action. But self-knowledge and the knowledge of others are two sides of the same coin. They happen together and they work together. The humanities in general, and literature in particular, enable you to think about yourself by asking you to think about others. Which means that when you read, you should do so not to entrench your identity, but to expand your humanity. "I place my faith in fiction," says the novelist and philosopher Rebecca Goldstein, "in its power to make vividly present how different the world feels to each of us." Its power, in other words, to enable you to imagine scenarios outside your own reality.

And that's a power that you need to have before you can responsibly make use of any other kind of power, before you can have an impact or change the world—phrases that speak of power. So yes, when college students graduate, they should take their moral passion forth into the world. But in the meantime, their primary job is to think. Before you change the world, you have to change your mind.

[2018]

WHY I LEFT ACADEMIA
(SINCE YOU'RE WONDERING)

If I care so much about college—about students, about teaching, about the humanities, about the transformative potential of the undergraduate experience—then why did I leave? Why, in 2008, after ten years on the faculty at Yale, did I say goodbye not only to that institution but to the profession as a whole? A lot of people have asked me that question; a lot more have assumed they know the answer. Did I quit in disgust at the corruption of the academic enterprise? Could I no longer bear to participate in the perpetuation of the class system? If I didn't get tenure at Yale, did I regard it as beneath my dignity to work at a less prestigious institution? No, no, and no.

Here's why I left: I didn't have a choice. I not only failed to get tenure at Yale—which was completely expected—I failed to land another job anywhere else. Let me explain how it works. When you are hired as an assistant professor, after you complete your PhD, at a leading research institution like Yale, the hope is not that you'll get tenure down the line. That almost never happens; for tenure at a top school, you need to stand among the foremost leaders in your field, and very few people are capable of establishing that kind of reputation in the space of six years. No, the hope is that you'll stay awhile, publish, then jump to another job somewhere else, somewhere that *will* tenure you. That's exactly what I saw among the junior faculty who preceded me in the English department. They got jobs at places like Northwestern, Northeastern, Smith, UNC, and the University of Kentucky. And that is what I thought that I would do, as well.

That I failed was not for lack of trying. Once I had finished a book and gotten it accepted for publication (this was in my sixth year), I went back on the job market. I received a few interviews, but no offers. Then I went back the next year. And the next year. And the next. (Yale had an anomalous system; you could stay for a maximum of ten years rather than the usual seven, with promotion to untenured associate after the sixth.) Here is a list of the schools I applied to:

Brown (twice)
Bryn Mawr
BU
Dartmouth
Davidson
Eugene Lang (The New School)
Holy Cross
Johns Hopkins (twice)
Kenyon
Macalester
McGill
Notre Dame
NYU (twice)
Ohio State, Mansfield
Ohio University
Penn State
Queen's University
Rutgers
Saint Louis University
Scripps
Stony Brook
SUNY Albany
Tulane
University of British Columbia (twice)
University of California, Davis
University of California, Irvine
University of California, San Diego
University of Chicago
University of Colorado
University of Illinois
University of Maryland
University of Michigan
University of Oregon (twice)
University of Pennsylvania (three times)
University of Portland

University of Toronto Mississauga
Vanderbilt
Western Washington University
Williams

That's thirty-nine schools and forty-six applications. Prestigious universities, public and private; non-prestigious universities, public and private;
Canadian universities; liberal arts colleges. Institutions in the Northeast,
Midwest, South, West, and north of the border; schools urban, suburban,
and rural. I would've gone just about anywhere. But with all that work and
all that hope, I got a total of five interviews, two callbacks (the final stage in
the hiring process), and zero offers.

With a name like Yale on my CV, plus a decent publication record, I must
have really screwed things up to have experienced such dismal fortune. And
I did. Oh, I did.

Let's go back. I hadn't followed the usual route to graduate school. I had
majored in science, not English (although, by the middle of college, I dearly
wished that I *had* majored in English). That meant that when I got to graduate
school, I was several years behind my classmates—a handicap, but not a fatal
one. More importantly, it meant that I entered the doctoral program without having been socialized into the profession to even the slightest degree. I
entered like an undergraduate, with an undergraduate's idealism and naïveté.
For me, graduate school, which I didn't begin until four years after finish-
ing college, was a way of finally doing that English major that I'd always
wished I'd done. I went, in other words, because I wanted to read books:
because I loved books; because I lived my deepest life in books; because art,
particularly literary art, meant everything to me; because I wanted to put
myself under the guidance of teachers who would inspire me and mentor me;
because I hoped someday to be such a teacher myself.

Anyone in the academic humanities—anyone who's gotten within smell-
ing distance of the academic humanities these last forty years—will see the
problem. Loving books is not why people are supposed to become English
professors, and it hasn't been for a long time. Loving books is scoffed at (or
would be, if anybody ever copped to it). The whole concept of literature—
still more, of art—has been discredited. Novels, poems, stories, plays: these
are "texts," no different in kind from other texts. The purpose of studying

them is not to appreciate or understand them; it is to "interrogate" them for their ideological investments (in patriarchy, in white supremacy, in Western imperialism and ethnocentrism), and then to unmask and debunk them, to drain them of their poisonous persuasive power. The passions that are meant to draw people to the profession of literary study, these last many years, are not aesthetic; they are political.

I was dimly aware, when I got to graduate school, that the experience would be different from the few college English classes I had taken—I knew that "theory" was big, though I didn't much know what it was—but I had no idea what I'd be up against. Fortunately (or not), it didn't take long to find out. The first week of my first seminar—it was a "proseminar," designed specifically for entering students—the professor said this: "The most important thing for a first-year graduate student to do is to figure out where they stand ideologically."

"I know where I stand ideologically!" the young man next to me burst out. "I am a marxist with a small m." He was pounced upon by two or three of the women. "But Marxism has nothing to say about feminist issues!" one of them said. "That is why I am a marxist with a *small* m!" he replied. The professor smiled benignly; her pupils were apt. I cowered beneath the table (metaphorically), understanding immediately that, like a dissenter in a marxist (small m or large) regime, I would need to speak my true beliefs behind closed doors, and only to those I could trust.

Gradually, over the next few years, I got the lay of the professional terrain I'd entered into. It was marked not only by a relentless animus against the works of the past (and the "dead white men" who wrote them), but by a constant effort to enlist them in contemporary battles; by an enthrallment with jargon, a commitment to verbal opacity, and a suspicion of clear, conversational prose; by intellectual dishonesty and flabbiness and sloppiness, all implicitly excused by the alleged rightness of the cause; by an adolescent sense of moral superiority; by a pervasive atmosphere of ideological surveillance.

But what disgusted me the most was not the intellectual corruption. It was the careerism. It was the sense that all of this—all the posturing, all the position-taking—was nothing more than a professional game. The goal was advancement, not truth. The worst mistake was to think for yourself. People said things that they obviously didn't believe, or wouldn't have believed if they had bothered to subject them to the test of their own experience—that language is incapable of making meaning, that the self is a construct—but that the climate forced them to avow. Students stuck their fingers in the air to see which way the theoretical winds were blowing, designing their dissertations to catch the swell of the latest trend. Names of departmental stars—"Franco," "Gayatri"—were dropped in the graduate lounge like aces in a poker game. The whole enterprise seemed completely self-enclosed. People claimed to aim to change the world, to exert some influence outside of the academy, when it was perfectly clear that their highest ambition was tenure. One of the students I started with, among the smartest and most well-read, was a strong feminist who really did want to change the world. She left after a year to go to law school, where she felt that she actually could.

So why did I stay? Because I still loved books. Because I found some teachers to inspire and guide me, mostly by taking classes with people over fifty (there were still enough professors of the old school hanging on, though they were increasingly embattled). Because, as I'd suspected I would and discovered I did, I loved to teach. Because I thought that if I faked it long enough and hard enough—published enough articles, with enough footnotes—then I could slip through the cracks, get a job somewhere, then tenure somewhere, before I was found out. Because I believed in doing things the right way— reading the right way (to learn from books, not lecture them), thinking the right way (with both feet on the ground), writing the right way (like an actual human being), and teaching the right way (helping students to be better versions of themselves, not little versions of me)—and I wasn't going to yield the field without a fight. I wasn't going to let the bastards grind me down.

The strategy worked for a while. A long while, really. There were some potholes, to be sure, especially to do with the fact that I could never bring myself to read much theory, or to write the way that the discipline wanted me to, with that generic, disembodied voice. One of the department stars, who agreed to read a couple of chapters of my dissertation on the condition that he didn't actually have to sit on my committee (i.e., make a real effort), asked me afterward if I'd been living in a cave for twenty years. Even my graduate adviser, generally sympathetic and encouraging, said that I sounded like I was writing for the *New Yorker*. One year, the school played host to the annual meeting of the American Comparative Literature Association, the second-most important conference in the field—a fact to which I had succeeded in remaining oblivious, though I should have known that something was up when a fellow student, abuzz with preprofessional pheromones, asked if I was going to "the plenary." The last day, I bumped into one of my professors headed in the opposite direction. She was someone who usually got a mild vicarious kick from my subversive attitude. "Where are you going?" I asked her. "To the *conference*?" she said. Like, *where else?* "What conference?" I asked. A look passed across her face that was as if to say, "How far are you planning to push this charade?"

Nonetheless, I managed to publish a couple of articles and get some decent recommendations from professors over fifty, and when I ventured on the job market, the year I finished my degree, I was offered interviews at five institutions (out of the twenty to which I applied). Four were lower-tier places—Auburn, the University of Montana, Georgia State, and Cal State Los Angeles—and the fifth was Yale. The explanation for this strange assortment is that Yale's was still a very conservative department—meaning, it was still run by people who shared my intellectual values. Being able to write, for example, was not considered a liability. And since junior hires, who were only supposed to stick around for a few years, were mainly valued for their teaching, the department also cared a lot about how well they thought you'd do it. I withdrew from the other searches before they concluded (Yale made its decisions early, without callbacks), but it's quite possible that if I hadn't gotten the position I did, I would not have gotten one at all.

After nine years in graduate school, uncertain the entire time about my future, I had been granted a new lease on my professional life. Given Yale's generous ten-year timeline, plus leaves of absence in the fourth and seventh years, I should've been able to make it work: publish, get another job, make it to Castle Tenure.

But there were problems. For one thing, I was still having trouble bringing myself to professionalize. The drudgery of it all! Slogging through a desert of secondary sources (as bad as it is to have to write academic prose, having to read it is brain death). Enduring the endless odyssey of scholarly publication: submitting, submitting, submitting (rejection, rejection, rejection), submitting once more, revising, revising, revising (six months, twelve months, eighteen months), all for a single precious line on your CV and a readership of approximately zero. And the conferences. Oh, the conferences. You fly across the country to sit in airless ballrooms, scented with the odor of professional futility, listening to airless talks. You shuffle from panel to panel, with your name tag and your conference folder and your shoulder bag, like a middle manager at a sales convention. You give your presentation—your tiny little contribution—only to have it picked and poked at in the Q&A. (One interlocutor, whom I'd never met before, began her question by announcing that she was going to "torture Bill.") That is, when anybody's even there to pay attention. I went to a single conference in graduate school, where my panel was attended by five people, two of whom walked out before I gave my talk because they'd only come to hear their friend's. I didn't go to another one for almost five years.

Yet it wasn't just the drudgery, which might have been endurable if I had thought it served a valid purpose. I was having trouble professionalizing because, fundamentally, I didn't care about the profession. I didn't believe in the profession. I didn't think that writing literary monographs and journal articles, or going to academic conferences, does much of any good for anyone. And I don't believe that I'm alone in that—I mean, not even within the profession. That is why, I think, so many literary academics need to imagine they're saving the world, and why so many end up writing about anything, it seems, but literature: Houdini, Hitchcock, *Buffy* (this is known as "cultural studies"), law, history, human rights (subjects that are felt to have more gravitas). I was just less interested than other people in participating in the pretense.

Besides, there were things I did believe in, things I thought more worthy of my time. Above all, teaching. Books had blown my mind open when I was a young adult, they had literally changed my life, and I wanted to enable that for other people—college students in particular. Graduate students are there to be professionalized. College students come to you because they're hungry for enlightenment; books, for them, are still about life. Graduate students need to demonstrate how much they know; they've settled into their intellectual position, and they'll defend it to the death. College students are open, fluid, still exploring, still being formed; they have not yet learned what they're supposed to think, and they don't mind saying, "I don't know." They are still alive, in a way that many of my colleagues, and many of the adults I knew in general, were not. But teaching, for me, was also about developing relationships. It was about office hours, and the open-ended conversations that can happen there, as much as it was about the classroom. It was about having a student freshman year, then seeing them again—in other classes, or as their adviser, or just because they felt like dropping by—for the next three years, then continuing to hear from them after they graduated. It was, in other words, about mentorship.

The other thing I believed in was writing for a general audience: partici-pating in the wider culture, sharing my love of art, sharing my understand-ing of art. Communicating with people beyond the narrow circle of fellow subspecialists. I had done this in graduate school, as a dance critic (one of the reasons it took me nine years to finish). I continued to do it, at Yale, as a book critic and, eventually, an essayist. I thought that it was something academics ought to do, a way of contributing to society, but mainly I did it because I liked to. I liked to write: to tinker with sentences, to make sounds and patterns with words, to give myself, and hopefully others, a thrill. I liked the chance to read like a reader, not a professor, the way I used to read, and, since my specialty was nineteenth-century literature, to read contemporary fiction, to find out what novels were saying about the world that I was living through. I liked having a presence in that world. It certainly seemed a better use of my ability than writing another journal article.

The problem with spending time with students, or on students, or writ-ing book reviews or essays is that none of those activities do anything for you professionally. Academics are rewarded for one thing and one thing only: research. Scholarly publication. Nothing else counts; anything else is a step toward professional suicide. I knew this, of course, and it tormented me. But, to quote a phrase, I could do no other. I believed in what I believed in, and if I had to do it the other way, the way you were supposed to—shaft my stu-dents by doing the minimum for them, enclose my mind completely within the profession—then I would rather not do it at all. Besides, I didn't think that I could put my soul aside for ten or twenty years and still be able to find it at the end.

So I tried to have it both ways. I did my scholarly work with one hand and my teaching and nonacademic writing with the other. I tried to beat the system; I tried to write my own rules. And I came pretty close to succeeding. I got those five interviews my last four years on the job market, all of them, essentially, at liberal arts colleges, the kinds of schools that place a greater emphasis on teaching and that I was hoping to work at in any case. But in the end, I came up short.

And maybe that was for the best. Maybe the truth is that academic life—not as I imagined it going into graduate school, but as it actually is—was not the proper place for me. Certainly, in terms of my intellectual life, I'm much happier doing what I've been doing since I left: writing the kinds of essays that appear in this book, and other things besides, but doing it full-time. Following my curiosity wherever it leads, unconstrained by disciplinary boundaries, academic shibboleths, or the crotchets of peer referees. Back when I was still an academic, whenever I got an idea that didn't pertain to my research or teaching—an idea about the world around me, about something that I'd noticed in the culture—I would tear off a strip of paper, jot it down, and stick the paper under the stapler on my desk. Once a year, after spring semester and before I returned to my scholarly work for the summer, I would gather up the strips, take a seat in the garden, and transcribe them into a notebook, expanding on them as I went—letting my mind off its leash, dreaming of essays to come. Those were some of the best hours of my year. Now it is the way I make my living.

And maybe my fate was also just. If there are any academics reading this, I'm sure that's what they're saying to themselves. Who am I to think I'm special? Who am I to think that I can thumb my nose at the profession and get away with it? And that's fair. I'm not special. I just made different choices, and I need to live with them. But let me just say this, now that professors approach me and tell me that they want to "write"—want to do what I do (though without, presumably, losing their jobs). To do what I do, you had to have done what I've done. A writer isn't something you decide to be one day; becoming one takes as much work, as many years and tears, as becoming a tenured professor. Our paths diverged a long time ago, and now they're very far apart. There's no going back, for either of us, and no way of getting from one to the other. You can no more expect to be able to "write" now than I can expect to be offered a faculty job. You also made your choices, and you also need to live with them.

No, I didn't play by the rules, so I can't expect to have won. Unless the problem is the rules. Because it wasn't so much that I wanted to be treated differently than everybody as that I wanted everybody to be treated differently. I wanted the rules to change; I played by the ones that I thought we should have. I insisted on behaving as if I existed in an environment that valued teaching as much as scholarship and intellectualism as much as specialization. Where opening the eyes of a hundred undergraduates was worth as much as supervising one more dissertation, and publishing an essay in a periodical that's read by tens of thousands was as valuable as adding one more item to the pile of disregarded studies.

For this isn't just my story, and if it were just my story, then it wouldn't be very important. It's a story of misplaced institutional priorities. And beyond that, it's a story of a profession that is eating its young. You see, I could have done everything I did, and not done everything I didn't, and managed to survive, if not for a reality that far transcended my individual choices. I could have spent too much time on my teaching and writing, I could have published academic work that refused to clothe itself in jargon or to pay obeisance to the latest trends, I could have even had a white penis (which put two strikes against me on the job market), and still have found another position, were it not for this: there were fewer and fewer positions to find. Institutions were shifting their teaching to adjuncts on a monumental scale. They were destroying with one hand the professoriate they were creating with the other. And, of course, it's only gotten worse since then: worse and worse and worse. Which means that while the particulars of my story may be unique to me, the outcome is not. Thousands of people are driven out of the profession each year (and thousands more agree to settle for the adjunct life). And the ones who get screwed, as the general level of undergraduate instruction continues to be abysmal, tend to be the dedicated teachers, the ones who made the same mistake that I did, of caring about their students. Ultimately, the reason I left academia (since you're wondering) is the same that many others have. My story is a personal disappointment; the larger story is a tragedy.

[2021]

HEAL FOR AMERICA

America faces a growing shortage of primary care physicians, especially in chronically underserved inner-city and rural communities. By 2032, according to a recent report, the shortfall will amount to as many as fifty-five thousand providers. Yet fewer and fewer medical school graduates elect to enter primary care. Deterred by poor reimbursement rates, low income relative to other specialties, and increasing patient loads—not to mention high levels of student debt—new MDs are opting instead for more lucrative fields.

I'd like to propose a solution. Each year, thousands of students graduate from America's most prestigious colleges without a clear vocational direction. They are brilliant, hardworking, and eager to contribute to society. What better way to address our shortage of physicians than to organize these new graduates into a corps of energetic, idealistic young doctors and dispatch them to those same underserved areas? I envision a competitive application process, five-week summer training program, and two-year initial commitment. Sure, recruits are likely to feel overwhelmed at first, but what a life experience for them, out there on the front lines of the healthcare crisis, making a real difference in people's lives!

I can already hear the objections. With little training and no experience, our new providers won't be "real" doctors. What will they possibly have to contribute? But a lot of experts say that medical school is a waste of time. Poorly taught classes in tedious subjects like anatomy and physiology are no match for the enthusiasm, enterprise, and general awesomeness that our novice physicians will bring to the clinic. In medicine, after all, knowledge and skill are less important than a can-do spirit. Besides, these kids are the best and the brightest, as their colleges are always telling them, quick studies in any subject to which they choose to turn their scintillating intellects. They'll be up to speed in no time.

Will there be resentment from the other doctors—the ones who have been toiling in obscurity for years, unvalued, ignored, and underpaid—about having to work beside these Ivy League celebrities? Perhaps, but what matters here are the patients, not the sensitivities of a bunch of careerist hacks who have always been more interested, quite frankly, in protecting their professional prerogatives. If our new physicians help to break the power of the AMA, then so much the better. And if they accept the two years that society invests in them and then decide to take their talents to a different field, like finance or consulting—well, I'm sure they'll be a friend to healthcare for the rest of their successful lives.

Besides, what is the alternative? Funding medical services for low-income communities at anything like adequate levels would take a lot of money. Not compared to what we give the Pentagon, but you know what I mean. America's job creators aren't going to stand for higher taxes, not when the share of income that goes to the top 1 percent amounts to a measly 23 percent. Our aggregate tax burden is already over 25 percent, more than half of what it is in western Europe. We need to be realistic here.

Similar proposals have been made with respect to our educational system, but those are ridiculous, of course. Everybody understands that it takes years of training and experience to become a good teacher, and that students and schools need continuity, not a pack of self-congratulatory dilettantes who parachute in for a couple of years, then go off to Goldman or McKinsey with their newly burnished résumés. I could see it working for lawyers, though.

[2013]

ON THE BEACH

My first semester in graduate school, one of my professors told us a story. This was from his own days in graduate school, at UCLA. A classmate had failed his orals. Now he was trying again; if he failed the second time, he'd be out of the program. When my professor ran into him on his way out of the building after the exam, the guy had a grin on his face.

"How did you do?" my professor asked.

"I failed!" he said.

"Then why are you smiling?" my professor asked.

"Because I'm going to the beach!"

It took me fifteen years to understand that story. I had thought it was about those silly Southern Californians—that they're always happy, no matter what else is going on in their lives, as long as they can make it to the beach. It was only once I had survived my own oral exams, humped my way through a dissertation, played the game of job market roulette (which starts to feel like Russian roulette), endured a couple of performance reviews, ventured back on the job market, and thought about the endless succession of humiliations that was still stretching out in front of me that I understood what the story was really about. He was out. They couldn't touch him anymore. He was going to the beach.

When I left academia and set about to try to make it as a full-time writer, I was dreading the commercial side of my new profession. Like every good leftist and many an academic, I looked on the market as evil, a place that would besmirch your values and destroy your soul. But it didn't take me long to realize that I preferred the discipline of the market to the discipline of the disciplines.

Here's the incident that, in retrospect, brought things into focus for me. My final academic article (it was on *Jude the Obscure*) had been returned by the editor with a profusion of niggling comments. What especially galled me was her insistence that I "fix the pronouns." In other words, I had committed the cardinal sin of using the word "we," long discredited in right-thinking circles as an instrument of repressive liberal universalism (as in "we think" or "we believe"). Never mind the fact that I had employed the pronoun in a different sense entirely, merely to refer to "we" readers of the novel, Hardy's implied audience. Now I'd have to mar the piece—it was for a Festschrift for my graduate adviser, so the prospect was especially painful—and for no good reason other than the imbecilic crotchets of one individual. Who was this person, anyway? I knew that she taught in a prestigious department, but when I looked her up, I discovered that what she mainly was was an academic bureaucrat, the kind of figure who doesn't publish much but manages to climb the ranks by sitting on lots of boards and committees.

This is a trivial instance, but I had seen far graver versions of it all the time: people who were blocked from getting jobs or keeping them, people whose work was rejected for publication (a body blow in academia, of course), and only because a single individual decided to stand in their way, a single human bottleneck, and often for motives that were purely personal, or self-interested, or just plain arbitrary. The market is indeed no respecter of higher values, but at least the transactions are honest. If an editor thinks your book will sell, they'll buy it. There are no hidden agendas. They aren't going to care if it conforms to the latest intellectual fashions, or whether you've cited their friends. You're also shooting at a vastly bigger target. Millions of people buy books in this country; only a tiny fraction need to purchase yours to make it a success. In academia, where job openings are scarce and only a few journals exist in any given field, a handful of gatekeepers decide your fate.

They also treat you as an equal in the market. It isn't just an endless series of hazing rituals. You are a potential partner, and there are always other people you can work with. In academia, though, you are forever trembling, like a figure out of Kafka, before the next tribunal: graduate admissions, graduate courses, orals, chapter conferences, dissertation committee, hiring committees, peer reviews for publications and grants, promotion reviews, tenure review, more peer reviews and promotion reviews. And because it's always up or out, at least until you get tenure, you can't just muddle along at the same level, the way you can in other occupations. Everything is always on the line; every test is existential.

The reason that academic politics are so vicious, the old joke goes, is that the stakes are so low. But that is not entirely the case. The power of senior figures over graduate students and junior colleagues is quite complete, and quite routinely abused. You are at their mercy, and mercy is in short supply. (The stakes for the decision makers, to be sure, are small. They have job security and no bottom line to worry about.) The longer you are in, what's more, the worse it gets (at least, again, until the moment of tenure), because the fewer your options outside the walls. The more the academic job market continues to implode, the fewer your options in any case. One thing seems certain, as the crisis in higher education proceeds: the way that people treat each other is only going to get worse.

For graduate students, however, the barrier to leaving the profession is more psychological ("I'm going to the beach!") than anything else. You're made to feel, if you even contemplate it, as if you were thinking of renouncing holy orders—another survival, like its feudal hierarchy, of academia's origin in the Middle Ages. I saw it many times, in my department, with students who had chosen, usually with many agonies of self-reproach, to drop out of the program: the shame, the sense of failure, the sense, even, of pollution, as if these decent young people—diligent, earnest, goodhearted—were descending from Parnassus to the dirty world. But academia already is the dirty world. What judgment shall we pass on a profession that, in the name of high ideals, so betrays the trust, so trifles with the conscience, of its children?

[2012]

In Memoriam

Iwrite this on the second anniversary of the death of my graduate school adviser—my *Doktorvater*, as the Germans say. The fact I even know this ought to give you some idea of my feelings for the man. As it happened, I didn't receive the news for several weeks. The book that I was writing at the time was going to have a chapter that was constructed around our relationship when I was in school. Really, in some sense the whole thing was an homage to him, and one of my deepest hopes for the project was that he would get to see it before it was too late. He was old, and he'd been sick, very sick, for several years, yet I was sure, somehow, that he would hold out long enough. Which was nothing but magical thinking, of course. But I'd begun to correspond with him again a few months earlier, and I was simply unable to imagine that he would die before the book was ready. I was unable to imagine that he would die at all.

The day that I sat down to start the chapter, I decided to check his Wikipedia page. I knew that I would talk about his energy, his productivity, and I wanted to remember exactly how many books he had written. I didn't even get that far. As soon as I googled his name, I saw it there, under the link: "Karl Kroeber (1926–2009)." Even now as I write this I still can't comprehend the finality of that second number. My own father's death, the previous year, had not been as difficult. Not because I loved Karl more, but because our conversation wasn't finished. But then, it never would have been. It seizes me, suddenly, still. Something crosses my mind, and I call to him in thought, needing to hear what he thinks. And then I remember: he isn't there anymore. I know that he's dead, but I still can't quite accept that he is really *dead*.

A memorial was held a few months later. A lot of people came. It made me jealous to be forced to realize just how many students had loved him over the years—to realize that I wasn't even in the inner circle, in the long run—but larger than the jealousy was simply gratitude that I had been allowed to know him at all, along with awe that one man could have blessed so many. Our minds were asleep, and he awoke them at a touch.

I had a dream about a year ago. I was standing in a wide but shallow room, a kind of auditorium or hall, a little elevated on a set of bleachers that ran along one of the longer walls. Other people were about. Then I spotted him walking across the length of the room in front of me. He was bearing a sheaf of papers before him, and his eyes were fixed ahead. There was something stately about his presence, and something inhuman, as well. I called to him, then called again, but he could not hear me, or he would not hear me, only kept on walking with that steady, almost trancelike purpose. He approached the farthest wall, and before my disbelieving eyes, and to the swell of unappeasable grief, he disappeared right through it.

If I believed in God, I would say that Karl was bringing Him his final manuscript. But I don't believe in God, and neither did he. He believed in the future. He believed in us.

I think of Socrates and Jesus, if only to think of something else. I multiply my grief at losing Karl by a thousand, and imagine what their students must have felt—what Plato must have felt, and Xenophon, what Peter and Thomas and James. And so, to keep their teachers with them, they committed their words to writing, preserving the memory of their sweet discourses. And we've been straining for the echoes of them ever since.

My book was done—too late. My book came out. And to my fellow students, to the members of his family, I inscribe it thus: *His spirit lives in all of us who knew him.*

[2011]

THE SOCIAL IMAGINATION

GENERATION SELL

Ever since I moved to Portland, Oregon, that hotbed of all things hipster, I've been trying to understand the meaning of today's youth culture. The style is easy enough to describe—the skinny pants, the facial hair, the wall-to-wall tattoos. The question is, what does it signify: what kind of idea of life, what stance with respect to the world?

To bring the question into focus, I've tried both to simplify it and to think about it comparatively. The hipsters have taken their place in a line of youth cultures that dates back, at least, to the late 1940s: beatniks, hippies, punks, slackers. Each, I've decided, can be understood in terms of two related attributes: the emotion or affect they valorized (the thing you were supposed to feel) and the social form they envisioned (the way they wanted the world to look).

For the hippies, the feeling was love: love-ins, free love, the Summer of Love, all you need is love. The social form was utopia, understood in collective terms: the commune, the music festival, the liberation movement. The beatniks aimed at ecstasy, embodied as a social form in individual transcendence. Theirs was a culture of jazz, with its spontaneity; of marijuana, arresting time and flooding the soul with pleasure (this was before the substance became the background drug of youth culture as such); of the flight, on the road, to the West; of the quest for the perfect moment.

The punks were all about rage, their social program nihilistic anarchy. "Get pissed," Johnny Rotten sang. "Destroy." (Hip-hop, punk's younger brother from another mother, was all about rage and nihilism, too, at least at first.) As for the slackers of the late '80s and early '90s (Gen X, grunge, the fiction of David Foster Wallace), their affect ran to apathy and angst, a sense of aimlessness and pointlessness. Whatever. That they had no social vision was precisely what their social vision was: a defensive withdrawal from all commitment as inherently phony.

So what is the hipster affect—or let us say, more broadly, the millennial affect? The thing that strikes me most about young people now is how nice they all seem to be: polite, pleasant, moderate, earnest, friendly. Rock and roll-ers used to be snarling rebels or chest-beating egomaniacs. Now the presentation is low-key, self-deprecating, post-ironic, eco-friendly. When Vampire Weekend appeared on the *Colbert Report* to plug their album *Contra*, the host asked them what they were against. "Closed-mindedness," they said. In Jonathan Franzen's *Freedom*, an aging rocker, surveying the crowd at a club, thinks, "they seemed . . . to bear malice toward nobody . . . gathered not in anger but in celebration of their having found . . . a gentler and more respectful way of being." A former colleague of mine is said to have told his students that they belong to a "post-emotional" generation. No edge, in other words: no anger, no ego.

What is this about? A rejection of culture-war strife? A principled desire to live more lightly on the planet? A matter of the way that kids today are raised—all, everybody's special and everybody's point of view is valid and everybody's feelings should be taken care of? Perhaps a bit of each, but mainly, I think, something else.

Consider my other interpretive criterion. What is the millennial genera-tion's ideal social form? Here is what I see around me, in the city and the cul-ture: food carts, twentysomethings selling wallets made from recycled plastic bags, boutique pickle companies, boutiques, techie start-ups, Kickstarter, urban-farming supply stores, bottled water that wants to save the planet, website ventures. Today's ideal social form is not the commune or the move-ment or even the individual creator as such; it is the small business. Every artistic or moral aspiration—music, food, good works, what have you—appears to seek expression in those terms. Call it Generation Sell. Bands are still bands, but now they're little businesses, as well: self-produced, self-published, self-managed. When I hear from young people who want to get off the careerist treadmill and do something meaningful, they talk about opening a restaurant. The objective is not to get rich. Nonprofits are still hip, as well, but students don't dream about joining one; they dream about starting one. In any case, what's really hip is "social entrepreneurship"—companies that try to make money responsibly, then give it all away.

None of this is bad, necessarily, but it is striking. Forty years ago, even twenty years ago, a young person's first thought, even second or third thought, was not to start a business. That was "selling out"—a phrase that has rather tellingly disappeared from our vocabulary. Where did it come from, this change? Less Reaganism, as an old student suggested to me, than Clintonism—the heroic age of dot-com entrepreneurship that today's young people grew up amidst (and during which the hipster culture began to emerge). Add a distrust of large organizations, including government, as well as the sense, a legacy of recent years, that it's every man for himself. Because this isn't just millennials. The small business is the idealized social form of our time, full stop. Our culture hero now is not the artist or reformer, not the saint or scientist, but the entrepreneur. Autonomy, adventure, imagination: entrepreneurship comprehends all this and more for us. The characteristic art form of our age may be the business plan.

And that, I think, is the real meaning of the millennial affect—which, like the entrepreneurial ideal, is essentially everyone's now. Today's polite, pleasant personality is, above all, a commercial one. It is the salesman's smile and hearty handshake. (If you want to get ahead, said Benjamin Franklin, the original business guru, then make yourself pleasing to others.) I was recently contacted by a young woman who plans to launch a website to promote the need for reading and reflection to people of her generation. Not just promote it, though, of course, but market it. When she asked me for advice, I suggested that she start by pointing out the superficiality of social media. Well, she said, I agree with that, that's the whole premise of what I'm trying to do, but I wouldn't want to come across as negative, because that turns people off. If they think you're criticizing them, she said, they won't want to buy what you're selling.

That is precisely what I am talking about: the bland, inoffensive, smile-and-a-shoeshine personality—the stay-positive, other-directed, I'll-be-whomever-you-want-me-to-be personality—that everybody seems to have. It's said that people in Hollywood are always nice, in that famously fake Hollywood way, because they're never certain whom they might be dealing with. It could be somebody who's more important than they realize, or who might become important down the road. Well, we're all in showbiz now, walking on eggshells, relentlessly tending our customer base. We're all selling something today; even if we are not literally selling something (though thanks to the internet as well as the entrepreneurial ideal, more and more of us are doing just that), we are selling ourselves. We create a brand, and the brand is us. The self today is an entrepreneurial self, a self that's packaged to be sold.

Where did hipsters come from, and why have they proved such a durable part of the cultural landscape? In *Bobos in Paradise*, David Brooks describes how he returned to the United States in 1994, after five years abroad, to discover a new phenomenon, the class that he christened the bobos or "bourgeois bohemians": people with upper-class incomes but bohemian self-presentations, the demographic that gave us the latte, the Prius, Whole Foods, Restoration Hardware, et al. Now that the boomers had aged into power, in Brooks's analysis, the counterculture had gone mainstream, and '60s values had become the norm.

It was in that context that the hipster emerged. Boboism didn't only change the bourgeoisie; it also changed bohemia. It destroyed bohemia, by co-opting it. Hipsters are what bohemians look like after bohemianism has been commercialized. Hipsters have typically been understood as a category of consumers: "self-curators" who painstakingly choose the music, movies, clothing, and so on through which they construct their identities. It is more useful, I think, to understand them as producers and distributors. Hipsters create bobo culture. They make or sell or serve, or simply pioneer, what bobos buy. Try to picture Allen Ginsberg having a chat with Don Draper across the counter at the local coffeehouse, and you'll realize how far we've come.

Hipsters and bobos are symbiotic. In fact, the two states are often different stages of the same life. Hipsters are frequently bobos in training—graduate students or their equivalent in the arts, food, media, and so forth. Whether they turn into bobos depends on how successful they manage to be (or whom they end up marrying). Does your album take off? Do you get that tenure-track position? Does your food cart turn into a restaurant chain? And because the two stylistic categories overlap—because today's Allen Ginsbergs and Don Drapers are drawing from the same universe of cultural signifiers—the transition is seamless. Instead of having to get a haircut and a new wardrobe, not to mention a new set of friends, if you want to sell out, if you want to go over to the Man, now you just keep doing what you're doing, at progressively higher price points. ("The creatures outside looked from pig to man, and from man to pig, and from pig to man again; but already it was impossible to say which was which.")

Which means that the hipsters possess a relationship to mainstream society that is radically different from that of their youth-culture forebears. The beatniks stood in opposition to the company men, as the slackers did to the business boys. But the hipster ethos incorporates no element of rebellion, rejection, or dissent—remarkably so, given that countercultural opposition would seem to be essential to the very idea of youth culture. ("What are you against?" "Closed-mindedness.") And that, I think, is why the hipster has proven so durable. The heyday of the hippies lasted for all of about two years, from the Summer of Love in 1967 to Altamont in 1969. The punks and slackers held the stage for little more than half a decade each. That is the nature of rebellion: it needs to keep occurring. The punks rejected the mainstream, but they also rejected the previous rejection, hippiedom itself—which, by the late 1970s, was something that old people (i.e., twenty-eight-year-olds) were into. But hipsterism, which has been around for a solid generation now, appears to be a stable cultural configuration.

That is the reason I've come to believe that the particulars of hipster style are ultimately insignificant. Hippie apparel embodied hippie values; all those beads and loosely flowing garments meant love, meant openness and peacefulness. Slackers wore flannel and old jeans to show they didn't give a shit. Nor did it take a semiotician to figure out that when a punk shoved a safety pin through her eyebrow, she was expressing rage. But the beards, the hats, the tattoos? The skinny jeans and vintage dresses? Wherever it originally came from, the only message hipster style conveys, at this point, is "I am a hipster."

[2011]

HEROES

The long period of our "forever wars" that followed 9/11—especially those initial years, with their giddy rush of righteous aggression—reordered the national imagination in a way not seen for decades. No symbol became more sacred in American life than the military uniform. The cross remained divisive, the flag had become a bone of partisan contention, but the uniform commanded automatic, universal reverence. In Congress as on television, generals were treated with awed respect, service members spoken of as something close to saints. Liberals were especially careful to produce the right noises, obeisance to the uniform having become the shibboleth of patriotism, as anti-Communism once had been. Across the political spectrum, throughout the media, in private life as well as public, the pieties were second nature: "heroes," "warriors," "mission"; "our young men and women in uniform," "our brave young men and women," "our finest young people." "Thank you for your service," we intoned.

The cult of the uniform originated during the Iraq War with the call, issued from on high, to "support the troops." The slogan capitalized on our desire to avoid the mistake of the Vietnam era, when hatred of the conflict too easily became hostility to those who fought it. Now the logic was reversed: supporting the troops, we were told, meant supporting the war. (In fact, that's all it seemed to mean.) It was a bait and switch, an act of emotional blackmail: if you opposed the war or questioned the way it was being conducted, you were undermining "our brave young men and women."

As both Iraq and Afghanistan dragged on, other purposes came into play. The greater the sacrifice that fell on a single small slice of the country, the more we went from supporting the troops to putting them on a pedestal. In World War II, everybody fought. Soldiers were not remote figures to most of us; they *were* us. Now, instead of sharing the burden, we sentimentalized it.

It was a lot easier to idealize the people who were fighting than it was to send your kid to join them. This was also a form of service, I suppose: lip service.

The cult of the uniform also bespoke a wounded empire's need to reassert its masculinity. Iraq itself, that catharsis of violence, expressed the same emotional logic. We'd been hit in the head with a rock; like a neighborhood bully, we grabbed the first person we could get our hands on and beat them to a pulp. Mission accomplished: we were strong again, or so we imagined, and the uniform became the symbol of that strength. In the soldier and marine, we saw ourselves as we preferred to: stoic, powerful, focused, devoted.

All this surely helps explain why, even as both conflicts descended into stalemate, the military managed to avoid accountability. Did the fault really lie with the civilian leadership alone? Had the armed forces really ceased to be the big, bumbling bureaucracies they always were? Did "our brave young men and women fulfill every mission we ask them to," as the catechism went? At the very least, the generals ought surely to have come in for criticism—as they did, when appropriate, in every other war. And yet our worship of the uniform kept them from blame, and ourselves from thought.

There were other questions, too. It is probably safe to say that nothing on the order of My Lai took place in Iraq or Afghanistan, but there was Abu Ghraib. There was the brutal, premeditated gang rape of a fourteen-year-old girl, and the murder of her entire family, in Mahmudiyah, Iraq. There was the self-described "kill team" in Kandahar province that executed Afghan civilians for sport. Of these, only the first was widely reported, and only, no doubt, because of the pictures. How many other atrocities took place? Maybe none, maybe quite a few. Because we didn't ask—because we didn't want to ask—we'll never know.

As the national narrative has shifted from the War on Terror to the specter of decline, the uniform has come to play another psychic role. The military are the can-do guys, the one institution—certainly, the one public institution—that still appears to work. The schools, the highways, the post office; Amtrak, FEMA, NASA, and the TSA—not to mention the banks, the newspapers, the healthcare system, and above all, Congress: nothing seems to function anymore, except the armed forces. They're like our national football team, the one remaining sign of American greatness.

And here we come, I believe, to the deepest meaning of the new creed. The word most typically intoned, when the religion of the uniform is being celebrated, is "heroes." So what is heroism? What kind of psychological work does the concept do for us? Heroism is bravery and selflessness, but more than that, it is triumphant action, and in particular, morally unambiguous action. In most of life, especially in public life, there is scarcely such a thing on either count. Politics is a muddle of moral and practical compromise. Victories are almost always partial, ambiguous, and subject to reversal. Heroism belongs to the realm of fantasy—the comic book, the action movie—or to delimited spheres of action, like space exploration or sports. The marine who saves his buddies in a firefight, the policeman who rescues a child from a well—the challenges they face are clear and simple and isolated from the human mess. And note how frequently the element of rescue arises when we speak of heroism. Heroes are daddies and mommies: larger-than-life figures, unimpeachably powerful and good, who save us from evil and hurt.

"America needs heroes," it is sometimes said, a phrase that's often uttered in a wistful tone, almost cooingly, as if we were talking about a lonely child. But do we really "need heroes"? We need leaders, who marshal us to the muddle. We need role models, who show us how to deal with it. But what we really need are citizens, who refuse to infantilize themselves with talk of heroes and put their shoulders to the public wheel instead. The political scientist Jonathan Weiler regards the cult of the uniform as a kind of citizenship by proxy. Soldiers embody a notion of public service, he argues, to which the bulk of us are now no more than spectators. What we really need, in other words, is a kick in the pants.

When a version of the foregoing appeared in the *New York Times* (this was before we withdrew from Iraq), I thought I'd be hung from a lamppost. In the event, the response was far more positive than I expected. Yes, I got some hate mail ("sorry piece of human crap," "pseudo-liberal fascist asshole"), a few brickbats from right-wing websites, and an invitation (declined) to play the piñata on *Fox and Friends*. But the reaction was mostly supportive, and much of it came from veterans themselves. One correspondent, a retired navy captain, observed that our lionization of the military leads the country to charge the armed forces with missions—nation-building, broadly speaking—that they are not trained to carry out. Another, a Vietnam vet, remarked that the "support" in "support the troops" "is really a mile wide and an inch deep." A third pointed out that "saluting the troops" is good for business and included a link to a truly nauseating ad for American Airlines. Other people told me that being approached by total strangers and "thanked" for their "service" felt weirdly anonymous and dehumanizing. Quite a few insisted that only a draft can bring us back to reality.

I also learned that the rhetoric of heroism falsifies both many of the reasons that people enlist and the work that a lot of them actually do. According to the sociologist Jerry Lembcke, author of *The Spitting Image: Myth, Memory, and the Legacy of Vietnam*, some individuals do indeed enlist for idealistic reasons, but most of them do so because they need a job, or to get money for college, or to get away from the place they live. Every officer knows that soldiers fight to protect their comrades, not to keep the country safe.

Of course, it doesn't really matter why you joined or why you're fighting if you're now exposed to mortal danger (as well as to the moral danger of taking a life). But far from everyone in uniform is. Most people in the air force, as one of my respondents noted, have desk jobs. Sailors at sea are extremely unlikely, the way our wars now go, to find themselves in peril. There is nothing wrong with that. There is something wrong with slapping the label of "heroes" on a couple of million people and imagining that you are honoring them by doing so.

But the hardest thing to say in all of this is this: the people who fight for us, who die for us or have their minds or bodies shattered for us, are not keeping us safe or "preserving our freedom." They, and we, may certainly like to think they are, but how many of the wars that we have fought, say, since Korea, major or minor, have served that purpose? Vietnam was not the Revolution, and Iraq was not World War II. Mainly, we fight to preserve our empire—which means, to enrich the people who run our empire—and to enable politicians to get reelected. In other words, our service members do not fight "for us" at all. I am not a pacifist. I believe we need a military. But I am sickened by the reasons that we use it now. What I mainly feel for people who have served in combat is not veneration (or contempt). It is pity—it is sadness. Such a criminal waste of life.

[2011]

JUST FRIENDS

Can men and women be friends? We've been asking ourselves that question for a long time, and the answer is almost invariably no. The locus classicus is found in *When Harry Met Sally.* . . . The problem, Harry famously explains, is that "the sex thing gets in the way." That's the conventional wisdom. Platonic relationships are suspect, and they always have been. People of the opposite sex may claim to just be friends, the message goes, but count on it—wink, wink, nudge, nudge—something more is going on underneath. Or will be, once they figure out how they really feel about each other (which is exactly what happens with Harry and Sally). Popular culture enforces the notion relentlessly. In movie after movie, show after show, the narrative arc is the same. What starts as friendship (Ross and Rachel, Monica and Chandler) invariably ends up in bed.

There is a history here, and it is a surprisingly political one. Friendship between the sexes was more or less unknown in traditional society. Men and women occupied different spheres, and, in any case, women were seen as inferior. A few epistolary friendships between monastics, a few relationships in literary and court circles, but beyond that, cross-sex friendship was as unthinkable in Western society as it still is in many cultures. Then came feminism—specifically, Mary Wollstonecraft, one of the founders of feminism. Wollstonecraft, who published her great manifesto *A Vindication of the Rights of Woman* in 1792, was wary herself of platonic relationships, which could lead too easily, she thought, to mischief. But she did believe that friendship, "the most sublime of all affections," ought to be the mainspring of marriage. If marriage was ever going to be more than a relationship of domination and dependence, a flare of passion followed by a lifetime of indifference, then spouses needed to learn to think of themselves as friends—which meant that women needed to be recognized as equals and receive an education that would make them equals.

Easier said than done, of course. If anything, Victorian domestic ideology, with its "paterfamilias" and its "angel in the house"—the patriarchal husband, the saintly little wife—represented a step backward. But by the 1890s, when feminism emerged from the drawing rooms and genteel committees to become a mass, radical movement, friendship reappeared as a political demand. This was the time of the "New Woman," portrayed in fiction and endlessly debated in the press. The New Woman—Sue Bridehead, in *Jude the Obscure*, is the most famous fictional example—was intelligent, well-read, strong-willed, idealistic, unconventional, and outspoken. For her, relationships with men, whether or not they involved sex, had to involve mental companionship, freedom of choice, equality, and mutual respect. They had, in short, to be friendships. Just as suffrage represented feminism's vision of the political future, friendship represented its vision of the personal future.

Again, not so easy to put into practice. But the notion of friendship as the root of romantic relationships started to seep into the culture. The terms "boyfriend" and "girlfriend," which had begun to appear in the 1890s, were commonplace by the 1920s. We take the words for granted now, but think of what they imply, and how new an idea it was: that romantic partners are bonded by more than erotic passion, that the relationship incorporates equality and companionship, as well. A boyfriend is a friend, not just a lover—or at least is supposed to be. As for husband and wife, Wollstonecraft's ideal has long since become a cliché. Who doesn't think of their spouse—or claim to think of them, or want to think of them—as their best friend?

So friendship now is part of what we mean by love. Still, that doesn't get us to platonic relationships. For that we needed yet another wave of feminism, the one that started in the 1960s. Friendship wasn't part of the demand this time, but what was demanded—equal rights and opportunities in every sphere—created the conditions for it. Only once the sexes mixed on equal and familiar terms at school, at work, and in society at large—only once it was normal and even boring to see a member of the opposite sex at the next desk—could platonic friendships become an ordinary part of life.

And that is exactly what's happened. Friendships with members of the opposite sex have been an important part of my life since high school, and I hardly think that I'm alone. Consult your own experience, but as I look around, I do not see that platonic friendships are actually rare at all or, the conventional wisdom notwithstanding, worthy of a lot of winks and nudges.

Which is why you don't much hear the term anymore. Platonic frie..
now are simply friendships.

But doesn't the sex thing get in the way? At times, no doubt. It's harder
for the young, of course—all those hormones, and so many of your peers are
unattached. There was certainly sexual tension in some of my early friendships with girls and women. Sometimes it was acted on, sometimes it was
sublimated—neither of which necessarily made the friendships less real. In
fact, one of the most common solutions to Harry's dilemma may simply be
for people to have sex, then become or remain friends. If the sex thing gets in
the way, the answer often seems to be to just get it out of the way.

But it doesn't always get in the way. Maybe you're not attracted to each
other. Maybe you know it would never work out, so it's not worth screwing
up your friendship. Maybe other things are more important. Maybe that's just
not what it's about.

So if it's common now for men and women to be friends, why do we so
rarely hear about it? Why does Hollywood insist that such relationships
do not exist? Partly, it is a narrative problem. Friendship isn't courtship. It
doesn't have a beginning, a middle, and an end. Stories about friendship, of
any kind, are relatively rare, especially given the enormous place that such
relationships have in our lives. And, of course, they're not sexy. We don't get
stories about friendship because what we want, or what they think we want,
are stories about love. Put a man and a woman together on-screen, or in the
pages of a novel—any man and woman, friends, classmates, colleagues, boss
and worker, teacher and student—and we expect the sparks to fly.

Yet it isn't just a narrative problem, or a Hollywood problem. We have trouble, in this culture, with any love that isn't based on sex or blood. We understand romantic relationships, and we understand family, and that's about
all we understand. We don't understand mentorship, the asymmetric love
of master and apprentice, professor and student, guide and guided; we don't
understand comradeship, the bond that comes from shared, intense work;
and we don't understand friendship, at least of the intimate kind. When we
imagine such relationships, we seem to have to sexualize them.

I cannot think of another area of our lives in which there is so great a gap
between what we do and what we say we do. But maybe things are beginning to change, for reasons that are generational. Having grown up with feminism, people born in the '60s or later are apt to take equality between the
sexes, and all that it entails, for granted. Having grown up with the gay rights

movement, they are open to a wider range of emotional possibility. Friendship between the sexes may no longer be a political issue, but it is an issue of liberation: the freedom to love whom you want, in the way that you want. Maybe it's time that we all took it out of the closet.

[2012]

SEEING THINGS

In the eighth episode of the sixth season of *Mad Men*, Don Draper asks his underlings a rhetorical question: "What is advertising about?" He waits a beat, then answers the question himself. "It's about getting your foot in the door." Don, like most of the office, is in the middle of a manic, weekend-long freak-out triggered by amphetamine injections from a quack doctor. He isn't thinking of a product or a client; he is thinking of his neighbor's wife, who has cut off their affair. He has been spending a lot of time staring at her door, trying to will himself inside, and now he thinks he's figured out a way to do it.

Later in the episode, one of the junior creatives is having sex with a teenage hippie, somebody's daughter, who's been hanging around the office. The door is ajar, and one of the executives is leering at them through the crack. The scene recalls a flashback from the season's opening episode. The adolescent Don, a shy, shell-shocked boy who is being raised in a brothel, is peeping through a keyhole as the boss-man screws his stepmother. It also glances ahead to other doorways, other sights. The year is 1968: everyone is seeing things, at least on television, from which they cannot look away.

What is advertising about? The episode seems to be telling us: it's about voyeurism. It's about getting your eye in the door. We are plied, on our screens, with little dramas of the good life. A child is comforted with soup. A handsome couple relaxes on the beach. Some friends share a drink on the town. We gaze on, not just with longing but with envy. We get off, but not as much as they do.

Yet since the days of Don and company, over the last few decades, perhaps, and in the upper reaches of the income distribution in particular, I think—or maybe it is like this everywhere, and always was—there's something more, as well, something even worse. It isn't just the old equation of things equals happiness, so go and buy more things. I see it in the style sections and the upscale magazines. The artist with the groovy loft. The actor with the groovy art. The power couple with the groovy friends. The whole empire of bobo-hipsterism, with its premise of the self-curated life. Now your envy is directed not so much at what those people have as at the sensibilities that enabled them to acquire it in the first place—the eye, the taste, the touch, the sophistication.

You don't just want their stuff. You don't even want their life. You want their soul. And that, you know, you'll never have. Don and his ilk offered hope, at least, even if it was an empty hope. Your future could be better than the present. But now it's not about the future anymore; it is about the past. The emotion isn't lust; it is regret. You were born the wrong way. You have lived the wrong life. It's your nervous system. It's your heart. There's no injection that can save you, no drug that's going to make you who you want to be. You can stare all you want: the door to your desire is never going to open.

[2013]

THE TRUE CHURCH

I have been to Jewish services of all kinds, have seen Catholics, Lutherans, and Episcopalians at worship, Muslims, Hindus, Jains, and Sikhs, Chinese and Tibetan Buddhists—Golden Temple, Holy Sepulchre, Wailing Wall; Lhasa, Bodh Gaya, Santa Maria sopra Minerva—but the truest religion I have ever witnessed was a meeting of Alcoholics Anonymous. A friend had reached his twentieth anniversary of sobriety, and I came to a meeting to help him celebrate.

What I saw there was religion stripped to its bones, austerely beautiful like a piece of Shaker furniture. No priesthood, no prelacy, no special garments or sacred objects, no shibboleths of membership. A bare minimum of custom and formula. A congregation called by need, not duty. Meaning springing from the bottom up: not from mythology or dogma or scripture, language handed down by rote, but from the particularities of individual experience—words spoken for the first time, not the trillionth. One person said, "I don't wake up anymore feeling like I want to die. I may not always wake up feeling like I want to live, but I no longer wake up feeling like I want to die." Another said, "When I drank that first beer, I had no idea what was going to happen after that." A third replied, "When *I* drank, I knew *exactly* what was going to happen. I always wound up in the same place. Now that I don't drink, I have no idea, and it's wonderful."

Most of all, a sense that all this really mattered in the most immediate and urgent way. The overwhelming feeling that I've gotten from most of the religious services I've attended is that none of it had to do with anything other than itself. This time, instead of pulpit abstractions about "faith" and "service," or vague ideas about attaining some future blessed state, what I saw were people fighting for their lives—right here, right now. "Meeting," as in business meeting, is a good word for it: there was no room for anything but the most concretely practical considerations—that is, the most authentically personal ones. For most people, church is for Sunday; AA members go to meetings every day. The program is religion set down in the midst of life, not a special sanctum that we keep cordoned off in our brains. One of AA's acronyms is SOBER: "Son Of a Bitch, Everything's Real." Amen, selah.

[2011]

Arms and the Man

I was in Decatur, Georgia, for the annual book fair several years ago. Decatur is a prosperous and educated suburb of Atlanta. Agnes Scott College is located there; Emory is right nearby. But the South is the South, and as I am reminded every time I go, the South is memory. At the courthouse in the center of town is a Confederate monument erected in 1908 "by the men and women and children of DeKalb County." "After forty two years," it proclaims, "another generation bears witness to the future." I thought about that "men and women and children," the resonance of each word, when "people" would have done as well and spared the mason sixteen letters—got an image of the men that day of dedication, their womenfolk beside them and their children in front, absorbing the lesson. Seven years later, the Klan was refounded on top of Stone Mountain, ten miles away. Cross burnings were regular there until as late as 1970, a couple of years before they finished carving on its side a monumental bas-relief, three acres big, of Jefferson Davis, Stonewall Jackson, and Robert E. Lee.

Around the courthouse in Decatur are several freestanding panels, erected in the 1950s, that each narrate some minor skirmish or other during the siege of Atlanta. They go on at exorbitant length—some 250 words, in one case— like pages torn from a history book, and each recounts some temporary, partial, piss-ass little victory within the larger debacle. ("Wheeler's men . . . drove Sprague's troops . . . to the public square where, outflanked, they withdrew with the wagon trains to the North Decatur Road.") A friend who lives there now, with whom I discussed it all later, reminded me of Faulkner's famous lines on Pickett's Charge at Gettysburg, the so-called high-water mark of the Confederacy: "For every Southern boy fourteen years old, not once but whenever he wants it, there is the instant when it's still not yet two o'clock on that July afternoon in 1863 . . . and that moment doesn't need even a fourteen-year-old boy to think *This time. Maybe this time. . . .*" My friend also noted the shape of the courthouse monument, an obelisk—made me realize to what extent the South is driven by a sense of permanently wounded masculinity, how much its macho culture constitutes an endless compensation for defeat. It's like fucking Kosovo, I thought, that battle in the fourteenth century that the Serbs are still obsessed with. Winners move on; history belongs to the losers.

All this helped me make a different sense of our perennial debate about guns, specifically, of one of its strangest claims: that the Second Amendment is intended to enable citizens to take up arms against the government. It's ridiculous, of course, on two counts. No one ever quotes the second part of the amendment, right after "A well regulated Militia." "[B]eing necessary to the security of a free State," it reads. The *security* of the state, not its overthrow. Making war against the government? The Constitution calls that treason, and it is the highest crime the document envisions. And then there is the sheer absurdity of thinking you can go against a modern army with your tiny little rifles.

I had always assumed that the gun people, in making the argument, were invoking the Revolution. But now I wonder if some of them, at least, do not have a different war in mind. Tyranny, rebellion, just resistance to an unjust federal government, small arms against small arms in a fair fight. They are stockpiling guns for a battle they've already lost. They are dreaming of a second chance. Save your Confederate dollars, boys, the South shall rise again. *This time. Maybe this time.*

[2013]

LATTER-DAY SAINT

B ill Cunningham is an old man in a blue smock who stands every day on the streets of New York City taking pictures of passersby. Bill Cunningham is the producer, since 1979, of the "On the Street" column in the *New York Times*, a photographic record of the city's fashion life, and the subject of the 2010 documentary *Bill Cunningham: New York*. Bill Cunningham is tall, thin, boyish, eighty-three or thereabouts, painfully shy, inflexibly principled, secretive, sweet. His eyelids flutter. His face flickers between joy and pain. He smiles beatifically when he thinks of beauty.

He lives a life of almost unbelievable simplicity. His apartment is a small studio in Carnegie Hall filled almost entirely with filing cabinets. (They hold every photograph he's ever taken.) There is no kitchen, no closet, no bathroom. He sleeps on a cot—not even a cot, a board—and hangs his few clothes on the handles of the filing cabinets. He doesn't go to the movies, doesn't watch television, eats at the office or a diner, and gets around on bicycles (which keep getting stolen). What he does is work: out on the street every day, at a function or two in the evening (he also does a society column), downtown after hours, perhaps, to catch the more exotic creatures of the night.

He was born in 1928 or '29. He says his family was working class, but he dropped out of Harvard, and his accent sounds patrician. He doesn't seem to have a personal life. He treats everyone the same: drag queens, socialites, people on the street. He moves among wealth and glamour without being touched by a desire for either. "You see if you don't take money," he says in the film, "they can't tell you what to do, kid. That's the key to the whole thing." His only love is beautiful clothes. He's a "slob," he says, searching for "stunners."

Later on, we see him in Paris. The famous blue smock, it turns out, is the uniform of the Parisian street sweepers—the lowest of the low, as it were. He is being inducted as an officer into the Order of Arts and Letters. At the reception, he wears a blue smock and takes pictures, as if it were some-body else's event. The man who will bestow the award tells the camera, "He doesn't want to be honored. He doesn't want anything. Very deeply, I think, he doesn't believe he deserves it." Accepting the award, Cunningham says, "It's as true today as it ever was: He who seeks beauty"—his voice begins to break—"will find it."

The French appear to think that this man is an artist. I think he's some-thing else. The asceticism, the self-erasure, the monkish cell and monkish habit, the deep humility and high principles, the otherworldliness: Cunning-ham has shown me what it means to be a saint. It's not about morality; it's about devotion to the absolute. He doesn't create beauty; he does exactly what he said: he goes out in the world and seeks it. He chases epiphanies. He waits for visions. He enacts a purity the world does not possess. He insists on God.

Late in the film, the director asks him two questions. The first is the one we've been waiting for. "Have you ever had a romantic relationship?" Cun-ningham laughs: "Do you want to know if I'm gay?" He's coy, but the answer appears to be yes. As for the original question, that answer is no, never. "You do have body urges or whatever. You control it as best you can."

Then comes the second question. "I know that you go to church every Sunday"—Cunningham drops his head and, stricken, seems to give a sob—"and religion, is that an important part of your life?" Cunningham keeps his head down, face frozen, for nearly thirty seconds. You almost think he's going to stay like that until the crew packs up and leaves. At last he simply says, "It's something I need."

[2012]

Arts

THE MAKER'S HAND

A COMMENCEMENT ADDRESS DELIVERED AT THE
OREGON COLLEGE OF ART AND CRAFT

Let me begin by offering my congratulations to all of you who are graduating today. I do so not only, as is customary on such occasions, because you have completed your respective degree programs, but also because you chose to start them in the first place. In doing so, you already began to demonstrate the kind of independent mindedness that will serve you so well as you go forward into your lives by rejecting the current conventional wisdom about what education ought to be.

Education, say the pundits and the politicians, must be above all practical, by which they mean, narrowly vocational. "Top 10 Majors" means the most employable, not the most interesting. "Top 10 Fields" means average income, not job satisfaction. Major in something, we tell our young people, that's the name of a job, like nursing or business or engineering. And whatever you do, don't study the liberal arts—still less, God forbid, the fine arts.

So I know that it probably took a lot of courage, and a lot of stubbornness, to get here in the first place. You had to stand up to the grown-ups, and maybe even to the peers, who said things like, "What are you going to do with that?" or, "Oh, so you decided to go for the big bucks." Or who just kind of looked at you a certain way. Who questioned the value, in other words, of what you want to try to do. "Value," a word that is worth coming back to.

You also rejected the option of going to a different kind of art school. Because art schools haven't been immune from the pressure toward this sort of narrow practicality any more than colleges and universities in general. Across the country, we see art schools and arts programs, at both the bachelor's and master's levels, contorting their curricula in the direction of that which is thought to be most immediately negotiable in the marketplace, which generally means, that which can be done on a computer. Graphic design, illustration, animation, video. We see them, in the name of efficiency and cost cutting, loading up on adjunct faculty, stinting on studio space, and turning their arts programs into cash cows for their larger institutions. We see them teaming up with corporations to provide the kind of graduates businesses want rather than the kind of education students need. We see them rebranding themselves with "innovative" degree programs, adorned with trendy names, that no one seems to know the purpose of, least of all the people who created them. We see them expanding too fast, assuming too much debt, and being forced to hike enrollment, or tuition, or both.

But you chose to attend a different kind of school. A school that doesn't exist to serve a larger institution or a set of corporate patrons. A school that, rather than chasing the siren song of growth, has maintained its allegiance to the intimacy of the studio and the irreplaceable value of the pedagogical relationship. Above all, a school that remains committed, if I can put it like this, to the centrality of the hand in the making of art.

You learned to work with a range of materials—that's how your curriculum was structured—but, at bottom, you were learning how to use your hands. In an age when we are turning into pairs of eyeballs staring at screens, when the prophets of technology are dreaming of a future when we'll leave our bodies altogether and unite with our computers, you were learning how to *think* with your hands. Which means that you were learning how to be an artist in the most basic and most ancient sense. The word "art," as some of you may know, derives from a prehistoric verbal root that means "to fit together." That is why the concepts of "artist" and "artisan" were indistinguishable until a relatively recent point in human history. An artist, a craftsperson, is someone who engages in the elemental human act of taking hold of the raw material of the physical world and shaping it into a form that is useful and beautiful. Of making something, we might say, from nothing: something that wasn't there before, from materials that seemed too unpromising to bother with.

It is a capacity, it is *the* capacity, that the ancient mind understood as that in which we most approximate the divine. In Genesis, man is made in the image of God, but he is made in the image, precisely, of God the maker: God who forms Adam, like a potter, from the dust of the earth, and Eve, like a sculptor, from the rib of Adam.

Now that's all pretty cool, and reason enough to be proud of yourselves, and thankful that you didn't do what everyone was telling you to do and go to a "real" college and major in business. And, indeed, the capacity to work skillfully with your hands will stand you in good stead not only as you engage with your chosen materials, but any time you have reason to interact in a mindful way with the physical world, whether that means building out a studio space or fixing a bike or cooking a meal for friends or making a Halloween costume for a child.

But it also means more—beyond the magic, the prestidigitation, of manual dexterity. By learning to make, you were learning, more broadly, to *make do*. To use, as we say, whatever is at hand, whatever *comes* to hand. To piece together everyday materials, as you do in the studio, into unexpected forms, into unexpected things, even when those materials aren't material at all, when they are ideas or images or emotions or relationships. You were learning, in other words, how to bring new things into the world, how to make something from nothing: how to create.

And that is a very valuable thing to be able to do, perhaps now more than ever. We live in the great age of creativity: not necessarily creativity as an act (I'm not sure just how great an age it is for that), but creativity as an idea, a desire, an object of veneration. Everybody wants to be a creator today, or at least, a "creative." Every business wants to harness creativity, especially by *hiring* creatives. Every college and university wants to teach creativity, so its graduates can enter the "creative industries." Every city wants to attract the "creative class."

So actually being *able* to create, to make it and not just fake it, is really valuable. I said that we'd get back to that word, "value." Creativity is a value because it is felt to be valuable, valuable in the sense in which everyone implicitly means the word "valuable," valuable in the market. Which is certainly a good thing, and ought to come as some relief. Creativity makes you employable. More importantly, it makes you viable in an age when employability is a less and less relevant issue. One of the problems with going to school just to get a job is that there are fewer and fewer jobs to be gotten. More and more people are making a living by piecing together a life, by making do with whatever comes to hand. By being, not affable and obedient, the old employment values, but stubborn and courageous and resourceful. By being creative not just *in* their work but *with* their work.

But I do have a problem with this fetish that the marketplace has made of creativity. Actually, I have a lot of problems, as you can probably tell, but one, for now, in particular. Let me approach it by quoting a passage I just came across in one of those books that extol the virtues of our new technological economy. "Many young users" of the internet, the authors say, "are digital 'creators' every day of their lives. When they write updates on social media or post selfies, they are creating something."

Now I don't know about you, but anyone who looks on status updates and selfies—things that involve neither knowledge nor effort nor originality nor skill—as forms of creation has a very different idea of creativity than I do. And so, indeed, the authors do. They do not say, after all, that *taking* a selfie is a creative act; they say that *posting* one is. Creativity, here, means creating what is known as "content." And content means something you can click on, and therefore something that is capable of generating revenue, of creating value, for the tech industry.

Content exists exclusively online, and it is the act of putting something online that creates content. *Hamlet* may be art, but it is not content: not until the text is digitized and uploaded or a performance is videotaped and posted. A bracelet, a sculpture, a pot: none of these count as content, none of the physical objects that you guys have been making in the studio with your hands. Only their images, put on the internet, are content, which means that only those are visible as value, as "creativity," in the online world that is increasingly coming to dominate our lives, our economy, and our imaginations. Anything that can be put online is creative, in that sense, and anything that can't is not. Painting a painting is not an act of creativity. Snapping a picture of someone else's painting, and putting it on Instagram, is.

This is how Tim Kreider, the writer and cartoonist, has described the situation: "The first time I ever heard the word 'content' used in its current context, I understood that all my artist friends and I . . . were essentially extinct. This contemptuous coinage is predicated on the assumption that it's the delivery system that matters, relegating what used to be called 'art' . . . to the status of filler, stuff to stick between banner ads."

But that isn't, after all, the whole story of creativity in the contemporary world. The creeping digitization of everything is being met by a vigorous counter-response in the form of a new flourishing of craft production. The idea of the artisan—most conspicuously in its adjectival form, "artisanal"—has risen to an unprecedented level of cultural salience and social prestige. People are hungry to restore their connection to the physical world, the sensual world, the world of objects that display the marks of time and of the human touch, the world of things made by hand—the world the hand makes.

Which means that you are doing something people want and need. And that you *aren't* doing what everybody else is doing, or trying to do. And that you aren't doing what everybody *can* do, like posting a selfie or starting a podcast or putting videos on YouTube. And that you're doing something that, by definition, no computer or machine can ever replicate. All of which is emi-nently practical, and thus, again, should come as some relief.

But you are also doing something more. You are remaining loyal, like your school, to other, higher values. That word again. You are giving form—literally giving form—to the proposition that value isn't only to be measured in money, or creativity in clicks. You are teaching us to value beauty, thought, care, presence, uniqueness: to value them for their own sake. To insist on their survival in the world.

And by doing that, you're doing something further still. In her book *Art Thinking*, the writer and educator Amy Whitaker remarks that the reason it is hard to put a value, monetary or otherwise, on a work of art before it is created is that, to adapt a definition from Heidegger, "a work of art is some-thing new in the world that changes the world to allow itself to exist." That is why it's always such a risk to make one: because you're not just asking people to think that what you've done is good; you're asking them to alter their *idea* of good. Every original artist, to paraphrase Wordsworth, must create the taste by which they are appreciated. Creative works come into being by reor-dering existing values. They propose new values. They exist in the future. They bring the future into being.

The highest thing you learned to do here is to decide for *yourself* what is valuable, to define for yourself what value is—indeed, what art is, what cre-ativity is. And that is the ultimate *form* of creativity: to question the world as given, to insist on asking questions of the world. And that is the ultimate freedom that creativity endows you with: the ability to liberate yourself from other people's definitions.

I wish you all the best as you go forth into the world, and I urge you to do so with confidence. The future is in your hands.

[2017]

UPPER MIDDLE BROW

In "Masscult and Midcult," his famous essay in cultural taxonomy from 1960, Dwight Macdonald distinguished three levels in contemporary culture. At the top was High Culture, represented most recently by the modernist avant-garde but already moribund in Macdonald's day. At the bottom was Mass Culture ("or Masscult, since it really isn't culture at all"), also known as pop culture or kitsch (or, more recently, entertainment). In between was the insidious new form that Macdonald labeled Midcult. Midcult is Masscult masquerading as art: slick and predictable, like Masscult, but varnished with ersatz seriousness. For Macdonald, Midcult was *Our Town*, *The Old Man and the Sea*, *South Pacific*, *Life* magazine, the Book-of-the-Month Club: all of them marked by a high-minded sentimentality that congratulated the audience for its fine feelings.

"Masscult and Midcult" was published at the dawn of a new era. In his introduction to a recent collection of Macdonald's essays, Louis Menand writes that the culture that was about to emerge in the ensuing decade, a hybrid of pop demotics and high-art sophistication—Dylan, the Beatles, *Bonnie and Clyde*, Andy Warhol, *Portnoy's Complaint*—would render its categories obsolete. Perhaps, but Masscult and Midcult are certainly still with us. Masscult today is Justin Bieber, the Kardashians, *Fifty Shades of Grey*, George Lucas, and a million other things. Midcult, still peddling uplift in the guise of big ideas, is *Tree of Life*, Steven Spielberg, Jonathan Safran Foer, *Middlesex*, *Freedom*—the things that win the Oscars and the Pulitzer Prizes, just like in Macdonald's day.

But now I wonder if there isn't also something new. Not middlebrow, not highbrow (we do not have an avant-garde to speak of), but halfway in between. Call it upper middle brow. The new register is infinitely subtler than Midcult. It is post- rather than pre-ironic, its sentimentality concealed behind a veil of cool. It is edgy, clever, knowing, stylish, and formally inventive. It is Jonathan Lethem, Wes Anderson, *Lost in Translation*, *Girls*, Stewart/Colbert, the *New Yorker*, *This American Life*, and the movies that *should* have won the Oscars (the movies that you're not sure whether to call "movies" or "films").

The upper middle brow exhibits excellence, intelligence, and integrity. It is genuinely good work (as well as being most of what I read or watch myself). The problem is it always lets us off the hook. Like Midcult, it is ultimately designed to flatter its audience, approving our feelings and reinforcing our prejudices. It stays within the bounds of what we already believe, affirms the enlightened opinions we absorb every day in the quality media, the educated bromides that we trade on Facebook. It doesn't tell us anything we don't already know, doesn't seek to disturb—the definition of a true avant-garde—our view of ourselves or the world. (Think, by contrast, of truly unsettling works like *The Wire*, *Blood Meridian*, or almost anything by J. M. Coetzee.)

There is a sociology to all of this. As Clement Greenberg pointed out in "Avant-Garde and Kitsch" (1939), a forebear of Macdonald's essay, high culture flourished under the aristocracy, while mass culture came in with mass literacy. Midcult is a product of the postwar college boom, a way of catering to the cultural aspirations of the exploding middle class. But now, since the 1970s, we have gone a step further, into an era of mass elite and postgraduate education. This is the root of the so-called creative class, the liberal elite as it exists today—in David Brooks's formulation, the "bobos" or bourgeois bohemians. The upper middle brow is the cultural expression of this demographic. Its purpose is to make consciousness safe for the upper middle class.

Brooks's term encapsulates the aesthetic problem. How do you make art that transgresses the assumptions of people who think that everything they do is transgressive? How do you create an avant-garde if everyone believes that they're a rebel? How do you dissent when dissent is already commodified?

Brooks traces the roots of boboism to the 1960s—the very decade, as Menand points out, when McDonald's old distinctions were being overrun in Pop art, rock and roll, and the New Hollywood. The culture of the '60s really was an avant-garde, and not only for its formal innovations or its violation of stylistic decorum, but because it embodied the moral revolt of the time: the sexual rebellion, the contempt for institutional authority, the insurgencies of socially marginal groups.

But all that's long since ossified by now. The baby boom has become the establishment; their morality has become the mainstream; and the sensibility of '60s art has become the upper middle brow, the house style of the upper middle class. Irony is taken for granted. Formal innovation is expected. A mixture of aesthetic registers is de rigueur. Ridicule is aimed at what's left of the cultural enemy. Nothing shocks, and nothing is designed to shock. Beneath the gestures of transgression there exists a moral consensus that is every bit as unexamined, as immobile, and as self-congratulatory as that which girded the ruling class the bobos displaced. Somehow, the rebels of a half a century ago have grown up to become the new Victorians. There's a right way now to eat, speak, think, laugh, make love, raise your children, spend your money, vote.

Which means it really shouldn't be that difficult to create, or at least to define, a revived avant-garde. Here are some of the pieties that it might undertake to profane. That people are basically good. That freedom is the chief ingredient of happiness. That we control our fates. That society is slowly getting better. That we are more virtuous than those who came before us. That the universe coheres in a mystical whole. That it all works out in the end. In short, the whole gospel of self-improvement, progressive politics, ethical hygiene, and pantheistic spirituality. The upper middle brow is as committed to the happy ending as is Hollywood. Tragedy is inadmissible: the recognition that loss is loss and cannot be recuperated, that most people's lives end in failure and emptiness, that the world is never going to be a happy place, that the universe does not love us.

A new avant-garde would be not only experimental, but difficult. The upper middle brow is always inventive, but it is never difficult. Difficulty tells us there is something that we do not know, something that evades our mental structures. Instead of cutting the world to our measure—rendering it manageable, comfortable, and familiar, as the upper middle brow is meant to do—difficulty makes us recognize the narrowness of our experience, here on our little island of middle-class American normalcy. It starts with the truth and seeks to bring us to it, not the other way around. It isn't fun, it isn't soothing, and it isn't marketable. It is only art.

[2013]

Food, Food Culture, Culture

I used to think, back when all the foodie stuff was gathering steam—this would have been about 1994, when everyone was eating arugula and going on about, I don't know, first-press organic broccoli rabe—that our newfound taste for food would lead, in time, to a taste for art. Americans were discovering their senses—learning to value pleasure, distinguish subtle differences, and make fine judgments—and sensual responsiveness is the first step toward aesthetic sensibility. Maybe we were finally on our way to Old World sophistication. Today tapenade, tomorrow Tintoretto.

What has happened, in retrospect, is not that food has led to art, but that it has replaced it. Foodism has taken on the sociological characteristics of what used to be known—back in the days of the rising postwar middle class, when Leonard Bernstein came to us on television and Mortimer Adler was peddling the Great Books—as "culture." It is costly. It requires knowledge and connoisseurship, which are themselves costly to develop. It is a badge of membership in the upper classes, an ideal example of conspicuous consumption. It is a vehicle of status aspiration and competition, an ever-present occasion for snobbery, one-upsmanship, and social aggression. Nobody cares if you know about Mozart or Leonardo anymore, but you had better be prepared to discuss the difference between ganache and couverture.

Young men once headed to the Ivy League to acquire the patina of high culture that would allow them to move in the circles of power—or if they were to the manner born, to assert their place at the top of the social heap by parading what they already knew. Now students at elite colleges are inducted, through campus farmlets, the local/organic/sustainable fare in the dining halls, and osmotic absorption via their classmates from the Upper West Side or the San Francisco Bay Area, into the ways of food. More and more of them also look to the expressive possibilities of careers in food: the cupcake shop, the pop-up restaurant, the brewery or vineyard. Food, for many young people today, is creativity, commerce, politics, health, almost religion. It took me some effort to explain to a former student recently that no, my peers did not think about food all the time when we were her age, unless you mean which diner we were going to for breakfast. "But food is everything!" she said.

Like art, food is also a genuine passion that people share with friends. Many try their hands at it as amateurs—the weekend chef is what the Sunday painter used to be—while avowing their respect for the professionals and their veneration for the geniuses. It has developed, of late, an elaborate cultural apparatus that parallels the one that exists for art, a whole literature of criticism, journalism, appreciation, memoir, and theoretical debate. It has its awards, its maestros, its televised performances. It has become a matter of local and national pride, while maintaining, as culture did in the old days, a sense of deference toward the European centers and traditions—enriched at a later stage, in both cases, by a globally minded eclecticism.

I recently witnessed a heated discussion between two young proponents of food. One insisted that the lower orders be raised up, through programs in schools and the like, to an understanding of the finer points of enlightened consumption and appreciation. The other countered that the culture of food is elitist, that food must be brought down to where the people are. I told them that whichever side one plumped for, their argument exactly reproduced the kind of debate that an earlier age would have had about art.

As aestheticism, the religion of art, inherited the position of Christianity among the progressive classes during the decades surrounding the turn of the twentieth century, so has foodism taken over from aestheticism around the turn of the twenty-first. Now we read the gospel according not to Joyce or Proust but Michael Pollan and Alice Waters. *Eat, Pray, Love*, the title goes, but a lot of people never make it past the first. Nor need they. Food now expresses the ethical values and absorbs the spiritual energies of the educated class. It has become invested with the meaning of life. It is seen as a path to salvation, for the self and humanity both.

But food, for all that, is not art. Both begin by addressing the senses, but that is where food stops. It offers no ideas, proposes no meanings. It furnishes nothing to the imagination, nothing to the mind. An apple is not a story, even if we can tell a story about it. A curry is not an idea, even if its creation is the product of one. A good risotto is a fine thing, but it isn't going to give you insight into other people, allow you to see the world in a new way, or force you to take an inventory of your soul. Yes, food centers life in France and

Italy, too, but not to the disadvantage of art, which still occupies the supreme place in both cultures. Here in America, we are in danger of confusing our palates with our souls.

———————

When I published a version of the preceding in the *New York Times* in 2012, I was not prepared for the volume of vitriol the piece—specifically, the final paragraph—elicited. Word for word, I've never written anything as controversial. To assert that food is not art, I learned, amounted to a kind of blasphemy. One podcaster, with whom I've had a running argument about this ever since, could literally not believe that I would say such a thing. I had to be putting people on or, at least, being intentionally perverse. That the notion that food *is* art would not have occurred to anyone fifty years ago, even thirty years ago—still less, that that idea is self-evident—did not mollify him.

I had touched a nerve, it seemed. But why? Because, as I've realized since, this wasn't really about food—or rather, it wasn't only about food. One of the signal social developments of recent decades is the rise of amateur creativity, both on the internet and elsewhere: on YouTube and TikTok and Instagram and Medium, but also on Etsy, at art walks and crafts fairs, through food carts and food courts, in little shops and online stores. Yet it isn't enough for people to be creative, or to be recognized for being creative. No, they must be "artists": the coder, the baker, the candlestick maker; the exhibitionist on TikTok and the "personality" on YouTube. Because, as we are often told—and here's the article of faith, against which one must not transgress—"everyone's an artist" now. Which means, in practice, that everyone has a right, a kind of human right, to *call* themselves an artist. And thus their medium—food, crafts, code, dumb little videos, commerce itself—must perforce be art.

The result is that art can mean anything now—or so many things, at least, that the concept is becoming useless. When you can no longer say what something is not, you can no longer say what it is. So what is art? A famously difficult question, of course, but we can begin by clearing away some of the semantic confusion that surrounds the word. "Art," etymologically, historically, means simply "craft or skill," especially such craft or skill as comes from learning or practice, and part of the difficulty in talking coherently about art today derives from the fact that this older sense remains in circulation: in words like "artful" and "artless," in terms like "liberal arts" and "Bachelor of Arts," in phrases like "the art of war," "the art of self-defense," and, yes, "the art of the deal." When Julia Child called her famous instruction book

Mastering the Art of French Cooking, that is the sense she had in mind. She was not asserting that cooking belonged among the disciplines that were known by then as "the fine arts" or, simply, "the arts": painting, sculpture, drama, dance, poetry, fiction, music.

That notion of "the arts," as it developed across the eighteenth and nineteenth centuries—and with it, the notion of "art"—have left us with another reservoir of confusion. For it was then and only then that "art" became a thing: not just a unitary concept, one that gathered the disparate arts beneath a single umbrella, but also a kind of higher essence—"Art"—that ascended to the status of a cultural ideal, an object of esteem and veneration. "Art" was great; eventually, if you wanted to say that something was great—if you wanted to praise someone's skill, or the product of their skill—you called it "art." "That sports car is a work of art." "He raises basketball to the level of art." But those are statements of quality, not category. They are metaphors, just as, when we say that somebody is "poetry in motion," we don't literally mean that they're verse. When my podcasting acquaintance insists that food is art, what he really means is that it *can* be.

But if art is art—if it is a thing, not merely a superlative—then it is art if it is good or not. Bad art is still art, just as bad food is still food. Being good does not make something art; being art does. "I've had some memorable meals," the podcaster protested. Yes, I replied, and I've had some memorable sex acts, but that doesn't make them art. Not everything memorable is art; not everything intentional is art; not everything beautiful is art; not everything creative is art. Not even everything that's all of those at once.

There are many definitions of art, but the best, I believe, comes from Arthur C. Danto, the great aesthetician and critic. Art, he said, is embodied meaning. Art makes meaning, in other words, but it does so not explicitly (as, for example, I'm doing it here) but through form. Ursula K. Le Guin, in the introduction to her novel *The Left Hand of Darkness*, puts the matter like this: "The artist deals with what cannot be said in words"—what cannot be stated explicitly. "The artist whose medium is fiction," she adds, "does this *in words*. The novelist says in words what cannot be said in words." Says it through the form, that is, her words assume, the forms her words create. Just so, the painter says in paint what cannot be said in words, the musician says in notes what cannot be said in words, and so forth.

The key word here for us is "says." Art has meaning; art speaks. Art is not necessarily representational, but it is always referential. It always points outside itself. It always claims to speak, however enigmatically, the truth. And that is why food is not art. Food does not speak. We do not ask, of a bouilla-baisse, what does it mean. We do not sit around the kitchen table, as we do around the seminar table, debating our interpretations of the thing that lies in front of us. We do not ask of a chef and her pasta, as we do of a painter and her canvas, what she is trying to say. She isn't saying; she is doing. She isn't proposing meanings; she is offering sensations. That is why art can be ugly and still be good, but a dish that tastes bad is a failure. That is why we criticize the artist who repeats himself—creates a work that's too much like his old ones, that "doesn't say anything new"—but repeating himself—making that dish we loved so much the last time, and making it the same—is one of the things that we want from a chef. Art can be ambiguous, mysterious, even mendacious, but terms like those, applied to food, are incoherent. There is no such thing as a false meal, only a lousy one.

Why does all this matter? Because art's ability to embody meaning—to speak to us, to speak of us—is what gives it its value and force, its power to shape our souls and change our lives, its claim on our attention, our allegiance, our support. The pleasures of food, however intense, are no substitute. Man does not live by bread alone.

[2012, 2021]

THE PLATINUM AGE

In 1970, CBS appointed a new vice president for programming. Within a year, in a move that became known as the "rural purge," he had canceled *Hee Haw, Lassie, Green Acres, Petticoat Junction, The Beverly Hillbillies*, and *Mayberry R.F.D.*, some of them among the network's most popular shows. In their stead, he introduced, among other offerings, *The Mary Tyler Moore Show, All in the Family*, and *M*A*S*H*, three of the most esteemed programs in the history of television. By the middle of the decade, he had added *Maude, Rhoda, The Jeffersons*, and *Good Times*, shows that likewise helped to bring a new sense of social relevance to the small screen.

In 1975, ABC appointed a new president of its entertainment division. Within a couple of years, he had greenlit *Charlie's Angels, Three's Company, The Love Boat, Fantasy Island*, and *Battle of the Network Stars* (satirized by *Saturday Night Live* as "Network Battle of the T's and A's"). Collectively, those shows and others like them earned the nickname "jiggle television" and represented a new low for the lowest common denominator. They also helped to catapult ABC, the perennial runt of the network litter, to the top of the ratings.

The first executive was Fred Silverman. The second executive was also Fred Silverman. His motive was the same in each case. The revolution at CBS was undertaken not, as the story often goes, out of a high-minded sense of social responsibility, nor from a commitment to artistic excellence. Silverman cut the rural shows and introduced the hipper ones because he wanted CBS to pivot from the aging segments of the audience to the more desirable young-adult demographic. When he got to ABC, where he also revived the fortunes of *Happy Days*, spun off *Laverne and Shirley*, and oversaw the creation of *Roots*, the executive that *Time* would dub "the man with the golden gut," continuing to surf the zeitgeist (and no doubt knowing that he couldn't vie directly with the brand he'd built at CBS), sensed the opportunities for market share that lay in new directions.

Television, like movies and popular music, is often portrayed as an ongoing battle between the artists and the suits. The artists want creative freedom; the suits want profits. Both propositions are true, but the latter doesn't mean the suits are evil. It simply means they're businesspeople: it means that they're doing their jobs. And that is what we—and more importantly, the artists—should want them to do, if only because it enables them to give the artists something else that artists want (and need, and deserve): a paycheck. When television is at its best, as it's so often been in recent years, that is not because the suits capitulate. It is because they're smart enough, or confident enough, or desperate enough, to bet that creative freedom, at least in certain circumstances, can itself conduce to profit.

Which means that the protagonist of this drama is neither the artists nor the suits. It is the people who enable creative freedom to be profitable and garbage to be profitable, too, who made a hit of M*A*S*H as well as *Charlie's Angels*, the people whom the artists and the suits are both appealing to. The protagonist is us. If TV is so much better than it used to be, that's because we're better (believe it or not). What's more, we were always better. It's just that television had to change before we could see that.

How we got from there to here—as its subtitle puts it, *From* I Love Lucy *to* The Walking Dead—is the subject of David Bianculli's encyclopedic new volume, *The Platinum Age of Television*.* Bianculli, who has been a television critic for over forty years (he wrote his first review about a new program called *Saturday Night Live*), attempts to throw his arms around it all, the whole of scripted television. His table of contents alone runs to half a dozen pages: eighteen generic categories (crime, legal, variety, soaps, four different kinds of sitcoms), with five key series focused on for each (and many others mentioned along the way), plus interview-based profiles of twenty-five creators or creative teams, everyone from Mel Brooks to Amy Schumer.

It's a lot, and as someone who has always enjoyed Bianculli's work on NPR's *Fresh Air*, where he has served as television critic ever since the show went national in 1987, I expected the book to deliver a lot. So it gives me no plea-

---

* *The Platinum Age of Television: From* I Love Lucy *to* The Walking Dead, *How TV Became Terrific* (New York: Doubleday, 2016).

sure to have to report that *The Platinum Age* is not only quite a bit less than the sum of its parts, its parts aren't all that great to start with.

Bianculli does provide some interesting material along the way. "[I]f one TV series inspired more of the people interviewed in this book than any other," he tells us, "it was *The Twilight Zone*." The now-familiar concept of an "arc," in which an outside character is featured in a story line that spans the course of several episodes, was invented, we learn, on the crime show *Wiseguy* (1987–90), where the guests included a couple of neophytes named Kevin Spacey and Stanley Tucci. Bianculli also gives us information, albeit in scattershot form, about the kinds of technical and regulatory changes that have always played a crucial function in the evolution of the medium. Cable networks became possible in the 1970s after the development of geosynchronous communications satellites. The rise of the national morning news shows (and the cancellation, after twenty-nine years, of *Captain Kangaroo*) was tied to a relaxation of federal programming requirements in the early 1980s. In a rare extended discussion, Bianculli explains how the creators of *I Love Lucy* pioneered the still-standard three-camera format for sitcoms—which involved enlisting the German cinematographer Karl Freund, whose credits included *Metropolis*, to design the lighting that enfolds a set in that familiar shadowless illumination—incidentally making possible that pillar of the network business model, and of everybody's childhood, the rerun.

But for the most part, Bianculli's book is little more than a long, unenlightening slog, a Bataan Death March through a jungle of minutiae—heavy on factual detail, very light on context or analysis. With ninety series to cover, plus extensive connective tissue within each genre, stock publicity photos that don't do much but take up space, and all those individual profiles, Bianculli seldom gives us more than a couple of pages of text on any given show. Even then, it's mainly who, what, and when, not how or why. The creators and their backgrounds, the basic premise and the leading actors, a memorable episode or two, Emmys won and ratings earned, at best the briefest stab at an idea—that's usually pretty much it.

The Platinum Age is less a study, a connected series of insights bound together by an argument, than it is a catalogue. The problem isn't helped by Bianculli's governing conceit—both what it is and how he handles it. The idea is Darwinian: for each of his eighteen "species," he will undertake to trace the evolution that has brought us to the present moment. In every case, he tells us, "both the programs and the characters become significantly more complicated" (just as biological species evolve, the implication is, in the direction of increased complexity). The plan sounds promising, but Bianculli doesn't try to execute it more than intermittently. He would have needed to tell us a great deal more about each of his "individuals," his programs—a great deal more of genuine substance—before he could have connected them in ways that went beyond the mere chronology of this and this and this. *If* he could have connected them: *The Bob Newhart Show* happened, and then, eleven years later, *Seinfeld* happened, and then, twelve years after that, *Louie* happened, but is there any reason to believe that one grew out of the other, that they even all belong to the same kind of show? So busy is Bianculli counting leaves and sketching acorns that he scarcely notices the trees, let alone the forest.

Is evolution, what's more, especially as Bianculli thinks of it, the best way to explain what's happened to the art form since it started in the 1940s? For one thing, complexity is not the same as quality, and quality is what we really care about. *Modern Family* is unquestionably more complex than *All in the Family*, but is it really better? More importantly, television genres are not really species, in the sense of being self-contained. Bianculli's evolutionary links are so often weak or tenuous or absent because developments in television freely cross from one type of program to another. He tells us that the daytime soaps are disappearing, but he doesn't notice that the genre's themes (and attitudes, and audience) have migrated to reality shows like *The Real Housewives of Beverly Hills* and *Keeping Up with the Kardashians*. He rightly praises CBS's early '70s sitcoms for finally bringing a sense of social reality to scripted television, but he forgets that issues like gender equality, racial conflict, and the Vietnam War were not new to the small screen, because they'd long been staples of the set of programs that we call the news. Aaron Sorkin creates dramas, "but the show that has informed everything that I've ever written," he tells Bianculli, is *M*A*S*H*.

There is a broader issue, too. The evolution Bianculli traces, for example, in the "single working woman" sitcom—from *Mary Tyler Moore* to *Murphy Brown* to *Girls*—is a growth not in complexity so much as in feminism: the ways that women's lives were changing, and the extent to which those changes could be represented on the screen. But feminism didn't happen only on the working woman sitcom. Mary Richards and Murphy Brown and Hannah Horvath are part of a larger change that has included female characters on shows like *L.A. Law*, *Roseanne*, *The West Wing*, *The Good Wife*, and many, many more. More to the point, feminism didn't happen only on TV. The biggest flaw in Bianculli's evolutionary framework is that evolution doesn't take place in a vacuum. Species change because their environment changes, and the environment that television programs struggle to survive in is the culture—which is another name for us. Bianculli's genres have evolved in the direction of greater complexity—and for the most part greater quality—not each out of some sort of inner necessity, some innate teleological drive, but because the medium has as a whole. And TV has changed, for the most part, because the audience has changed—although the process, at least until not long ago, was far from linear.

We call the early days of television the "Golden Age," though I wonder if it wasn't really just a Stone Age gilded by the glow of our nostalgia. In any case, much of what was good about it—much about it, period—was drawn from preexisting media. Variety shows, as Bianculli tells us, came from vaudeville. Westerns, which ruled the ratings in the late 1950s, came from Hollywood. Anthology series like *Kraft Television Theatre* and *Playhouse 90*, which consisted of self-contained, single-episode dramas, often of very high quality, came from theater. And the sitcom, plus a great deal more, came from radio.

Once television was standing on its own two feet, it proceeded to fall on its face. Already by 1961, Newton Minow, chairman of the FCC, was inveighing against the "vast wasteland." TV in the 1960s was abysmal: "hillbillies, cowboys, and spies," as one executive put it, not to mention, as Bianculli reminds us, Martians, genies, and talking horses. Like Hollywood, which also did a lot of sucking in the '60s, scripted television tried to act as if the counterculture—which increasingly meant the culture—did not exist. There were exceptions, such as Bianculli's beloved *Smothers Brothers Comedy Hour* (which was canceled after three tumultuous seasons in 1969), but the '60s, by and large, did not show up on television till the '70s, with Silverman's coup de main at CBS. By 1974–75, the top eleven shows included three programs that centered on black characters—*The Jeffersons, Good Times*, and *Sanford and Son*—plus *Chico and the Man, Maude, Rhoda, The Mary Tyler Moore Show, All in the Family*, and *M*A*S*H*.

But like the New Hollywood, a movement that had gotten underway a few years prior to Silverman's revolution, the heyday didn't much outlast the middle of the 1970s. In movies, all was crushed beneath the juggernaut of *Star Wars* and its progeny, escapist blockbusters that traded in juvenile fantasies and crypto-nationalist myths. In the living room, it was jiggle television, the retrogressive nostalgia of *Happy Days* and *Laverne and Shirley*, and the reactionary chic of *Dallas*. A vast cultural retrenchment was underway, soon to find political expression in the ascendancy of Ronald Reagan.

In retrospect, the 1980s and '90s can be regarded as a slow, halting climb from out of those depths toward the high plateau we stand upon today. In 1981 came *Hill Street Blues*, a major aesthetic advance; in 1989, *Seinfeld*, a comparable earthquake in comedy. The great shows were exceptions, though, and some of them disappeared quickly. *My So-Called Life* (1994–95) came and went within a year; *Twin Peaks* (1990–91), in little more than that. Bianculli has sections on *St. Elsewhere* (1982–88) and the brilliant *Larry Sanders Show* (1992–98), the first important scripted cable program, as well as on *The Simpsons* (1989–forever), *NYPD Blue* (1993–2005), and a few others. But as late as the start of 1999, it remained possible to feel that if you weren't watching television at all, you weren't missing very much—that TV was still basically garbage, if now more slickly packaged garbage, and that it was never going to get much better.

And then, quite suddenly, everything changed. Bianculli pegs the last year of the century as the start of his Platinum Age, and he will get no argument from me. It was the year that HBO began to televise *The Sopranos*. (It also saw the debut of *The West Wing* and of Jon Stewart's version of *The Daily Show*.) By 2002, *The Sopranos* had been joined on HBO by *Six Feet Under* and *The Wire*—none of them like anything that anyone had ever seen before, and all of them better than anyone could have imagined. A new complexity, yes, but also a new depth, new daring, new wit, new moral seriousness, new psychological and social realism, new sense of tragedy—new artistic brilliance. The floodgates had opened, Showtime, FX, AMC, and other networks joined the fun, and everything seemed possible, because everything was.

How did we get there? The first answer is obvious: the advent of cable. Broadcast networks, it's been said, sell viewers to advertisers, but HBO sells programs to viewers. It took chances the established networks wouldn't or couldn't. But while that explanation tells us how the first great programs got to viewers, it doesn't tell us how they were created to begin with, or why the audience embraced them. The answer to the first is everywhere in Bianculli's book, especially those profiles. James L. Brooks (*Mary Tyler Moore*), Larry Gelbart (*M*A*S*H*), and Norman Lear (everything else) had either grown up watching television or started as writers in the new medium. Today's creators grew up watching *them*, and a few others like them. Television got good, or good again, as soon as there were enough people making shows who had come of age with the medium and felt it in their bones; it got great as soon as there were enough who had grown up steeping in the work of that earlier generation.

But the creators haven't been the only ones who have been watching. We've been watching, too; we've been training up. Every aesthetic advance—*Hill Street*'s overlapping dialogue, *Seinfeld*'s quick-cut scenes, the tendency of characters on Platinum Age programs, as Bianculli points out, to leave the most important things unsaid—has prepared us for the next. We can take in more, better, faster than ever before, and as a result, we also expect more. A great audience, Fran Lebowitz has said, is more important for the creation of great art than great artists are: great audiences create great artists, by giving people the freedom to take chances. "The thing I knew going into *Louie*," Louis C. K. tells Bianculli, "was that the American palate, the ear, was tuned better and that people were willing to go anywhere you wanted them to."

We're also vastly better educated now. In 1950, the share of young American adults who were graduating from college was 8 percent. By 2000, it was 29 percent. In 1950, scarcely half of all adults had even finished high school, as compared to about 90 percent in 2000. Our cognitive training, on average, is incomparably more demanding, and more and more of us are also using that training at work. The "creative class"—not just artists and designers but scientists and engineers, teachers and professors, high-tech workers, legal and medical professionals, and more—roughly doubled as a share of the workforce from 1950 to 1999 (to 30 percent), and roughly quadrupled in absolute numbers. This is not to say that high school dropouts can't appreciate *Transparent*, or that every doctor watches *Breaking Bad*, but it does mean that television is addressing itself to a radically different population than it was in 1950, even 1970.

Yet it may not be as different as it seems, because we were probably never as bad as TV made us look. The best thing that cable has done for the quality of scripted television is also the thing that everyone laments about the media landscape today: it has chopped up the audience into smaller and smaller pieces. Of course television was a wasteland in the days when there were only three networks; executives could only program shows that they thought would appeal to a sizable chunk of the country. Yes, America shared a common frame of reference back when everyone was watching Walter Cronkite, but everyone was also watching *The Beverly Hillbillies*, the top-ranked show the year that Cronkite took the anchor's chair, with a rating of 36 (which means that 36 percent of households with a set were tuning in). *NCIS* and *The Big Bang Theory*, last year's highest-rated scripted programs, clocked in at all of 11.1.

Cable has enabled us to see just how diverse—and therefore, how sophisticated—the audience really is. There may have always been a few million people who would have been interested in something like *The Wire*, which is all that ever watched it when it aired, but we were never going to find out. Now there are creatively daring, commercially viable series that attract far smaller audiences even than that. In three seasons (with at least two more on the way), *Broad City* has yet to crack a million.* There's still a lot of crap out there, of course—really, it's still mostly crap, but why shouldn't it be? It's mostly crap in every medium: crap fiction, crap movies, crap music, crap magazines. Pop culture has been mostly crap since it began, which means pretty much since Gutenberg. The very first form of mass entertainment— the bloated, turgid chivalric romances of the sixteenth century—is what Cervantes invented the novel by writing against. The only difference, when it comes to television, is that the crap is much more visible to everybody else. Readers of serious fiction are at best only dimly aware of sewage merchants like Nora Roberts or Dan Brown, but Kim Kardashian is right there on the same device. What cable has really done is make TV like every other medium, one whose range reflects the true breadth of American tastes.

All of which means that the critical commonplaces that earlier generations took for granted, whether of the "boob tube" or "medium is the message" variety, are long since obsolete. Which in turn makes David Thomson's *Television: A Biography* so deeply disappointing.** Thomson, who has written many books on cinema, is widely regarded as our greatest living film critic. But here, attempting to conquer an adjacent medium, he badly misfires. The book has its pleasures, especially when Thomson focuses his movie-critic eyes on individual moments: Angie Dickinson flirting with Johnny Carson; James Garner and Mariette Hartley flirting their way through some three hundred Polaroid commercials, an entire movie thirty seconds at a time.

---

* It never did.

** *Television: A Biography* (London: Thames & Hudson, 2016).

But *Television*, for the most part, is a rambling farrago of secondhand McLuhanisms and self-important sociocultural bloviation, the general purport of which is that television is eating your soul and the world is going to hell. If Bianculli misses the forest, Thomson's book is all forest, less a consideration of specific programs than a sermon on the evils of a demon known as Television. Thomson tells us that he has been thinking about the medium his whole life, and that may be part of the problem. His book exists within a conceptual framework that might have been assembled thirty years ago, if not fifty years ago. Nowhere is there any hint that television today is significantly different than television in the 1980s or the 1960s. Thomson manages to get through an entire chapter on the news (or, as he calls it, "the News," another large abstraction) with just a couple of passing mentions of the twenty-four-hour cable networks. As for Bianculli's Platinum Age—that is, everything since 1999—it is largely ghettoized within a single chapter, and despite the fact that its most recognizable character type is the masculine sociopath (Tony Soprano, Don Draper, Walter White, et al.), its existence doesn't prevent Thomson from saying things like "[t]elevision seldom strays far from likable people." The medium may be the message, but the medium has changed.

Far better, though briefer, is Clive James's *Play All: A Bingewatcher's Notebook*.* James, as canny a critic as one could desire, and as elegantly smooth a writer, places at the center of his book a figure Bianculli omits and Thomson condescends to: the viewer. Specifically, himself, as he works his way through boxed sets of *The Good Wife*, *Breaking Bad*, *Game of Thrones*, and other Platinum Age standards. I don't agree with all his judgments. (I still don't understand how he or anybody else can fail to see the ludicrous *House of Cards* for what it is: "prestige television" at its worst, an overinflated balloon of high-concept flatulence.) But vigorous dispute—loud and personal and unselfconscious—not pious worship of canonical relics, is the hallmark of a living art, which means an art that ordinary people love enough to fight about.

James, unlike Thomson, actually likes television—likes it more than film, in fact. For Thomson, seriality is the guarantee of triviality. "[R]eal acting and catharsis depend on danger and the prospect of closure," he writes. For James, the very length of long-form television—even shows, like *The West Wing*, that might have continued indefinitely—gives it a superior ability "to search souls," its actors greater scope for the virtuosic display of emotional

---

* *Play All: A Bingewatcher's Notebook* (New Haven: Yale University Press, 2016).

range. (He is thinking in particular of Allison Janney as C. J. Cregg.) Thomson expresses a prudish horror at the thought that anybody in the business might be interested in making money. James understands that good television "serves the producer, but only because it serves the consumer first: capitalism the right way up." What's more, he knows that great popular art appeals to the lizard brain as well as to the monkey brain: the former not only with nudity, violence, cursing, and beautiful actors to look at, but most of all with story. Thomson and James are both in their seventies, but while Thomson exudes the sour fatalism of the superannuated, James envisions a bright future stretching out beyond his death, especially for television. His book concludes with his ten-year-old granddaughter, already fluent in the language of the medium, a member of the generation growing up amidst the riches of the Platinum Age.

Thomson thinks the TV era is already yielding to the era of the internet, but this is manifestly false. The two are perfectly compatible, because television will still be television—linguistic inertia being what it is, I suspect we'll still refer to it as "television"—even once we no longer watch it on televisions. Assuming that the people who create it can continue to come up with ways to make us pay for it (and let us hope they do), I don't see much "disruption" taking place. A good television show is not the kind of thing that amateurs can make in their garage. It costs a lot, and the thing that costs the most is talent: talented writers, actors, directors, makeup artists, set designers, music supervisors, and many, many more.

Talent doesn't simply happen, either; it needs to be developed. David Chase grew up, as Bianculli tells us, watching programs like *The Twilight Zone* and *The Untouchables*, but he also worked in television for almost thirty years—on series such as *Kolchak: The Night Stalker*, *The Rockford Files*, and *Northern Exposure*; as a writer, writer/producer, and executive producer—before creating *The Sopranos*. The television business, in its Florence by the ocean there in Southern California, has evolved a modern version of the workshop system, where talent ripens through collaborative work under the tutelage of established creators. That's why even mediocre or conventional programs are valuable in the larger scheme of things. They give creators experience, and they also give them a paycheck, so they can stick around to work another day. Chase earned his first writing credit on something called *The Bold Ones: The Lawyers*.

If anything, the new distribution models, including online streaming, are giving the artists more freedom than ever. Without specific time slots to fill, episodes can find their natural length. So, it seems, can series, with creators now at liberty to plot a tightly woven narrative, spanning a specific number of seasons, from the inception of a project, rather than dragging the story out for as long as the audience is willing to sit still. The very flux in which the medium now finds itself creates more room to operate. "There's no system in place anymore," the comedian and podcaster Marc Maron, who just concluded a series of his own, remarked not long ago. Executives at networks like FX and IFC, he added, "can't pretend to know the answers, so they trust in the creatives."

Are there too many programs these days? Bianculli asks the same question, noting that "the total number of prime-time scripted series on broadcast, cable, and streaming services" came to 409 in 2015, up from 280 in 2010—itself undoubtedly a huge increase from just a few years earlier.* A reduction of the herd, such as always follows overpopulation (to speak in Darwinian terms), would not be a catastrophe. In the meantime, television is the only art form I'm aware of where the "middle class" is thriving. There may be fewer people in the business who are making Seinfeldian fortunes today, but there are many more who earn a decent living, and that is much to be preferred.

As for us, it's truly something to be living through the efflorescence of a great new art. The wasteland, unexpectedly, has bloomed.

[2016]

---

* By 2019, it was 532.

MERCE CUNNINGHAM:
CELESTIAL MECHANICS

To walk into the Cunningham Studio on the eleventh floor of Manhattan's Westbeth Building is to understand more about the work of Merce Cunningham than can be contained in any number of reviews. Set like a ship's bridge atop this massive accretion of masonry and steel, an entire square block of apartments and galleries abutting the Hudson River at the edge of Greenwich Village, the studio seems a glass goblet brimming with force and light, as if the river's energy were pouring into it on the back of the steady wind. Perception of scale, sense of direction, quality of sound, the very feeling of your body: all are as suddenly, radically transformed as when you watch a performance by the Merce Cunningham Dance Company. As removed from ordinary specificity as in its extreme distillations it always seems, Cunningham's choreography is grounded, one realizes, in the dimensions and rhythms of a particular place. The chamber of dreams to which his dances always refer turns out, with the logic of dreams, to have a street address.

The walk to Westbeth takes you through the most densely charming parts of the West Village. Past Bleecker Street, though, the island opens up like a tired partygoer unlacing her stays. A bus steams toward you on the wide flood of Hudson Street, then, like a curtain being pulled, fixes your gaze on the scene it uncovers as it glides past, a clutch of early diners at the White Horse. Past Hudson, the traffic quiets down enough to remind you that the birds chirp even in New York. Greenwich Street would be nearly empty at this hour but for a couple of rollerbladers flick-flacking along in the complex syncopation of their slightly different tempos: flick–flack, flick-flack, flackflick. Shadows of fire escapes bar the luminous honey that the westering sun slathers on old brick buildings. The slanting light becomes a slope that leads you toward the river; the river's immensity, sensed before it's seen, impels you forward. The streets, cobblestone now as they approach the water, as if in echo of its wind-roughened texture, seem to offer up the space they have collected to this largest of all spaces.

It is only at the final moment that Westbeth rises before you, almost frightening in its mass, almost comical in its miscellaneousness. A nine-story hunk of doughty beige brick, elegantly ornamented, perches on concrete piers above a two-story facade of steel-fenced industrial windows. To the south, a collage of catwalks, water towers, and huge square chimneys defines an irregular region of grim, dark, empty air. Facing the river, a monumental iron gateway—arched, braced, bolted, and spiked—looks designed to repel a Viking invasion. Westbeth is never the same building twice.

Then you're up on the eleventh floor. To the left, a little maze of dressing rooms and offices, all sudden turns and sliding plywood doors, that makes you feel like the quarter in one of those disappearing-coin-trick boxes. To the right, what all the space has been saved for: the main studio. Like a parade on the next avenue, it sends out a force field that draws you toward it even before you know that it's there. And that force is, first of all, the energy of its light. Light pours into it through rows of seven-foot windows along either of its longer walls. Island light and river light, solemn light and playful light, light heavy with darkness and light that seems itself shot through with light meet and alchemically combine under the gently arched ceiling. By late afternoon, everything seems perfused by the light in which it has been soaking all day. The light perfuses *you*, as you step inside: you feel translucent, made of a more buoyant medium.

The very dimensions of the studio alter your sense of proportion. There are two kinds of monumental spaces, those that make you feel tiny and worthless and those that make you feel large and exalted. It's a question of shapeliness. Here, the qualities of the space—breadth, clarity, just proportion—become the qualities of your body. The dance floor, a sprung-wood platform that occupies all but one edge of the room, is only a couple of inches high, but it feels about two feet tall when you sit on the side to watch a class. When you step onto it to take class, those two feet seem to add themselves to your height, and to your wingspan. The "open field" that Cunningham has made of the traditionally closed stage you are now in the middle of. When the music begins—synthesized sounds that seem to come from every direction at once—you become a creature of the field as well.

After class, just after sunset, it is almost impossible not to step out for a few minutes onto the patch of roof that lies adjacent to the elevators. The western sky is a wash of acid greens that seem to dissolve the passions of the day. Airplanes arrange and rearrange the space against the horizon as they head south from LaGuardia over the church spires and office buildings of New Jersey. The sky's colors deepen: the brick red of nostalgia, the dark purple of sorrow. Birds fleck the air. A steamboat chuffing north makes the Hudson seem suddenly small and friendly, a gentle cove. Ringed with lamp-light, the river glows from within, like a fragment of bottle glass washed ashore from its waters.

Does Cunningham's work take its shape from the environment in which it is created, or does this world appear the way it does to me because his work has taught me to see it?

After its physical attributes, the thing that most strikes you about the Cunningham Studio, and that explains so much of what you see onstage, is the quality of the activity that goes on inside. The best name for it, I think, is silence: an absence not of sound but noise. There is a sense of decorum about this place that sets it apart from other studios I've been to, a sense of dignity, a sense of respect for one's peers. And also a sense of common purpose. The most reticent of men, Cunningham has required those around him—company members, teachers, students—to create a self-sustaining community for the propagation of his art, of their art. Having set the basic classes, he has left his teachers free to order and elaborate them as they will. Tempo and emphasis vary significantly from class to class with the temperament and experience of the teacher. Some teachers are company members, some former members, some apprentices; it's not unusual to see a dancer who has finished taking one class stay to teach the next. Amidst the variation, however, the essential remains constant. For Cunningham, dance is as much a spiritual discipline, a form of meditative practice, as it is a medium of expression. He has dis-tilled certain values into a technique—rigor, serenity, intellect, beauty—and the technique has instilled them in his dancers. The man and his method have become the center, not of a cult but of a culture.

After taking classes at the studio twice a week for about a year, I have come to believe that the essential principle of Cunningham technique is reduc-tion. Just as Cunningham's choreography begins by stripping away story, music, and decor, his technique begins with a severe limitation of the body's possibilities. The purpose is to permit the conceptualization of movement as a series of binary or ternary choices. In Cunningham technique, the torso is either tilted or upright, twisted or straight to front. The lower back is either

curved or flattened, the upper back, curved, arched, or straight. The working leg touches the standing leg at ankle or knee, never in between. Other
binaries are common to most techniques: plié/straight, parallel/turned out.
Still others follow from the nature of space: right/left, front/back. The most
important of all the binary divisions in Cunningham technique, and the
focus of much of its training, is the disarticulation of hips from torso, the
lower from the upper body.

There are several things to note here. The technique's reductions exclude
many conceivable binaries altogether. The head never moves independently
of the upper torso in any direction. The free foot is never flexed. There is no
épaulement, and the arms do not change shape. (Cunningham's choreography is more liberal, it should be said, than the letter of his technique.) But
more important than the details is the entire tenor of the analysis that pro-
duces them. Cunningham's reduction is not only more severe than that of
other techniques; it is fundamentally different. Ballet recognizes, for example, four possible heights to which the standing foot can rise, as compared
to Cunningham's one (quarter pointe, half pointe, three-quarter pointe, and
pointe), but even those are understood as convenient approximations of a natural continuum. For Cunningham, there is no continuum and no nature; the
body becomes, at this point, a set of numerical abstractions, of +/– or +/0/–
switches. Ballet's approach to the body is organic. Cunningham's is analytic.
Ballet, coeval with the Enlightenment, seeks to refine nature by the light of
order and reason. Cunningham technique, born in an age of abstract art and
digitalized information, leaves nature behind for the realm of pure numbers.

This analytic process, however, is only the first step. Having reduced the
body to an array of precisely delimited choices, Cunningham proceeds to
make those choices, and to make them in any possible combination. The
contrast with academic classicism is again illuminating. Ballet positions and
movements are conceived as harmonious wholes (which is why they have
names that describe them as wholes: fourth arabesque, pas de basque). But
if Cunningham has freed his thinking about dance from the constraints
of convention, he has also freed it from the constraints of anatomy. Under
his method, the conceptually discreet entities into which the body and its
movements have been disassembled can be treated, for purposes of reas-
sembly, as autonomous. The ways in which the body naturally fits together
and moves together do not need to be considered. In passing from analysis
to synthesis, radical simplification becomes radical complexity, and radical constraint, radical freedom.

Again, these are only my inferences about the way that Cunningham goes about putting movement together. Nor am I suggesting that he combines possibilities haphazardly; they are rather the raw material to which he applies his remarkable compositional gifts. But the principles I've outlined do make sense of some of the most prominent features of Cunningham's work. For one thing, they help explain its tremendous complexity, for they suggest that its possibilities multiply exponentially: ten binary choices (and there are quite a bit more than that) mean 1,024 possible positions. For another, they help explain its difficulty, as well as its frequent awkwardness and strangeness. And so they also help us to appreciate the extraordinary virtuosity that it requires. From this perspective, in fact, Cunningham's drive for ever-greater levels of technical ability only makes sense: he wants to open all his options up.

Finally, these principles point us to what is surely among the philosophical sources of Cunningham's art. The discovery that the movements of the heavenly bodies can be expressed in mathematical terms led philosophers as far back as Pythagoras and Plato to the belief that those bodies, that all of material reality, are merely emanations of a higher, numerical order. Matter changes; numbers are unalterable. Matter decays; numbers are inviolable. Prime movers unmoving, pure form: a kind of god. But if numbers are the god of Cunningham's art, complexity and chaos are the nature of the world that they bring into being—just as they are outside the theater. The achievement is remarkable, really: it is one thing to reduce the complexity of experience to the simplicity of numbers, quite another to run the process in reverse. The architects of the computer do it one way; Cunningham does it on his own. And in so doing, he brings his art—and we who watch it—into simultaneous contact with the twin faces of reality: mutability and permanence, chaos and form, the uniqueness in change and the identity through change of every body that moves.

All this has helped me better understand the experience of taking a Cunningham class, as well as that of watching the Cunningham company. In class, far from feeling disassembled, your body feels remarkably unified and "clean," all straight lines and simple relationships. The technique's spareness permits an unusual intensity of focus: with no need to worry about adding ornamentation in the neck, shoulders, or arms, you can attend very closely to the muscles that are centrally active, those of the pelvis, abdomen, and upper thighs. Such focused attention is strictly necessary, for there's no room to hide in this technique, no chance to "cheat" positions and no value placed on mere brio. Thus, even more than concentration and strength, Cunningham technique demands and develops a unique sense of calm. The absence of noise that strikes you at the Cunningham Studio begins on the dance floor, inside the bodies at work there.

The qualities developed in class shine forth luminously onstage, but with this difference: we see their obverse sides—the front, as it were, of the tapestry. The cleanness that you feel in class becomes a preternatural clarity of shape. In their extraordinary precision and purity of line, Cunningham's dancers appear as if lit up by the flash of a strobe; their images etch themselves onto your retina. Nor, again, do we get the impression of modular, disjunctive bodies. In fact, Cunningham can allow himself to conceptualize the body segmentally because in physical reality it is unalterably one. He can make the body assume unnatural shapes precisely because we will always see it as one. As the energy of his meanings derives from the imaginative tension created by the union of heterogenous elements in a single work, so does the energy of his forms derive from the physical tension created by the union of conflicting lines of force in a single body. As for the calm his technique instills, it reads onstage as serenity, the outstanding temperamental characteristic of the Cunningham dancer. What is in fact an inward attentiveness seems to us an imperturbable attention, like the gazing of a star upon the sea.

After a number of years of stability, the company's roster has undergone a lot of alteration in the last three years. Some of its most splendid dancers have departed, including Victoria Finlayson, Alan Good, Helen Barrow, and Patricia Lent. (Good has left since the company's annual season at City Center in New York.) Chris Komar, a veteran of twenty-two years and now assistant artistic director, appears to have retired from the stage. Other than Komar and Cunningham himself, only one dancer, Robert Swinston, has more than seven years' seniority, and six were performing at their first City Center this year. Their relative lack of experience showed in a certain hesitancy onstage, but these new and recent additions promise the same abundance of aesthetic bliss as was supplied by the company of the 1980s.

The most immediately striking of the new women is Banu Ogan, a long-limbed, long-waisted dancer. Ogan has aristocratic features and a blithe manner that suggests the preoccupied delight of a fine lady arranging a bouquet of tulips. Cunningham immediately put her physical and temperamental qualities to use to create one of the most beautiful passages in *CRWDSPCR*, a new work that is full of them. The piece reflects, it seems, on city life: we see street performers, perhaps, and people sitting on benches, and we also see a lot about what happens in crowded places to the body, its movement, and its loves. But there is also a long section, beginning with a solo by Ogan, that seems to take place in a park. The music's roaring, traffic-like sounds quiet to a distant murmur as, with little elastic movements of the instep and knee, her body begins to rise and fall, pliant yet weighted, a flowering branch lifting and subsiding in the wind. Her long back arches and tilts, her free foot curves sur le cou-de-pied; she seems lost in a reverie of sunlight and sweet air. It's very much like watching someone do tai chi in Prospect Park, and it is the secret center of this dense and rushing work.

Cheryl Therrien, also new this year and also tall, is in more important ways the opposite of Ogan. Where the latter gives the impression of lifting away, in both the physical and spiritual senses, from the earth and its things, Therrien's dancing seems deeply rooted in both. Her strong ankles and big, expressive feet give her movement a solidity and a largeness that read as steadfastness and frankness and generosity. But her most striking qualities emanate from hands and face. There is a lack of refinement about the way she holds her hands—straight out from the wrist, fingers apart, flattish—that make them seem outsized and animate and, somehow, incredibly wise. In both *Touchbase* and *Enter*, she has inherited roles that capitalize on this quality with passages of isolated arm movements, messages written in the language of dreams. And in Therrien's expression, the company's characteristic serenity passes into a wisdom that seems born of a hundred years of equanimity before the procession of desire and change. No wonder Cunningham has seized on her for a number of symbolically important roles, including figures of fate in both *Change of Address* and *Enter*. Therrien is a performer who is just beginning to reveal, or discover, the depths of her expressive ability.

Then there are the dancers who just blow you away with their virtuosity. If there are greater technicians in modern dance than Frédéric Gafner and Jenifer Weaver, I have not seen them. Of Gafner's many excellences, one of the most pleasurable is his deftness of release in getting off the ground; he's soaring before you even notice the preparatory plié. His petit allegro is a marvel of precision and fluidity—*Sounddance* (1974), revived this year, gave him a minute-long burst of it—and also underscores his cool efficiency, his air of getting the job done. Gafner's relationship to his body is like a concert pianist's to his fingers. But if Gafner is cool, Weaver is almost absent. Her physical perfection is astonishing—torso sculpted and lithe, feet beautifully articulate, legs that move without visible resistance in the hips—but her emotional investment appears to be minimal. Nothing ripples the surface of her infallibility: this is at once her greatness and its limitation.

Jean Freebury, by contrast, is all puckish vivacity. Her features are so animated that you expect her to break into laughter at any moment (sometimes I actually wished she would cool it), and this same vividness and love of movement energize her whole body. She is also so sure-footed that her full force can flow through allegro combinations without abating for the divisions of the steps. At rest, she makes you think of an idling sports car. As for Thomas Caley, one of the new men, he is simply the most beautiful young stallion to come along in fifteen years. Tall and handsome, with puppy-dog eyes and fullback shoulders, he disports himself with the carriage of a danseur noble and the happy irresponsibility of a prince. One cannot look at him and simultaneously believe in the reality of suffering. This may not be the whole truth, but it is part of the truth, and it is one of the things that beautiful young people are for.

All this variety of excellence, together with the nine marvelous dancers I haven't discussed, makes it quite incredible to hear the charge that's sometimes made, that Cunningham's dancers all look the same. As much might be said about Cunningham's dances, as it once was said of Balanchine's. But to these charges, the rejoinder is clear: it depends how carefully you look. A strenuous attention to experience—intense, sustained, comprehensive—is the essential quality of all cognitive excellence: scientific discovery, artistic creation, critical insight. By making dances that repay such attention, Cunningham teaches us, teaches us all, to achieve that kind of excellence. The spiritual training that begins in the studio so that it may continue onstage continues onstage so that it may terminate in the audience. Westbeth is a portable phenomenon.

[1994]

MARK MORRIS: HOME COMING

Only a couple of years have passed since Mark Morris brought his dance company back from Brussels, but already his stint as director of dance at the Théâtre Royal de la Monnaie has developed a compelling little mythology—part wandering in the wilderness, part anni mirabiles, part rite of passage. Wilderness: the Belgians, having been steeped in a couple of decades worth of Maurice Béjart's ponderous Ballet of the XXth Century, proved themselves unready to enter the XXIst, tossing Morris's company more brickbats than bouquets. Wonder years: in Belgium, Morris enjoyed the resources of a lavishly funded state opera house, an opportunity unheard of in modern dance, and he used them to create works on a scale that was likewise unheard of in modern dance. Coming of age: as Joan Acocella wrote last year in *Vogue*, Morris went to Brussels, at age thirty-two, "the most important young choreographer in the United States" and returned three years later "simply one of the foremost artists in the United States."

I call these notions myths not because I do not think them true, but because they have acquired in many minds, including mine, a truth more significant, more luminous, than the mere facts on which they are based. Together with the other myths that have attached themselves to Morris's career, they make up a kind of symbolic biography, one that bespeaks the degree to which this brilliant young artist has captured our imaginations.

Yet whatever legends they engender, the life and work move on. Morris's four-handed productivity continues unabated, his output now including works for his company, the Mark Morris Dance Group; works for the White Oak Dance Project (the high-profile touring venture launched three years ago with Mikhail Baryshnikov); ballet-company commissions; and occasional choreography for opera. MMDG's most important affiliation has remained with Dance Umbrella of Boston, under whose aegis it holds a four-week residency and two-week season each spring, but the company's visits to New York have been sporadic, stealthy, and brief. Last year's season lasted two weeks, but this year's (all but smuggled into BAM, so minimal was the publicity) only four days. As for White Oak, a loose and fluctuating collection of veteran stars, it hasn't performed in the city yet and doesn't look like it ever will. Whatever the mystique that surrounds it—terpsichorean supergroup, Mark-Misha mind-meld, buck-naked romps through enchanted Floridian glades—White Oak is basically a barnstorming operation. And no one makes a profit dancing in New York.

So this year's season, brief though it was, offered a rare opportunity. Billed as "Dances to American Music," it was the first engagement to present both MMDG and (members of) White Oak—in other words, the two very different ensembles for which Morris now creates most of his work—on the same stage. Among other things, the juxtaposition affirmed what might be called the Monnaie Principle: what you make depends on how you make it. If the material circumstances in Brussels exerted their pressure on Morris's imagination, manifesting in the scope, shape, and tone of the works that he created there, the same appears to be true, in rather different ways, of both the post-Brussels MMDG and White Oak.

That much may seem obvious, but if Morris possesses the most articulate imagination in dance today—and it says here that he does—then what he makes matters a great deal. What he makes tells us about how we live. But *how* he makes is *part* of how we live. The conditions of our lives structure what we can say about them, and the outermost frame of a work becomes as meaningful as its internal form. The postmodern soloist performing in a small loft space tells us as much with her isolation as she does with her choreography. The traditional ballet company, with its hierarchy and its opulence and its sex roles, necessarily affirms an entire system of values. One of the most interesting things about Morris's work these days is that he creates it under such a wide array of conditions. And one of the most interesting things about "Dances to American Music" was its suggestion that he's quite aware of the issues and opportunities that that circumstance presents. The interplay of frame and form in the two works premiered at BAM was complex and at times remarkable.

The White Oak contingent appeared in *Mosaic and United* (set to Henry Cowell's String Quartets nos. 3 and 4, *Mosaic* and *United*), the five of them joining five members of MMDG. One can guess that the work was rehearsed in bits and pieces, since it couldn't have been easy to get everyone in the same place at the same time (especially Baryshnikov), which is undoubtedly one reason the dance never does get everyone in the same place at the same time. The cast is divided into two groups that never meet, alternating in both the "Mosaic" and "United" sections. The first group dominates "Mosaic," a gloomy landscape filled with images of illness and isolation. An eerie trembling movement breaks out periodically like a disease. The opening passage turns ninety degrees and repeats exactly to a repeat in the score, a variation without a difference, a matter not of musical fidelity but of mechanical repetition, inertia, futility. Later, the first group atomizes completely, the women crawling about, the men hugging themselves like lonely children. Configurations don't so much assemble as accrete, interpersonal connection reduced to mere proximity. The movement, like the music, is impersonal, hard-edged, and harsh, with none of the rounded or sustained or sensuous qualities characteristic of Morris's style.

"United" gives more to the second group, whose choreography is generally warmer and more interactive, though scarcely brighter. In one passage, the men move quietly from woman to woman, lifting or guiding them with a sad tenderness. Another passage is folklike—tripping rhythms, a relaxed carriage—yet maintains the sober mood. Transitions between passages are uncharacteristically absent, as throughout the piece, and, in any case, all this is bracketed by the doings of the first group, who open the section with a set of five solos—actually only two solos distributed among the five, as if to underscore the sense of loneliness with an ironic commonality—and end it with what seem like images of war: a V-formation that resembles a flight of bombers, versions of marching and mimed combat.

I'm not sure what it all added up to, but I'm also not sure that that wasn't a part of the point. Images of isolation, structures of futility, missing connections: the piece seemed to be about the process of not adding up, of social disintegration giving rise to a disintegration of meaning. But when, where? The program's title, "Dances to American Music," suggested an answer. Morris seems to have intended something deeper with it than a simple reference to the scores. *Mosaic and United*: America, too, is a fragmentary whole. We are atomized, warlike, occasionally generous, at times immensely tender, lonely, ill—a gloomy landscape of oppressive and enigmatic images, a total picture that doesn't exactly add up, at once a mosaic, as is often said, and yet, United.

But in speaking of America thus, Morris speaks also of an entire emerging world. What Gertrude Stein remarked at the turn of the century will be as true of the next. Americans are the oldest people in the world, because we've been living in the twenty-first century for a hundred years. Economic forces now are rearranging whole societies, shifting populations, altering the nature and pace of work. We work part-time, short-term, ad hoc, as temps and replacements, consultants and adjuncts. Relationships form and as quickly dissolve, enterprises start up, strip down, merge, and move on. It is under such conditions that ventures like the White Oak Dance Project arise. "Project": the word captures the notion precisely. You stay together only as long as it takes to accomplish the task. No commitments, no continuity, no overarching vision—very temporary but very convenient. Whether this is good or bad is not the point; the point is that these are the circumstances under which a great many things get put together these days. Things like *Mosaic and United*, a work whose making had to accommodate, and whose form bespeaks, the exigencies of a "project."

The dance is thus a rarity in Morris's canon, for that there are compelling and viable alternatives to postindustrial anomie and postmodern fragmentation is a central thesis of his work. Morris's output is enormously diverse, but at its core is the will to imagine human relations more honest, more deeply felt, and more satisfying than those that we are generally given to live. Sometimes this impulse manifests directly in mood and theme (*L'Allegro, A Lake*), but more often it operates as the implied point of view from which a given situation is seen—that is, from which it's seen as problematic. The light of a profoundly responsible humanism illuminates Morris's work, now at a greater, now at a lesser angle of refraction. In this sense, the horrors of *Lovey* and the degradations of *Dogtown* are every bit as humanistic as *A Lake*. In this sense—and it is only this sense that is meaningful. Those who find dances like *Lovey* and *Dogtown* vulgar must look to their own notions of decorum to discover true vulgarity. And those who find Morris's parodies frivolous or disrespectful might endeavor to distinguish between petrified modes of expression and the living emotions they arose to express. No less than the others, such pieces emanate from Morris's commitment to the truth of feeling, for it is by dismantling those petrifications that he clears the stage for fresh expression.

And in all the works that he makes for his company, the company itself becomes an agent of this underlying humanism. If the White Oak Dance Project is a "project," the Mark Morris Dance Group is a "group": egalitarian, communitarian, committed to the common realization of common ideals. (Of the roughly four hundred modern dance companies listed in *Stein's*

Catalogue, by the way, only three use that word to describe themselves.) I am not referring to the group's private relationships, which are irrelevant in this connection, but to the ones that they project onstage. The frame, again, is part of the meaning. In the alertness and courtesy and unity of purpose with which its members dance together—that is, in the style that Morris has instilled in them—the Mark Morris Dance Group embodies its director's humanistic sensibilities. As long as it is present on the stage, they will be, as well, commenting silently—now in harmony, now in counterpoint—on the choreography's explicit meanings.

Nowhere is this interaction more significant, perhaps, than *Home*, the second of the BAM premieres. At its most obvious level, the dance depicts the kind of rural life described in its score, which consists of three commissioned songs by Michelle Shocked and Rob Wasserman. Shocked, a young singer-songwriter from Texas, is known for colorful, intelligent lyrics and a sound that fuses country/western twang with the introspective tenderness of folk-rock. The songs for *Home* describe the simmering desperations of rural life—a pretty hackneyed theme, and one that's therefore suited to displaying her storytelling gifts. Instead of "the man from the bank" and "you done me wrong" and "save me Lord Jesus," Shocked offers vivid, unfamiliar stories of three precisely realized characters: a "widow at thirty-five" living alone on her farm ("Homestead"), a midwife who delivers a stillborn child ("Stillborn"), and a farmer waiting for the "custom cutter" to show up to harvest his wheat ("Custom Cutter"). Each is told through cunningly chosen details—hobos sleeping on the porch, the sudden crushing of a cicada—that serve as the dramatic index of emotions at once intense and understated. Listening to these narratives, we are forced to construct our feelings from the ground up (how many of us even knew what a "custom cutter" is?), unable to rely on the responses that we've been habituated to provide.

The choreography works in a similar way. Rather than building up large-scale patterns of movement, as he typically does to orchestral scores, Morris offers one simple image at a time, many of them held in tableau. Some are almost embarrassingly literal: wheat bending in the wind, fingers touching lips in pity on the word "stillborn." The difference between Morris and other choreographers isn't that he makes no room for virtuosity, as is sometimes claimed, but that he insists on subordinating it to aesthetic purpose. Here, knowing how delicate his theme is, he avoids sentimentality through a studied artlessness, allowing no exaggeration or prettiness to make room for false feeling. But though there's not a shred of sentimentalism about this or any of his works, in their largeness of emotion, they often verge on melodrama. Sometimes, indeed, he seems to run straight up against the melodramatic so as to drive back its limits, expanding our ideas as to how much feeling may legitimately be felt.

The strategy requires a counterbalancing tact at the level of composition—here, the casting of a group of six women against the single characters of the stories, a multiplication that both intensifies and objectifies the dramatic situations. In "Stillborn," the tactic also allows Morris to comment on the story through some beautiful images of womanly solace—ambiguous comment, since this is just the kind of solace that the midwife usually provides, but that she feels she's failed to offer here. In the other songs, dealing as they do with solitary figures, the tactic is frankly ironic. The communal meanings always present on MMDG's stage function, once again, to amplify the communal or anti-communal dimensions of a work.

In *Home*, Morris also brings those meanings in at a completely different level with an audacious compositional choice. Between the songs, a second group of six lines up on stage in street clothes and the kind of big leather tap shoes used for clogging. Shocked and Wasserman strike up a tune on mandolin and fiddle, and the dancers *just start clogging*. There's nothing extra about it; both times, Morris and his pals do just the sort of bouncy, joggling heel-and-toe moves you can witness anywhere from Appalachia to Texas. It was tight, energetic, and fun as hell. Morris looked as casual and content as a young uncle who'd just finished off his third helping of peach cobbler—I even caught him wiping his nose at one point—while June Omura, the freshest and most vivid woman in the company, glowed like a little girl taking her first pony ride.

But what really struck me was the way the audience reacted. Here we were at BAM—the penthouse suite of High Seriousness, the place where you go when you're hip *and* rich—and all they were doing was folk dancing, and the audience was going nuts. It was so telling, so clear an illustration of why Morris is seen as the choreographer of the age, the choreographer of the future. After a hundred years of modernist machismo, of Decadence and Dada and Brutalism and Punk, people want to feel again. It's been a long century. Home—that's where people want to go.

The question is, where is it? The title's most immediate reference points us to the small town, that mythic down-home home that we all carry around in our heads. But what it points us to is poverty and sadness—what's really there today. For while it might be argued that the clogging, in its brightness and vitality, is intended to display another side of rural life, that interpretation misses who it is who's actually doing it: emphatically *not* the dancers representing that life, but ones in fact "representing" no one but themselves. And it was surely no coincidence that Morris cast this group to have as multicultural, as it were, as non-down-home a look as possible: among others, Kraig Patterson, a delicately boned African American; Guillermo Resto, that dreadlocked Latino stud who looks more like a bear every year; Omura, whose sly New York wit darts out from Asian American features; and Morris himself, one of the most famously gay men in American art.

Watching those folks do that folk dancing, we learn a thing or two about how culture, multi- or otherwise, works. The small town may be collapsing, Morris is telling us, but its best energies are embodied in its art forms, and its art forms are available to all. Clogging expresses certain things, we all feel those things, so there's no reason that we can't all express them through clogging, no matter who we are. The only requirement is that we do it right. Authenticity isn't about wearing the right badge; it's about a rigorous and excellent application of craft. Virtuosity is virtue.

Still, the more that this pan-ethnic clogging asserts its own validity, the more it emphasizes the distance between the culture depicted in *Home* and the culture that performs and watches it. After all, the women who dance the work's dramatic sections are not any less remote from the world they're representing than the cloggers are—it's just that their remoteness is submerged in the act of representation. But by bringing members of the Mark Morris Dance Group onstage as themselves, *Home*, so to speak, blows the women's cover, making visible the frame that surrounds those stories, making us see them as fictions enacted by members of the Mark Morris Dance Group. And in the dance's final section, in yet one more involution of structure, that fictional world collapses altogether. After "Custom Cutter," the lights dim, the music grows pensive, and the women are folded back into the group as a whole. The entire cast concludes the work with a passage of melancholy circling and weaving, a kind of elegaic folk dancing.

The effect is like that of the cast of a play dropping character and quietly folding up the scenery. Here it turns the meaning of the work, the significance of its title, decisively away from the ruined or threatened homes described in Shocked and Wasserman's songs. Home is right here, Morris is saying, or it is nowhere. Understood in reference to the rural world that is the work's ostensible subject, the title is thus doubly ironic: it is not a home, and it is not our home. But understood in reference to ourselves, it is doubly hopeful: our world can be a home if we are strong enough to make it one, and insofar as we allow ourselves access to the cultures of our old homes, our new home can contain what's best in them, as well.

At its deepest levels, then, *Home* shows Morris pondering the nature of his art with new self-consciousness. He has painted the country/western reaches of the American landscape before, but here he both represents that world and marks the limits of his representation. His imaginative engagement is stringent and deep, but it remains, he reminds us, irreducibly imaginative— arising not from direct experience but from contact with the cultural forms of folk dance and popular music, terminating not in direct experience but in the creation of works of art. Morris's honesty in this regard makes our response more honest, too, urging us not to confuse aesthetic contemplation with immediate engagement, prompting us to ask not where to send the check, but what we know about that rural world and how we know it. *Home* leads us, finally, to think about the ways that any dramatic work brings us together with the world it represents. In an age when our experience is at once so wide and yet so elaborately mediated, this is no small thing.

"Bringing together": it is, finally, the central effort of Morris's art. There is his ostentatious collegiality, his cultural eclecticism, his inquisitiveness about all aspects of human movement. Most of all there is his company itself, its image not only communitarian but also instinctively inclusive: of all races, sexualities, bodily types. But as "Dances to American Music" insisted, that ideal is only half the story. The world of the "group" that Morris posits and so convincingly maintains exists beside the world of the "project," that more massive and less lovely reality. It is in this sense that his humanism is pro- foundly responsible. He does not reject the world of the project for the world of the group; he seeks to bring the two together, to enable the ideals of the one to suffuse the actuality of the other. The one maintains a necessary grounding; the other acquires a radiant moral significance. It is by keeping one foot in each that Morris achieves his fabulous agility.

[1993]

STUDIES SHOW ARTS HAVE VALUE

A recent article in the *New York Times* proclaimed the gladsome tidings. "New support for the value of fiction," it announced, "is arriving from an unexpected quarter: neuroscience." Our brains light up like Christmas trees, it turns out, when we are exposed to narrative language. Not only that, but reading fiction increases our ability to empathize with others. Writers, grateful for anything that might relieve their Dostoyevskian sense of wounded insignificance, rejoiced at the support; I saw the article whizzing past me several times on Facebook.

Me, I thought, *Here we go again.* Reading fiction increases our ability to empathize with others? Did we really need science to tell us that? But we need science, apparently, to tell us everything. I remember seeing a story in *Time* about thirty years ago: scientists show that urban life is stressful. Oh, *scientists* show? Writers showed us that 150 years ago and more. Balzac, Dickens, Gaskell, Zola. But that isn't good enough, at least for *Time*.

In *The Prisoner of Sex*, Norman Mailer remarked that he was "sufficiently intimate with magazine readers to know the age of technology had left them with an inability to respect writing which lacked the authority of statistics." I don't know about readers, but I do know about editors, and most of them don't like it when you rest your argument on literary sources. They want numbers, studies, sociology. Aristotle, Montaigne, and Emerson are not valid authorities on the topic, say, of friendship, but a study of fifty college students is enough to convince an editor of anything.

Oh, those studies. They always have a lot of data, but they so often miss the point. Their focus is too narrow, or they ignore the important factors, or they simply fail to grasp the underlying questions. They are either jaw-droppingly obvious or head-clutchingly misguided. Science is bad enough, where it doesn't belong, but the social sciences are even worse, precisely because they pretend to scientific rigor. When the social sciences committed themselves to the principle of measurement, as Allan Bloom remarked, they surrendered the ability to talk about anything that cannot be measured.

The problem, all around, is scientism: the belief that science represents the only valid form of knowledge. To accept as much is to deny the authority of one's own experience. Never mind Dickens; every city dweller understands that urban life is stressful. And it is upon nothing other than experience that art stakes its claim: the experience of the individual creator, and their ability to give it a form that resonates with our own experience. Art is a rebuke to the cult of the spurious expert. It is allied with citizenship, that other domain of the passionate amateur. In both, we stand upon our right to speak from the self.

That is why I found that article to be so galling. It's not enough for science (or "science") to tell us things that art figured out a long time ago. Now it presumes to validate art itself in scientific terms—which is to say, to invalidate it, by implicitly denying its status as an independent way of knowing. But we don't need neuroscience to tell us that reading fiction is valuable. We all know it, because we all feel it.

[2012]

LETTERS

ALFRED KAZIN:
FIERY PARTICLE OF SPIRIT

I have a dream of an infinite walk," Alfred Kazin told himself in 1947, "of going on and on, forever unimpeded by weariness or duties . . . until I in my body and the world in its skin of earth are somehow blended in a single motion." He was thirty-one, and just beginning *A Walker in the City*, his celebrated memoir of youth in darkest Jewish immigrant Brooklyn. Not sitting and studying, not looking or reading, but walking: going out, going through, the self in motion, in the world and with the world and being breathed on by the world—this was Kazin's master metaphor. And not just walking, but walking in the city, in that city, in his city. Kazin knew that walking in New York is not the idle stroll of flânerie, aestheticized, detached. A moral pressure everywhere surrounds you, streaming from the urgency and clamor, the sirens and the grime, from faces alert, beset. You are implicated; you are called upon. You do not float—you press. That is how Kazin moved through the world—*A Lifetime Burning in Every Moment*, he called a later memoir—and that is how we can begin to understand him as an exemplary American intellectual.

Kazin was the author of over a dozen books; over a thousand essays and reviews; of *On Native Grounds*, the massive, pathbreaking study of modern American prose that made his reputation at the age of twenty-seven; of *Starting Out in the Thirties* and *New York Jew*, sequels to *A Walker in the City* and together a dazzling group portrait of the generation of American intellectuals who came of age in the Depression and the war and bestrode American thought in the '50s and '60s. Himself among that generation's signal members, he was perhaps the country's leading critic, a mainstay on radio and television as well as in the highbrow press. It was the right time to be a public intellectual. In 1961, he interviewed the new president, for the *American Scholar*, at a private luncheon at the White House. In 1966, he was invited to Truman Capote's Black and White Ball as one of the "five hundred most famous people in the world." But all along his deepest work was being done in private, in the journals he started at age seventeen and would continue writing for the next sixty-five years, some seven thousand pages all together. If his life was an "infinite walk," his journals were the record of that walk.

Here's a rough summary, based on the lovingly edited selection by Richard M. Cook: Reading! Writing! Sex! New York! America! Jews! Words, books, books, life, life!* The journals' overwhelming note is passion. Kazin wrote with his whole being, from a ferocious intensity of hunger and joy. "The problem," he told himself, "is to bear oneself up, to go through to the end, to *be* and to grow and to deepen with everything one *has*." Note "the problem." Ideas, for Kazin, were nothing less than "instruments of salvation"—a pretty good definition of what it means to be an intellectual. His never-ending struggle was to understand himself and the world and himself in relation to the world.

He was a writer, he insisted, not a critic. "They are critics and have good taste," he wrote of a pair of acquaintances; "I am a writer and interested in everything I can see and read and feel and touch." Writing, as the journals are uniquely fit to show, meant integrating one's whole experience, one's whole personality, moving fluidly between thinking and feeling until they were a single thing, moving among the holy trinity of books, the self, and the world as ways of understanding each, and expressing it all, creating it all, discovering it all, in the daily, private act of laying down words.

Writing meant taking it personally, too. "I have always approached all literary and critical questions with the instinctive quick sympathy of the writer," he said, "not with the objectivity and heaviness of the critic." Kazin's greatness as a reader lay in his remarkable ability to get to the writer behind the writing, to understand literature not as an isolated realm of aesthetic exploration, but as a way of coming to terms with the world, of addressing "the problem," of expressing a stance about life. The writers that he dwelt with down the years—"these presences, these menaces, these taking-overs"—he imagined "walking, breathing, crowding, loving, talking to me . . . talking back to the constant reader, the lovelorn reader, the nudnick reader." Blake, Emerson, Henry Adams, Edmund Wilson, Hemingway: he had them in his heart and on his fingertips, carried their photos in his wallet.

For Kazin, all this was not only his own way of being an intellectual; it was the Jewish way. "New York Jew" this child of poverty and fervor defiantly

---

* *Alfred Kazin's Journals* (New Haven: Yale University Press, 2011).

declared himself: prophetic, angry, ironic, dispossessed; gauche, emotive, intemperate, rude. Writing from need, writing from hurt, writing from the margins, writing to pick a fight with the world. Thinking of Augie March, and of Augie's creator, and of himself and many others, he unfurls a bravura passage evoking the young Jew in America as "this eternal traveler . . . innocent and tough, skeptical and lyrical . . . a *force* . . . a stir in the world . . . a living and fiery particle of spirit." WASP writers like Adams and Wilson and Van Wyck Brooks he envied for their aristocratic equipoise and effortless possession of America. (Of his beloved Wilson he wrote, "EW thinks he is writing history whenever he sits down to his diary.") Jewish writers like Lionel Trilling, Kazin's bête noire, who aped, he felt, the Anglo-Saxon style, he couldn't hate enough. "T. cannot stand my temperament," he wrote. "[H]e cannot stand the ghetto Jew in me . . . L.T., the would-be gentleman—the little gentleman."

Kazin was not an observant Jew, but his Jewishness filled him to bursting. "The problem, as always," he wrote, "is how to be a 'Jew' without 'Judaism'"—that is, without traditional belief and practice or even communal affiliation. Kazin was not an American Adam. He did not believe in self-invention: he believed in self-discovery, in the sense of figuring out what history had already made you. What does it mean to be a Jew? What does it mean to be an American? These were his lifelong questions. *On Native Grounds* was followed by four more books on American literature. Unlike Trilling and other postwar critics, interpreters of the European tradition to a rising middle class that felt itself in need of culture, he did not look to England and the Continent. Unlike other progressive intellectuals of his generation, he embraced American values. "I love to think about America," he wrote, "to remember the kind of adventurousness and purity, heroism, and *salt*, the best Americans have always had for me."

Most of all, as time went on, he marveled at the conjunction of his two identities, of what had become of the Jew in America. "The beggarly Jewish radicals of the 30s," he wrote in 1963, "are now the ruling cultural pundits of American society." It filled him with ambivalence, "*the Jewish success*," the ambivalence of the outsider become an insider, of the person who has gotten what they feel they never should have wanted. It also filled him with sheer awe at what his generation had done. Thinking one day in 1968 of Norman Podhoretz's *Making It*, he sings an epic catalogue of notable Jews, sixty-one names that begin with himself and end with Susan Sontag, everyone from Mailer to Marcuse to Mike Nichols.

But something, he would later feel, had changed, as mention of Pod-horetz ("The brutal, little mind of Norman Podhoretz") suggests. "What excuses we do find," he writes in 1985, the depths of Reaganism and the heyday of the Jewish neoconservatives, "(we who once had no trouble exe-crating everyone in power) for those in power." It was a betrayal of origins, spirit, mission, history: "There really is no continuity between the 'sacrificed' (whether in the Holocaust or under slavery) and those who, in their name, are very busy sacrificing others." Kazin was never a Marxist, hated ideologies, always did his own thinking, but he never lost faith with the impulse that ani-mated the '30s, and the Hebrew prophets. "*The cry for justice* is eternal," he writes, "because it comes from the condemned, the pariahs, the proscribed, the forgotten, the homeless, the dissidents, the outlawed."

The farther one gets in Kazin's journals, the more salient does the word "power" become. The story of the postwar years, as we can see him live and watch and write it day by day, was the asymptotic ascent of Ameri-can power. "Everywhere today," he wrote in 1967, "the American who has any imagination and conscience tries to relate himself to the superpower we have become, and fails." For Kazin, steeped to saturation in American his-tory, this was a new version of an old story, the first flush of American might in the last, industrializing decades of the nineteenth century, witnessed at one end by Emerson, at the other by Adams. The charge for the intellectual remained the same: not to succumb to that power, not to become its accom-plice, but to make it accountable to the moral intelligence. Quixotic, he knew, to be sure—the quest of the mind in the world, the walk as long as life itself.

[2011]

Harold Rosenberg:
The Individual Nuisance

A single sentence sufficed to seal my veneration for Harold Rosenberg. It appears in the midst of the bravura conclusion of "The Intellectual and His Future," an essay from 1965. "One does not *possess* mental freedom and detachment," it reads, "one participates in them." Here was a dictum worthy of adoption as a creed. "Intellectual" is not a title, an honorific, or a job description. It is a daily aspiration.

Rosenberg is remembered, if he's remembered now at all, as one of the leading American art critics of the twentieth century, coiner of the term "action painting" to describe the work of Jackson Pollock, Willem de Kooning, and other Abstract Expressionists, and it was for that reason, several years ago, that I turned to his work. What I discovered was not an art critic but a full-spectrum intellectual who thought about art. He also thought about poetry, politics, theater, fiction, society, sociology, Marx, Marxism, Judaism, the media, and the nature of the intellectual himself.

And he did it all better than just about anyone I had ever encountered. He was Trilling without the solemnity, Kazin with a wider, more ironic mind (to name two earlier infatuations among the New York intellectuals). His point of view was comic in the deepest sense. An outsider by temperament as well as conviction, he looked at everything from the outside, accepting nothing—no movement, figure, social fiction, educated formula—at its own estimation. His most potent rhetorical weapon was satire—the whiff of caricature, the gust of common sense. "Far from being goaded to their parts by police agents hidden in the wings"—this in reference to the vogue of self-confession among postwar ex-radicals—"the guilty here had to force their way onto the stage. [Whittaker] Chambers himself, that witness of witnesses . . . describes how close he came to breaking under the ordeal of getting the notice of people whose vital interests he was determined to defend." But Rosenberg was not merely a debunker. He believed in things: in art, in the struggle to come to terms with reality, in the individual. He was skeptical of "thought," but he believed in thinking.

Other intellectuals saw through collective illusions. Rosenberg saw through the illusions of other intellectuals. The criticism of kitsch art (i.e., popular culture), a highbrow hobby in the new age of mass entertainment, was nothing, he wrote, but another form of kitsch—kitsch ideas. "There is only one way to quarantine kitsch: by being too busy with art." Notions of the "other-directed" "organization man," promulgated in the 1950s as descriptions of the new American type (and clichés of thought to this day), were in reality projections, he explained, on the part of the new caste of intellectual placemen who were swarming the postwar bureaucracies. "Today Orgmen reproduce themselves like fruit flies in whatever is organized, whether it be a political party or a museum of advanced art." As for "alienation," that great midcentury bugaboo and talking point, not only didn't Rosenberg deplore it, he saw it as a virtue, a failure "to participate emotionally and intellectually in the fictions and conventions of mass culture."

He was fearless in the face of reputation. T. S. Eliot (then at his zenith), having made an idol of "tradition," had led American poetry into a cul-de-sac of academicism. *1984*, all but sacred at the time, was marked by "frigid rationality and paranoiacally lifeless prose." Auden and Spender, darlings of the cultural left for their politically "responsible" poetry, avoided responsibility for individual experience and social reflection alike. "When I first encountered the gravity of Lionel Trilling," Rosenberg wrote, "I did not get the joke; it took some time to realize that there wasn't any."

Upon his death in 1978, Hilton Kramer, chief art critic of the *New York Times*, eulogized him as "the quintessential New York intellectual." For the essayist Seymour Krim, reflecting on the same occasion, Rosenberg had been the most intelligent critic writing in English. As for his physical presence, Krim reported, "Harold looked and shone like the Lion of Judah. He was about 6'4", a really heroic-looking prince among the bookish intellectuals . . . a sort of matinee idol of the intellectual underground" who had passed "a lot of lean years bucking all the Establishments." His passing, Krim wrote, "sweeps a period with it."

Harold Rosenberg was born in Brooklyn in 1906. He spent a year at City College, then three at Brooklyn Law School, but he would later say that he'd received his education on the steps of the New York Public Library. After graduation, he plunged into Village bohemia, befriending artists (de Kooning was an early and crucial encounter) and inheriting the twin legacies of the New York intellectuals: Marxism and modernism. He joined the League of American Writers, a radical group, wrote for *New Masses* and *Art Front*, and dreamed of becoming a poet. (A small volume, *Trance Above the Streets*, appeared in 1942.) During the Depression, he kept himself afloat by writing for the WPA, moving to Washington in 1938 to become the art editor of its American Guide Series, then staying after Pearl Harbor to work for the Office of War Information.

After the war, and back in New York, Rosenberg became a stalwart of the little magazines: *Commentary, Encounter, Dissent*, and, of course, *Partisan Review*. He found an apartment on Tenth Street, a rotting Village block that sheltered tramps, a poolroom, and a collection of obscure American painters who were in the process of transforming art. "The Herd of Independent Minds," whose title became a catchphrase, appeared in 1948; "The American Action Painters," which birthed another, in 1952. His first collection, *The Tradition of the New* (its title soon a third), appeared in 1959. Within a few years, he was lecturing at Princeton and writing for *Esquire, Vogue*, and the *New Yorker*. "The beggarly Jewish radicals of the 30s," Kazin wrote in 1963, "are now the ruling cultural pundits of American society."

Eight more collections would follow in the space of fourteen years (the most important is *Discovering the Present*, which, with *The Tradition of the New*, contains his finest work). In 1966 (he was already sixty), Rosenberg became a member of the University of Chicago's exalted Committee on Social Thought and, the following year, art critic for the *New Yorker*, positions that he held until his death. (Most of the later collections consist of pieces from the magazine.) The bucker of Establishments had stormed them, but he never relinquished his outsider stance. American society, he wrote in "The Intellectual and His Future," is replete with obstacles to independent thought, including institutional ones. "The intellectual, however, is adept at finding the cracks in society through which to crawl around the obstacles, whether he eludes them in the university, on a park bench, or in an insurance office."

Marxism and modernism. From Marx, Rosenberg acquired a sensitivity to history—above all, to historical action, or, more precisely, historical acting. A touchstone was *The Eighteenth Brumaire of Louis Bonaparte*, the work in which Marx famously declares that everything in history happens twice, the first time as tragedy, the second time as farce. Louis Bonaparte assumes the costume of Napoleon and dubs himself Napoleon III. "Luther donned the mask," Marx writes, "of the Apostle Paul." Rosenberg develops the idea: those who wish to seize control of history—political figures, revolutionaries—invariably cast themselves as reenactors of a prior revolution. History becomes a play, with roles, scripts, sets, and above all a plot—a predetermined outcome, guided by a self-appointed hero.

For Marx, the final hero would be a collective one, the proletariat, which would free humanity from history, its nightmare repetitions, by dispensing with historical make-believe and acting in the sober consciousness of actual conditions. But "one hundred years after . . . the publication of *The Communist Manifesto*," Rosenberg writes in 1948, "the simplification of history has not been brought about." Instead, the players of the nineteenth century have been replaced by a new, more malevolent form of farceur.

> The heroes of our time [Hitler, Stalin, de Gaulle] belong to contrived rather than spontaneous myths—on that account often evoking even more fanaticism than formerly as a psychological protection against disbelief . . .
>
> The comic nature of the twentieth-century hero is instinctively recognized the moment he makes his entrance upon the stage: in the popular phrase, "At first nobody took him seriously." The clown-hero retaliates to the ridicule of the world by exposing the lack of seriousness of the rest of the cast, of all the existing historical actors. The leader without a program challenges all opposing classes, parties, governments, individuals, to live up to *their* programs. And since all are playing a comedy of pretense, "the adventurer who took the comedy as plain comedy was bound to win."

The notion of politics as theater remained salient for Rosenberg throughout his career—more and more so, indeed, as the media tightened its grip, and political events became performances contrived to hold its interest. For the most part, however, he turned the metaphors of drama—role, action, mask—in a different direction. For it wasn't only the statesman or revolutionary who aspired to play a part, in his conception; it was, of necessity, every modern person. To be modern is to be cut off from the past, from the traditions that told you who you are and where you belong. "Since he is not bound to anything given," Rosenberg writes, modern man "is capable of playing countless roles"—the many roles that society offers him—"but only as an actor," aware of his disguise. Not content to be an actor, though, "he takes up the slack between himself and social reality," between ego and role—who he feels himself to be and who he appears as to others—"by creating illusory selves," fantasy projections of (as we would say today) a "real me." And yet, like Louis Bonaparte, he copies those selves from available models: "Socrates, for example, or Christ, or some revolutionist clothed in the glamour of the times" (one thinks of Che Guevara, Johnny Rotten, Patti Smith, each with their legions of imitators). "Members of every class surrender themselves to artificially constructed mass egos."

But modernism demonstrated an alternative. Social roles, prefabricated selves, conformity, illusion: all these could be resisted. The problem of the modern self—the problem of identity—remained. The solution was to treat it as a problem. Rosenberg's artistic heroes made the search for self—the effort to create a self—the content of their practice and the subject of their art. But before they were painters, those heroes were poets (poetry, remember, was his youthful aspiration): Rimbaud, Mallarmé, and Valéry, the leading French Symbolists, together with their predecessors Poe and Baudelaire. "I is another," said Rimbaud, and, as Rosenberg explains the process in an early essay, those figures sought, through programs of spiritual experimentation enacted in verse, to conjure up that other.

"Whoever undertakes to create," Rosenberg would later write, "soon finds himself engaged in creating himself," and he found his greatest self-creators in the artists he would dub the action painters: Pollock, de Kooning, Adolph Gottlieb, Philip Guston, with Hans Hofmann and Arshile Gorky as important anticipations. Rosenberg did not evince much interest in what he referred to as "formal modernism, or modernist formalism," the run of work from the Impressionists through the early twentieth century (Manet, Cézanne, Picasso, Matisse). Formal exploration never engaged him as such. Rosenberg tunes in when art confronts the modern crisis, when art itself becomes a crisis. That is to say, with World War I, with Dada and Surrealism. By 1914, he writes, the formal tradition was moribund. The art that followed, "*modern modern art*," "arises from the conviction that the forms of Western culture . . . have permanently collapsed." Dada declared, he writes, "that anything can be art"; Surrealism, that "poetry is the substance of painting." Both were forms of anti-art, and both turned art in the direction of philosophy, psychology, politics, and metaphysics.

These developments were slow to register on this side of the Atlantic. The 1930s were, in any case, a time when art was flattened underneath the dictates of leftist political orthodoxy. But in the 1940s, painting started over, as it were, in the United States. In "Parable of American Painting," the piece with which he chose to start his first collection, Rosenberg, thinking of the War of Independence—when files of British infantry were picked off from behind the trees by scruffy colonials—distinguishes between "Redcoats" and "Coonskins." The Redcoats fall because they think they're still in England, fighting on the rolling greenswards, instead of looking at the landscape that is actually in front of them. They are victims of style: they see what they've been taught to see. The Coonskin starts with where he is and tries to act accordingly. "Coonskinism is the search for the principle that applies, even if it applies only once." Whitman was a Coonskin. "What have I?" he said. "I have all to *make*."

Until the 1940s, Rosenberg explains, the great majority of American painters were Redcoats, projecting European styles onto American landscapes and streets. But the action painters had absorbed the "*modern* modern" point: there were no styles anymore—none with any force or claim. They needed to begin from the beginning. At the same time, though, they "shared . . . the intuition that there is nothing worth painting. No object, but also no idea." All that was left was the self, which they couldn't so much paint as paint into existence. Action, says Rosenberg, of any kind, "embodies decisions in which one comes to recognize oneself." The action painter starts with no design or expectation, no subject or thought. He makes a mark—a stroke, a drip—and the action begins. Each mark begets the next within a kind of dance. The artist thinks in paint, with his eyes and his hand. The canvas talks back, "to provoke him into a dramatic dialogue. Each stroke ha[s] to be a decision and [i]s answered by a new question."

Rosenberg was fond of pointing out that many of the action painters were immigrants, people for whom the question of identity was especially urgent. (Pollock was an immigrant from Wyoming.) Nor was it an accident, he thought, that the movement arose in America, that land of immigrants, transients, and strangers, and in "a century of displaced persons, of people moving from one class into another, from one national context into another." Still, while the action painter lands upon the shore of each new canvas free of preconceptions or intentions, like the immigrant he does not land there free of the past. That past consists of everything he's seen, especially art. The *modern* modern artist "picks his way among the bits and pieces of the cultural heritage and puts together whatever seems capable of carrying a meaning." The action painter, in particular, "starts an action and observes what kind of image it will magnetize out of the formal accretions piled up in his mind." Tradition, like paint, becomes something to think with.

A painting so produced, says Rosenberg, is not an object but an event. It is a "fragment," a "sketch," not a whole so much as "a succession of wholes" (de Kooning's famous *Woman I*, he tells us, was "repainted daily for almost two years"), one whose end, the point at which the artist steps away for good, is as arbitrary as its beginning. "And after an interval," in "a civilization in which the cultures of all times and places are being blended and destroyed," these wholes, as well, perforce disintegrate. In modernity, says Rosenberg, there are no masterpieces, objects that endure—not for any dearth of creative energy, but because the conditions, the stable traditions, no longer exist. Indeed, as they circulate through reproductions in books and magazines, in the discourse of critics, journalists, and art historians, as they're taken up and set aside by curators, spectators, and artists themselves, as they lose or pick up speed and spin in their "passage through the social orbit," the masterpieces of the past are also now events. "The *Mona Lisa* arrives from Paris and is greeted at the dock like a movie star." "All that is solid melts into air," wrote Marx. "All that is holy is profaned."

"To be a new man," says Rosenberg, "is not a condition but an effort." ("One does not *possess* mental freedom and detachment, one participates in them.") Coonskins can turn into Redcoats, if they let themselves become a style—in fact, it happens more often than not. Just the initial breakthrough into newness can require an endeavor of years. "The American . . . who searched for genuine art has been fated to spend half his life in blind alleys," Rosenberg writes. "Often it required a second 'birth' to get him out of them. One thinks of the radical break in the careers of Rothko, Guston, Gottlieb, Kline"—or of that archetypal Coonskin, Whitman. The artists whom Rosenberg most esteemed were two for whom no question was ever settled, no label was ever sufficient, one-man avant-gardes who sustained their radicalism across a span of decades: his old friend de Kooning, "the foremost painter of the postwar world," and Saul Steinberg, a figure about whom the art world could never decide if he even counted as an artist.

They and other artists are the model individuals, in Rosenberg's conception; they show us what it means and what it takes to be one. And the individual, even more than art, was for Rosenberg the highest value. Not individualism, in the sense of libertarian conservatism, or of thinking that people aren't conditioned by their social context—he took leave of Marxism, but he didn't take leave of his senses—but the individual: the person who thinks for themselves, who acts on their own responsibility, who stubbornly insists upon their separateness and independence.

That figure, he believed, was everywhere under assault. First, in his early years, by Marxism, or by what it had turned into, Leninism. In Leninism, the Party supplants the proletariat as the hero of history. And the Party, with the omniscience granted it by the infallible methods of dialectical materialism and the sacred texts of Marx and Lenin, is in absolute possession of the truth. The Communist, says Rosenberg, is thus "an intellectual who need not think." The rest of society, as in other orthodoxies, is divided into two groups: the sheep and the wolves, the simple folk who know not and the evil ones who know incorrectly. To the sheep, the uninitiated, the Communist adopts a benignly pedagogical stance, one composed in equal parts of tolerance and smugness. In Lenin's words, he *patiently explains*. But to the wolf, the independent intellectual, the individual who dares to challenge the Party's monopoly on understanding, the Communist is ruthless. Such a person must be canceled, and since at stake is nothing less than the salvation of humanity, any means to do so is acceptable.

After the war, the assault came from other directions. In one lay not Communists but ex-Communists, ex-radicals and fellow travelers. Here began that vogue for self-confession of which Whittaker Chambers was the great exemplar. In *An End to Innocence*, the critic Leslie Fiedler went so far, to Rosenberg's disgust, as to indict the *anti*-Communist intellectual, to indict all intellectuals, for the sin of merely being intellectuals, for thinking and sounding like intellectuals and thereby separating themselves from "the Community," that idol of the 1950s. Rosenberg viewed with dismay (and sardonic amusement) the new generational style—"The Solid Look," the Brooks Brothers suit, the ideology of "babies, God and job"—especially as it was taking hold among the younger intellectuals. For society had discovered that intellectuals were useful—in government, in universities, in public relations and advertising firms—provided they agreed to stop being intellectuals. Which most of them happily did. Having donned the mask of Organization Man, "the gentlemen of the Left" became "hysterically antipathetic to whatever possessed its own physiognomy. The outstanding figures in modern art and literature were abused as 'mere individualists' unable to 'solve the problem of our time,'" and in the Cold War context, "'the end of innocence' meant, basically, an abusive goodbye to Karl Marx by shivering jobholders."

What bothered Rosenberg as much as anything about this *trahison des clercs* was its insistence on using the first-person plural. Fiedler was pointing his finger not at himself but at "us." Already by the late 1940s, writers like Trilling and Edmund Wilson were stepping forward to interpret the "Communist experience" of the 1930s—to speak, that is, for Rosenberg's generation. Rosenberg, who never spoke for anybody but himself, refused to be enlisted. There are common situations, he explained, but there is no common experience. Every person's is their own. His, for example, contained "all sorts of anachronisms and cultural fragments: the Old Testament and the Gospels, Plato, eighteenth-century music, the notion of freedom as taught in the New York City school system, the fantastic emotional residues of the Jewish family." For individual experience, he said, "it is necessary to begin with the individual . . . one will not arrive at it by reflecting oneself in a 'we.'"

The argument occurs in "The Herd of Independent Minds," his essay from 1948. The point of the title is not that the liberal elite is afflicted by groupthink (which is not to say that it isn't) but that it thinks of itself as a group. Mass culture, Rosenberg says, is predicated on the idea that everyone is alike, and it makes us over in its image, so that we come to see ourselves as alike. But there is also such a thing, he says, as "anti-mass-culture mass culture," the mass culture of the elite: "'significant' novels," "'highbrow' radio programs," "magazines designed for college professors"—the culture of "seriousness" and "social relevance." Characteristic of all mass culture is "the conviction that the artist ought to communicate the common experience of his audience." But since there is no common experience, the result is "contrived and unseeing art," rendered through a set of formulas, "by which the member of the audience learns from the author what he already knows"—"that together with others he is an exradical, or a Jew, or feels frustrated, or lives in a postwar world, or prefers freedom to tyranny."

By the same token, mass culture, including the anti-mass-culture of the educated herd, "must deny the validity of a single human being's effort to arrive at a consciousness of himself and of his situation"—must be hostile, that is, to genuine art. For "the genuine work of art . . . takes away from its audience its sense of knowing where it stands in relation to what has happened to it"—takes away, that is, the accepted versions of history, the official accounts of identity. It "suggests to the audience that its situation might be quite different than it had suspected." It brings us into a truer relationship to reality, but it brings us there, perforce, as individuals. "Along this rocky road to the actual it is only possible to go Indian file, one at a time, so that 'art' means 'breaking up the crowd'—not 'reflecting' its experience."

But, above all, Rosenberg discerned the impulse to negate the individual in the art world itself. The heyday of Abstract Expressionism—the action painters, plus figures like Rothko, Ad Reinhardt, and Barnett Newman, the movement's mystical wing, who sought to purify their art into an ultimate transcendent sign—did not outlast the 1950s. AbEx was deposed by Pop art—Warhol, Lichtenstein, Claes Oldenburg—succeeded, or joined, as the '60s wore on, by Op ("optical") art, kinetic art, and minimalism and other varieties of formalism. All involved for Rosenberg a retreat from the things he most valued in art. With Pop, he believed, art surrendered to the media; with Op art and kinetic art, to science. Formalism, which settled in as art-world orthodoxy, represented a rejection of content as such: of art's involvement with social, psychological, or spiritual questions, with anything outside itself. Gone in all these trends were the hand and the medium as instruments of discovery, the engagement of the self in the process of creation, the oppositionality and will to social transformation of the avant-garde.

Rosenberg viewed these developments—and this was characteristic of his thought across all its dimensions, part of what made him an intellectual who wrote about art rather than merely an art critic—in their historical and social context. After the war, the media itself had elevated both the profile and prestige of modern art. The result was the creation of what Rosenberg referred to as the "Vanguard Audience"—a mass audience for new art (an anti-mass mass, of course) that, priding itself on its sophistication, "could accept the new in its entirety, with all its conflicting assumptions or without any assumptions." The Vanguard Audience could not be shocked; it enjoyed affront and understood incomprehension. It did not embrace Cubism, or Surrealism, or Abstract Expressionism: it embraced them all indiscriminately. The new itself, in other words, became the highest value, became the only value. The new became a tradition: the tradition of the new, in Rosenberg's famous phrase, one that was "capable of evoking the automatic responses typical of a handed-down body of beliefs."

The artists who arrived in the '50s and '60s were happy to play to that audience. "Putting on a show developed a stronger appeal than the act of painting carried to a hesitant pause in the privacy of the studio." As for the audience itself, "after the strain of trying to respond to the riddles of Abstract Expressionism," "it preferred images taken in at a glance and 'glamorous' colors translatable into dress patterns." Warhol grasped that art, for them, was something not to scrutinize but be "aware of." Like Robert Rauschenberg and Jasper Johns (artists for whom Rosenberg had little use), he understood that people liked to see things they already knew: Brillo boxes, American flags, the collages of everyday objects that Rauschenberg rebranded as "combines."

Tending to the Vanguard Audience, as both a cause and beneficiary of art's new visibility, was a vastly expanded institutional apparatus: galleries by the hundreds, collectors large and small, arts councils, traveling exhibitions, university departments and museums, "editors, curators, art historians, archivists, biographers, publishers, columnists, TV and radio programmers, photographers, catalogue writers." The market, newly flush, turned art into a commodity, but the academics and museums turned it into something more insidious: a form of knowledge. A crowd of words surrounded the work: wall texts, exhibition catalogs, monographs, interviews. Never mind trying to feel your way, in silence and stillness, into a spontaneous aesthetic response. Artist, date, "period," style, expert interpretation: now you *knew*. Art was recruited for programs of public education, as the curator displaced the artist at the center of the enterprise. Shows turned into theses that you walk through, with paintings "function[ing] as illustrations to bring out the critical or cultural concept" (e.g., "The Nude through the Ages"). Exhibitions "more and more take on the character of art books, presenting wall-scale duplicates of the publications that will result from them." Art turned into "culture"—a form of living death.

As art became institutionalized, the artist became a creature of institutions: that is, a professional—respectable, well-groomed, a solid citizen. The Abstract Expressionists, the painters of Tenth Street—cranky, alienated, socially marginal, down at the heels—were the last in the line of artistic bohemians that stretched back to the Impressionists. Training in a studio gave way to training at a university, the half-a-lifetime's search in blind alleys to the smoothly ascendant career. The artist "abandon[ed] his shamanistic role, and the rites required to realize it"—Cézanne's anxiety, Surrealist self-estrangement, de Kooning's "failure"—all of which posed "an impediment to the good life of professionals," and to the characteristic goal of professionals, success. As art was drawn into the orbit of the university, its values drifted toward the academic, toward art conceived of as a set of problems and solutions, things you could rationalize, train, and explain—line, plane, form, color. Hence the reign of formalism and the emergence of the artist "who conceives picture making in terms of technical recipes, but who is entirely ignorant of the role of art in the struggles of the modern spirit." The avant-garde lived on, but only as a simulacrum of itself, a "socially reconciled avant-garde," sponsored by the NEA and sustained by "the myth of rebellion." Revolution, like the new, had become a tradition, and overturned nothing.

To the effacement of the individual in all its forms, Rosenberg offered no solutions, certainly no systemic ones. His only solution was to *be* an individual—or rather ("one does not *possess* . . ."), to try. That, at least, he thought, was always in our power. "For the individual," he said, "the last voice in the issue of being or not being himself is still his own." And to help us, there is art. One of the reasons that Rosenberg deplored the conversion of art into knowledge, of paintings into pictures in books, images on television, and slides in the classroom, is that "the direct experience of art"—up close, in person, just you and the work—"contributes a lively sensation of ignorance." Before a genuine work of art, one is left with questions, not answers. Which is to say, one starts to think.

There is art and, for us, there is the work of Harold Rosenberg. It should be obvious by now that my attraction to this man derives not only from his iridescent mind, his swooping prose, but from the relevance of his ideas to the present moment. I won't insult the reader's intelligence by drawing out the application of his picture of the "clown-hero" who "retaliates to the ridicule of the world," the "leader without a program" whose self-contrived myth "evoke[s] even more fanaticism than formerly as a psychological protection against disbelief." I will only note that we live in an age when the self-contrived myth has become a universal—as it were, a democratic—possession. Rosenberg wrote of the construction of illusory selves, devices to bridge the abyss between ego and role. Now, thanks to the wonders of social media and the miracles of the Instagram filter (not to mention of the plastic surgeon's office) that construction is literal. Yet it remains, overwhelmingly, an act not of creation but of imitation: of celebrities, "influencers," fictional heroes and superheroes, themselves copied one from another. We are everywhere invited to bullshit ourselves, and we everywhere comply. The clown-hero, in full theatrical makeup, calls his army of fanatics to the Capitol, and they arrive arrayed for cosplay. In seeking to understand our current existential malaise, our great contemporary deficit of being, we could do worse than start there.

Remember also that the artificially constructed egos that Rosenberg spoke of were mass ones, the self submerged within the herd. And the crisis of the individual, as he described it, has only deepened in the decades since his diagnosis. We need only think about the transformation, since the postwar years, of the meaning of the word "identity." Having once referred to a unique and hard-won self-conception wrested from experience—that which made you you and no one else—it now denotes the opposite. Your identity today is that which assigns you, at birth, to your group. Rosenberg said that there are common situations but only individual experiences. The identity-mongers also invoke experience (or "lived experience," as if there were another kind), but only to align it with collective scripts. Today we say "me too." To say "not me" is to invite anathematization.

The Party may be dead, but its functions live anew. Again today we have the orthodoxy of the left as Rosenberg described it: sacred texts and prophets (Foucault, Kendi, Judith Butler), omniscience conferred by a set of infallible formulas ("cultural appropriation," "white fragility"), pedantic smugness, messianic intolerance, consensus enforced by the standing threat of professional or social death. We certainly have no shortage of intellectuals who need not think, pundits and critics whose minds appear incapable of containing a thought that wasn't put there by the zeitgeist. If our public discourse has become so numbingly predictable, especially on the left, that is largely because it is dominated by individuals who can tell you their opinion of a thing before they've even heard of it.

In art, we are back to the '30s. Art must toe the ideological line. As for the mass audience, the herd, its demands are now explicit and belligerent. The artist must speak for the group (the one to which she's willy-nilly been assigned), never for herself as an individual, "a single human being." Which is to say, she must allow the group—or rather its self-appointed ideological commissars—to speak through her. The word today is not "reflect" but "represent": affirm rather than disrupt, as Rosenberg put it, the audience's "sense of knowing where it stands in relation to what has happened to it." Woe be unto those who dare to shock instead of pander, or who refuse the injunction to "stay in your lane." Anti-mass-culture mass culture is also still with us, the culture of the educated elite, with its fake rebellions and its moral self-flattery: NPR, the *New York Times*, the *New Yorker*, et al., together with the cultural products—always scrupulously woke—to which they give assent. One thing, though, has changed since Rosenberg's day. Elite mass culture hardly even anymore pretends to be interested in art—in art, that is, as opposed to entertainment, high art as opposed to kitsch. Art is too hard, too subtle, too complex, too time-consuming, altogether too recalcitrant. The professional would rather watch Netflix; the "cultural critic" would rather pontificate about the TikTok trend. Rosenberg didn't think that kitsch was even worth bothering to attack. Now it rules the world.

As for me, even more than his ideas, it is Rosenberg's example that is bracing. He was a thinker who maintained the stance, with respect not only to society but also to his fellow intellectuals, of the artist—or of the rare artist, like de Kooning or Steinberg, who never ceases to be a true one. Even bohemias, he wrote, become conformities. "The artist thus finds it necessary to exist on the edge of the edge," and that's exactly what he did. He kept faith with his estrangement. He was the greatest of the New York intellectuals, and also the least characteristic. He ran with no packs and subscribed to no schools—nor did he attempt to found any. And he stayed in the stream. He knew that culture—art, thought—if it is to live, must always be enacted: daily, continually, like de Kooning repainting a canvas. He faced the modern crisis, the disorientation of perpetual change, without swerving right or left, toward nostalgia for what was or utopian expectations of what will be. His only direction was forward: through problems, through questions, through doubt.

Late in life, Rosenberg composed the introduction to a volume of de Kooning's work. Its peroration, with a few adjustments, applies as well to its author himself.

> De Kooning has never attempted to attribute political meaning to his work.... Yet under the conditions of the ideological pressure characteristic of the past forty years, unbending adherence to individual spontaneity and independence is itself a quasi-political position.... Improvised unities such as de Kooning's are the only alternative to modern philosophies of social salvation which, while they appeal for recruits in the name of a richer life for the individual, consistently shove him aside in practice. De Kooning's art testifies to a refusal to be either recruited or pushed aside.... He is the nuisance of the individual "I am" in an age of collective credos and styles.

[2021]

HAROLD BLOOM:
THE HORROR, THE HORROR

With *The Anatomy of Influence*, Harold Bloom has promised us his "swan song" as a critic.* Fat chance. After some thirty original books and literally hundreds of edited volumes, after more than fifty years of brilliance, boldness, bombast, bathos, and bullshit, after Shelley, Blake, Stevens, and Yeats; anxiety, misreading, repression, and revision; Orphism, Gnosticism, Lucretius, and the Kabbalah; Shakespeare, genius, the canon, and *The Book of J*, after evidence of a logorrhea so Niagaran even death will be hard put to shut it off, there's little possibility that Bloom has given us his "final reflection on the influence process"—which in Bloomspeak means his final reflection, full stop, since everything he writes is wrapped around that fixed idea. *The Anatomy of Influence* is not only not his last book; it's not even his last one this year. Already in September comes an appreciation of the King James Bible, billed, inevitably, as the book that Bloom has been writing "all my long life" (or at least since his agent noticed that 2011 marks the translation's four-hundredth anniversary). "The culmination of a life's work": Is that the new one or the next one? Neither, it's the one he published thirteen years ago. The Harold Bloom Show, we can rest assured, is good for many seasons yet.

Before we get into this any further, I should mention that Bloom and I were once employed by the same academic department, though my years at Yale left me feeling little toward him one way or the other. I never even met the guy. Having fulfilled the dream of academics everywhere by renouncing as many obligations toward his home department as practically possible—meetings, committee assignments, duties in the graduate program, every responsibility except undergraduate teaching—Bloom has long since become,

* *The Anatomy of Influence: Literature as a Way of Life* (New Haven: Yale University Press, 2011).

as he likes to put it, "a department of one." I think I only ever saw him three times.

Which is not to say he wasn't sometimes on my mind. At a certain point during my sojourn at the institution, I started to develop what I thought of as the "*Heart of Darkness*" theory of the Yale English department. Conrad's novel is about colonialism and racism and the shadowed reaches of the human heart, but it is also a portrait of bureaucracy. My first clue to the analogy between my place of employment and the unnamed "Company" for which the novel's protagonist, Marlow, goes to work arrived when I realized that my department chairman was a perfect double for the manager of the Central Station, the creepy functionary who, we're told, has "no genius for organizing, for initiative, or for order even," who "could keep the routine going—that's all." Marlow himself, broken by his African ordeal, corresponded, I soon figured out, to any number of my senior colleagues, their spirits crushed by the tenure process. The "pilgrims," as Marlow calls them, that pack of hopeful fools who set off through the jungle in pursuit of a chimerical fortune, were the graduate students. But what finally clinched the theory for me was my recognition of the role played by Bloom. Bloom, I saw, was Mr. Kurtz.

I mean this in the best possible way. Remember that given the choice between Kurtz and the rest of the Company lot, Marlow plumps for Kurtz. Bloom, like Kurtz, freaked his colleagues out, all those people who were playing by the rules in hopes of clambering up the greasy pole. Bloom, like Kurtz, ignored the rules and had the moxie to impose his own. Bloom, like Kurtz, was a shadowy genius who, having ensconced himself in his private domain, was managing to produce, by methods however "unsound," more material—ivory in the case of Kurtz, books in Bloom's—than all his colleagues put together. (This was after the days of the Chelsea House series of critical collections, when Bloom and his "factory" of full-time assistants and freelance graduate students were cranking out as many as fifteen volumes a month.) Bloom, like Kurtz, was a legend, a rumor, a vaguely malevolent presence (or absence) to be spoken of in awed and envious tones. What was not to like?

In recent years, however, the parallel has taken a less flattering turn. Opinion has long been divided on Bloom. Some regard him as a blowhard, the promulgator, in indigestible prose, of theories both empty and obscure—a pontificator, a narcissist, a mountebank. Others—by far the majority in the popular press—have anointed him the critic of the age. One assessment ranks him with F. R. Leavis and Edmund Wilson as among the greatest English-language critics of the twentieth century. Another pairs *The Anxiety of Influence*, his major theoretical statement, with Northrop Frye's *Anatomy of Criticism* as the most original volumes of literary study since the war.

Both positions strike me as excessive. All alone with Leavis and Wilson? What about, to grab only the first handful, William Empson, Lionel Trilling, Frye, Frank Kermode, and Edward Said? The originality of Bloom's theoretical position is harder to gainsay, but originality is often nothing more than eccentricity, and the influence of *Influence* is easier to doubt. When I think of the most *important* works of postwar criticism, I think of Frye's *Anatomy*, Kermode's *The Sense of an Ending*, Stanley Fish's *Surprised by Sin*, Paul de Man's *Blindness and Insight*, Said's *Orientalism*, Sandra Gilbert and Susan Gubar's *The Madwoman in the Attic*, Stephen Greenblatt's *Renaissance Self-Fashioning*, Fredric Jameson's *The Political Unconscious*, and Eve Sedgwick's *Between Men*, books that launched or largely defined, respectively, myth criticism, narratology, reader-response criticism, deconstruction, postcolonial criticism, feminist criticism, New Historicism, contemporary Marxist criticism, and queer studies. *The Anxiety of Influence*—idiosyncratic, impacted, hermetic—launched nothing, except more books by Bloom. "Harold," as a professor of mine once said, "is a world unto himself."

Still, he really is brilliant, and I say this in full cognizance of the fact that "brilliant" is the most overused word in the academy. (The most underused is "boring.") Meeting Bloom in 1965, Alfred Kazin, sixteen years his senior and long established as one of the nation's foremost critics, was hit by a wave of intellectual insecurity: "Bloom . . . formidable to me, leaves me feeling like I know nothing and have read nothing of the English Romantics. . . . Fascinatingly gifted and fascinatingly complex man." But Kurtz is brilliant, too. What befalls Conrad's creation is what's befallen Bloom in recent years. Megalomaniacal excess, unchecked by external restraint, has collapsed into a kind of emptiness. "You don't talk with that man," says his acolyte of Kurtz, "you listen to him." "No one edits," says Bloom of himself. "I edit. I refuse to be edited." "The shade of the original Kurtz frequented the bedside of the hollow sham": the "public Bloom" of the last two decades, the celebrity critic who pronounces on everything under the sun, is basically a Wizard of Oz routine. "Kurtz discoursed. A voice! a voice! It rang deep to the very last": Bloom continues publishing with superhuman frequency, but he stopped saying anything new a long time ago.

Born in 1930, Harold Bloom grew up, the son of a garment worker, in the Yiddish-speaking Bronx. Precocious beyond measure—he has admitted to reading four hundred pages an hour and mentions having memorized a thirty-seven-line poem at first hearing—in another time and place he would have been an *illui*, a rabbinic prodigy, committing the whole of the Talmud to memory and unleashing his interpretive appetites upon the Law. Instead, at age ten, "already deep in Blake and Shelley, Whitman and Shakespeare," he discovered Hart Crane at the Fordham University Library. His conversion was sealed. Now it's much of English poetry, and a good bit more besides, that he's managed to house in his brain.

By twenty-five, after stops at Cornell and Oxford, Bloom was on the tenure track at Yale. It could not have been easy to be a Jew at the place in the mid-1950s, especially not a Jew as unassimilable as Bloom, and by his own account, it was not. "When I was twenty-four or thereabouts" ("a marginal graduate student and faculty instructor"), "this cohort among my students"—the Skull and Bones crowd—"seemed the enemy, if only because they assumed *they* were the United States and Yale, while I was a visitor." English as a field was notoriously anti-Semitic, and English at Yale, needless to say, was no exception. I have seen a photograph of the department from back in those days, and it looks like a game of What Doesn't Belong: a lot of WASPy guys, one woman, and Harold Bloom. According to a rumor that was still blowing around the halls when I got to the place, the department didn't want to tenure him, but he published so fast that he left them no choice.

Bloom made his bones as a critic of Romanticism. A book on Shelley was followed by *The Visionary Company*, a poem-by-poem explication, over 450 pages long, of the entire Romantic canon, and the first public sign of his vast ambition as a critic. Volumes followed on Blake and Yeats, then the strongest of his early books, *The Ringers in the Tower*, which includes a pair of seminal essays on the Romantic tradition, "To Reason with a Later Reason" and "The Internalization of Quest Romance." Along with his eventual colleagues Paul de Man and Geoffrey Hartman, Bloom was at the forefront of a critical movement that challenged the idea, still the popular view of poets like Wordsworth, of a Romanticism at home in Nature. Instead, Bloom argued, Romanticism registers a fundamental alienation of the mind from Nature: a desire to free the self, by means of the imagination, from what Milton called "the world of death"—from natural determinism, natural limitations. By Romanticism, moreover, Bloom meant not only the canonical figures of the Romantic period, but the main line of poetic tradition from thenceforth all the way through modernism and up until the present day—an idea first advanced by Frank Kermode but amplified by Bloom to displace Eliot and Pound from the center of modern poetry in favor of Yeats and Stevens, with Whitman as the crucial relay point between the centuries.

Bloom has offered two not necessarily incompatible explanations for the turn his work took next. In the first, he began to develop the theory that he would first sketch out in *The Anxiety of Influence* during the seven years he worked on *Yeats*. In the other, more humid one, he awoke from a nightmare on his thirty-seventh birthday in a "state of metaphysical terror" and spent the next three days composing a "dithyramb"—not a word one encounters very often outside of *Thus Spoke Zarathustra*—on the subject of poetic influence. This was after fourteen years of semiconscious brooding on the question ("I was a very emotional young man"). Working out the consequences of his inspiration would absorb him for many years more.

In Bloom's conception, literary influence is not the benign and occasional thing it is normally taken to be. Instead, poets necessarily struggle, consciously or not, with their greatest precursors—struggle to assert their voice, their originality, in the face of prior achievement. Most poets—"weak" ones, in Bloom's parlance—are defeated by the struggle. The "strong" ones wrest a partial victory (partial, since the contest deforms both poetry and poet) by "misreading" or "revising" their predecessor. The anxiety, Bloom insists, is in the poem, not the poet; poems, as he puts it, are achieved anxieties. Bloom is the Freud of criticism, putting poems on the couch and making them confess, often under a good deal of interpretive duress, their guilty secrets.

Lying behind the theory—which Bloom elaborated with a great deal of mettle, a great deal of learning, a great deal of exotic jargon (*clinamen, kenosis, apophrades*, etc.), and a conspicuous dearth of clarity (strange shapes moving in the mist, is my impression of much of his theoretical writing)—was the old Romantic need to assert the self in the face of anything that threatens its metaphysical independence: to establish, in Emerson's phrase, an original relation to the universe. The great enemy, in other words—embodied, for the poet, by the canon—was History, time, the Nietzschean "it was."

Bloom's ideas, developed across a half dozen more books, came to center on notions derived from Gnosticism, the ancient body of mystical beliefs. Gnosticism held that the world of matter, created by inferior gods, represents a fall from a condition of divine unity or fullness. Each of us contains a fragment of that godly fire, a spark trapped within our material selves—which means not only our bodies, but our minds or psyches, as well, our intellectual and moral beings. Our true soul is hidden to us, occulted: salvation consists of achieving Gnosis, experiential knowledge of that "*daemon*" (something very far from self-knowledge as we ordinarily understand it). Bloom finds Gnostic notions, which persisted well beyond the ancient world, to be ubiquitous in modern spiritual thought—not only at the heart of the Romantic tradition, but also in what he calls "the American religion," which emerged in the nineteenth century in sects like Mormonism, Southern Baptism, Christian Science, and others, and which, he says, bears little resemblance to Christianity.

Romanticism sought to overcome the world of death, in the wake of the loss of religious explanations and comforts, by creating what Stevens called "supreme fictions": new systems of symbolic meaning to redeem the cold universe of matter. Bloom sees Gnostic ideas, like Emerson's Over-soul or Whitman's "real Me," at the center of those efforts, but more to the point, Gnosticism serves as a supreme fiction for *him*. Beneath the jargon and the self-inflation, there is in Bloom an undersong of yearning, of spiritual hunger, a lonely person's need for solace and belief. What eloquence his writing has—its subsidence, sometimes, into calm simplicity—what claims his work to be the thing to which he says all criticism should aspire, wisdom literature, originates there. The pathos of his thought, as he wrestles the poetic angels for their blessing, lies precisely in the fact that he both believes and disbelieves his fables of redemption. Not for him the ecstatic certainties of Blake and Whitman—imagination's infinitude, the soul's immortality. Rather, Stevens's melancholy skepticism. Supreme fictions, but only fictions—held together, for the space of the verse, by poetic lines of force.

But if Gnosticism, and the poets he reads by its light, furnish Bloom with imaginative consolation, they do so for a very unattractive reason. Gnosis leads to freedom from time and nature and death, but it also leads to freedom from the final thing that most conditions us: other people. Anything that lies outside the self, in Bloom's conception, threatens the self. His career represents a long effort to negate that threat. Bloom must surely be the most solipsistic critic on record. Harold is, indeed, a world unto himself.

And as he piles up book on book, the problem's only getting worse. The corpus of the public or post-theoretical Bloom, which began in 1990 with *The Book of J* and which runs, at this point, to eleven volumes, represents a sort of creeping self-contraction. As the rigor has drained from his work, the sense of intellectual adventure, all that's left is self-assertion. *The Western Canon* introduced the notion of Shakespeare as the center of literary history. The prime influencer uninfluenced, the one man free of History, Shakespeare seemed to have rotated for Bloom into the divine position previously occupied by Gnostic entities. *Shakespeare: The Invention of the Human* confirmed the suspicion. The Bard, says Bloom, created us. Not played a leading role in shaping our consciousness, which is plausible, but him alone, and us entirely.

Since then, turning always in the same eddies, Bloom has offered little that is new, and often little altogether. Despite its author's claim "to render my appreciations fresh and not reliant upon earlier formulations"—a sadistic joke, in retrospect—*The Anatomy of Influence* is nothing but a roundelay of the same old terms, concepts, authors, readings. It is not, as promised, "a critical self-portrait," does not explain what it means to say that literature is "a way of life" or "is itself the form of life, which has no other form." "Why has influence been my obsessive concern? How have my own reading experiences shaped my thinking? Why have some poets found me and not others? What is the end of a literary life?"—none of these questions are answered or even addressed.

Instead we get the usual rundown, the form his books have mostly taken since *The Western Canon*, thin, rambling, largely disjointed remarks on a series of authors and works. The chapter on *King Lear* has no apparent point. Of Shakespeare's sonnets, we learn essentially nothing but that many of them "touch very near the limits of art." Fifteen lines from Mark Strand—supple, shifting, suggestive—are glossed in their entirety with the influence spotter's rhetorical question, "Is that final tercet Strand or Stevens?"—a query that surely means little, in either sense, to anybody else, and a typical example of the diminishing returns of Bloom's theoretical method.

Bloom, it seems, talks only to himself, employing a language of private terms he rarely bothers to explain: "cognitive music," "negative theology," "apocalyptic," "daimonic," "canonical," "sublime," "antithetical," "revisionary." Judgments are made, then made again a few pages later; anecdotes are told, then told again in a subsequent chapter. The argument turns to *Hamlet*, and all the extras take their marks: "woe or wonder," "free artists of themselves," "the prince thought much too well," "*Hamlet* centers the literary cosmos." But "argument" is not the word. Bloom's prose goes by free association:

What we know foremost about Hamlet-the-mystery is that he does not love us, or, indeed, anyone in the play, except perhaps the deceased Yorick. Iago loved Othello until that mortal God passed over him. Hamlet has a deep affinity with the loveless Edmund the Bastard. Criticism cannot sound Edmund to his limit, nor can it sound his half-brother Edgar, who is consumed by his love, both for Gloucester and for Lear.

Hamlet-Iago-Edmund-Edgar: a kind of literary Tourette's. None of these statements—none of which he hasn't made a dozen times before—proceeds from the one before it. ("No one edits.") It's like listening to your dotty Aunt Matilda, except she doesn't charge you $32.50 a pop. Or more to the point, like *Krapp's Last Tape*, a monomaniac's soliloquy, with Beckett's implicit meaning of "last" as merely "latest."

Bloom talks *for* himself, it seems, as well. How to explain all this, if not as an act of private communion? Avedon knew his business when he posed the critic with his eyes closed. Bloom doesn't explicate; he davens. His habitual assertions—Dostoyevsky's nihilists descend from Iago, Milton never shows us Lucifer unfallen, etc., etc.—must carry a special charge of meaning and feeling for him, the reason he can never utter them enough. His verbal touch-stones make a sort of litany. "Sublime," "canonical," "daimonic"—these, for Bloom, are a Catholic's "incarnation," "resurrection," "Christ the Lord," holy terms that trigger reliable emotional responses. When Bloom blurts out a sentence such as this (of which there are many in his recent work), "If you lived most of your life in the twentieth century, then the writers of your time were Proust and Joyce, Kafka and Beckett, or if you loved great verse more than fictive prose, the poets of your era were Yeats and Valéry, Georg Trakl and Giuseppe Ungaretti, Osip Mandelstam and Eugenio Montale, Robert Frost and Wallace Stevens, Luis Cernuda and Hart Crane, Fernando Pessoa and Federico García Lorca, Octavio Paz and T. S. Eliot," I think of a worshiper telling his beads. Except that Bloom, as he says, is a "sect of one." The reader is relegated to the keyhole. We watch him give himself a pleasure that we cannot share.

Finally, and most damningly, Bloom talks only of himself. Harold fills up everything with Harold. He speaks of Shakespeare, Whitman, Crane, but it's always of Harold he speaks. They are *his* Shakespeare, *his* Whitman, *his* Crane; *his* feelings, *his* enemies, *his* judgments. (Kurtz: "My Intended, my station, my career, my ideas.") Like the god of the Hermetics, Bloom in his work is a sphere whose center is everywhere and whose circumference is nowhere. One Harold fills immensity. In *The Anatomy of Influence*, he tells us not only that "Bloom" "seems to me the most literary of names," but that he insists on referring to Joyce's Leopold Bloom, the most important literary character of the twentieth century, as "Poldy" (Molly's nickname for her husband), because, essentially, this town isn't big enough for the both of them. Bloom describes the literary world as a labyrinth of interconnected texts, but at the center of that labyrinth is a figure with the head of Harold Bloom. Reading him reminds me of the scene in *Being John Malkovich* where the titular character enters the portal that leads to his own brain to find himself in a world where everybody looks like him and all they say is "Malkovich, Malkovich, Malkovich." In the world of Bloom, every author looks like Bloom, and all they say is "Bloom, Bloom, Bloom."

Bloom is fond of quoting a dictum from his mentor Kenneth Burke to the effect that one needs to ask what a writer, in composing a given work, intended to *do* for himself. Bloom's celebrated readerly omnivorousness can be understood as nothing less than a desire to defend himself from literary history by ingesting it. Everything that lies outside the self is a threat to the self. If all of History is Bloom—resembles Bloom, is ordered by Bloom, is contained in Bloom—then he is the original and only. Poetry and criticism, he has long asserted, both necessitate misreading or misprision. Both begin in a love for the work of the past—a "flooding of the soul"—that develops into a reactive need to protect oneself against it. This may be a good way of writing poetry, but it is no way at all to write criticism.

Marlow chose Kurtz above the Company men, and I much prefer Bloom—the old Bloom, not the hollow sham he's now become—to the general run of academic criticism, the kind of thing he used to call the School of Resentment and now refers to as the New Cynicism. His criticism is personal, passionate, spiritually urgent, knows that "literature is necessary if we are to learn to see, hear, feel, and think." It does not despise literature or seek to lecture at it from the glorious heights of political correctness. I listed some of the most influential works of postwar criticism before, but I didn't say I thought they were all necessarily worth a damn, still less the epigones they spawned. Yet Marlow only had a "choice of nightmares," Kurtz or the Company. We do not. Though he wouldn't have us think so—a mass of footling academics on the one hand, our great literary panjandrum on the other—Harold Bloom and the New Cynicism do not exhaust the universe of critical possibility.

I think instead of Frank Kermode. Kermode, who died last year, was every bit as learned as Bloom, every bit as wide-ranging, every bit as prolific, and certainly every bit as brilliant, and already by the 1980s, before Bloom's media blitz, he was regarded as the greatest living critic in the language. His temperament was circumspect, judicious, moderate, even modest, always open to new perspectives and new ways of thinking. He never placed himself above the books (or the reader), and he addressed both general and scholarly audiences with equal grace. His prose was lapidary, lucid—jeweler's work. He published to the last—a book on Forster in his ninety-first year— and since he didn't think he knew it all, he never lost his curiosity. *That* is my idea of a critic, and if the popular imagination has a different one, we know whom to thank. Bloom is fond of inveighing against the vulgarity of American culture, but by conjuring for himself the image of a literary holy man, issuing from the temple of his self-communion to announce his ex-cathedra judgments, he has done his part to vulgarize it.

[2011]

CLIVE JAMES:
LETTER TO THE TWENTY-FIRST CENTURY

Back when I was younger and more pretentious, I used to dream of founding something called the Boethian League. Boethius was the sixth-century philosopher who was put to death by the Ostrogothic king Theodoric the Great after spending his life in an effort to preserve classical learning following the collapse of Rome. I pictured him as the Last Man of antiquity, gazing out, as if on the edge of a dark sea, over the abyss of barbarism that followed in his wake. We Boethians would be the self-designated Last People of Western culture, leagued together to leave a record of that culture for the remote posterity that might someday rediscover it, as the Renaissance had rediscovered classical civilization eight centuries after Boethius. Our collective output would be called *Letters to the Fourth Millennium*.

What I didn't know at the time was that a one-man Boethian League was already in operation, and that his name was Clive James. *Cultural Amnesia*, forty years in the making and the summa of James's career as a cultural critic, may not be a letter to the fourth millennium, but it is explicitly one to the twenty-first century, from and about the twentieth and prompted by the suspicion that a new age of barbarism is indeed descending.* At the same time, this vast work, over eight hundred pages long, is also a kind of epic of the mind that produced it, an implicit record of its author's remarkable life and an argument for the intertwined values of humanism, liberal democracy, literary clarity, and moral courage.

Ever since Homer sang of the thousand ships that sailed for Troy, the catalogue has been a convention of Western epic, and James concludes his introduction with a catalogue of the cities in whose cafés he has sat, over the course of his long career as a journalist and television presenter—not to mention novelist, poet, lyricist, essayist, memoirist, travel writer, and literary and television

---

* *Cultural Amnesia: Necessary Memories from History and the Arts* (New York: Norton, 2007).

critic—working his way through tall stacks of books. The list begins with Sydney, his birthplace, wends its way across forty cities on six continents, and ends up back in Sydney, a symbolic circumnavigation of the geographic and literary worlds. The books were in German, French, Italian, Russian, Spanish, Latin, and English, languages he mostly taught himself, and *Cultural Amnesia* is a series of meditations on the writers and other figures, over a hundred of them, who have meant the most to him for reasons good or ill.

The book, then, is itself a kind of catalogue, alphabetically arranged—an abridged encyclopedia of twentieth-century art, thought, and politics: Marcel Proust and Jean Prévost, Aleksandr Zinoviev and Alexandra Kollontai, Thomas Mann and Josef Goebbels, G. K. Chesterton and Margaret Thatcher. The list is remarkable for its range: composers like Erik Satie and Duke Ellington; performers like W. C. Fields and Dick Cavett (James disdains the distinction between high and low art); heroic victims like Sophie Scholl and Heda Margolius Kovaly; discoveries like Paul Muratov, whom James refers to as "the most learned, original and stylistically gifted Russian art historian of his time" but whose work is now almost completely forgotten.

The Muratov essay typifies the book in a number of ways. There is the magisterial judgment I just quoted, which bespeaks not only breathtaking erudition but also supreme self-confidence. Elsewhere we are told that the Viennese wits Alfred Polgar and Egon Friedell wrote "the most successful full-length cabaret script of the years between the wars," that Enrique Santos Discépolo was the most gifted and prolific tango lyricist in Buenos Aires, and, with a rare qualification, that Abba Eban's *Personal Witness* is "perhaps the most remarkably sustained work of intricate diplomatic exposition ever published." Then there is James's bibliophilia (or bibliomania). He tells us he's assembled his collection of Muratov's work by ransacking bookstores worldwide, and throughout the book he lingers to describe the color or texture of particularly handsome editions. Rilke's are apparently especially beautiful, with the result that James's shelf of the poet's books ("let alone of books about him") now measures some five feet and counting. Where does he find the space?

Never mind the space—where does he find the time? Not by cutting corners. "At one stage I read all the way through [Saint-Beuve's] collected *Causeries de lundi* columns in a bunch of disintegrating paperbacks I bought from a *bouquiniste* on the Left Bank." ("It was one of the ways I learned French.") Either by reading fast or not sleeping. On the same weekend that he read Karl Tschuppik's book on the collapse of the Austro-Hungarian Empire in the library of a castle in Bohemia, "I worked through the two

imposing volumes of Metternich's *Denkwürdigkeiten*." James pays his audience the high compliment of assuming it shares his energy and appetite. His
imagined reader is a young intellectual making their start in culture the way
the author did himself a half a century ago, and he offers a steady stream of
advice on how to go about the business of self-education: must-reads and
how-tos, anecdotes and exemplars. Among his highest terms of praise is "he
figured it out for himself."

But James's vision of the life of the mind only starts with the individual.
He used to struggle, he explains, with the seeming paradox that culture
doesn't necessarily lead to humanism—witness Leni Riefenstahl or Bertolt
Brecht, both of whom made common cause with totalitarian regimes. Then
it dawned on him: "Humanism wasn't in the separate activities" that com-
prise culture, he realized, it was "the connection between them," "all the
aspects of life illuminating one another in a honeycomb of understanding."
Humanism, in other words, is the embrace of human creativity in all of its
variety. From this follows a complete aesthetics, politics, and sociology of
humanistic endeavor—though James would reject such lifeless terms for the
philosophy that he elaborates, unsystematically and in full-blooded contact
with the particulars of dozens of actual lives, across the length of the book.

The sociology comes first. Before he launches his symphony of voices with
Anna Akhmatova, James provides an "overture" on the café culture of prewar
Vienna. It is the place where his imagination seems most at home, precisely
because it was a time when the life of the mind was lived collectively and inter-
connectedly, by an astonishing array of wits and polymaths and artists and
journalists (like Friedell and Polgar and Peter Altenberg and Stefan Zweig, who
fittingly concludes the alphabetical procession). The cafés were their clubhouse,
their debating society, their stage, sometimes even their mailing address. They
were there, for the most part, because they were Jews, and were excluded, as
Jews, from university positions. The situation was humiliating, but the result,
says James, was that "whole generations of Jewish literati were denied the
opportunity of wasting their energies compiling abstruse doctoral theses."

As luck would have it, I started reading *Cultural Amnesia* on my way
to MLA, the annual convention of the Modern Language Association, the
professional organization of literary academics. Nothing in a long time has
focused my discontent with academic life more pointedly than James's asser-
tion that "Vienna was the best evidence that the most accommodating and
fruitful ground for the life of the mind can be something more broad than
a university campus." In James's cosmology, the university is the infernal

(and infertile) counterpart to the paradise of the café. If humanism means interconnection, the café gives that interconnection social form. But academia mandates specialization and militates against intellectual breadth (now more than ever, no matter how much lip service is paid to interdisciplinarity). The academic conference, where small groups of identically specialized professionals convene to debate narrow questions of interpretation and doctrine, is the café's demonic double.

But James's evocation of Viennese café society is elegiac, and not just because that society was destroyed by Hitler. James has also been a denizen of cafés, but he has haunted them alone. Friedell and Polgar and Altenberg were sitting on the table, not around it. Though James has led a richly social life, as he hints from time to time, still, he tells us, "most of [my] listening was done by reading." For a host of reasons—the expansion of universities, of suburbs, and of telecommunications, to name three—the kind of face-to-face intellectual-artistic life that Vienna exemplified, and that flourished in other twentieth-century cities, simply no longer exists. James's answer to this bereavement is the book itself. Here is the café that he's created in his mind, a convocation of voices that respond to one another across the barriers of language, outlook, expressive form, and, most of all, time.

If, for James, the café is humanism's ideal social context, its necessary political one is liberal democracy. The civilized life that humanism seeks to embrace in its totality is by its nature "provokingly multifarious" and "bewilderingly complex." Its preconditions are pluralism, tolerance, and freedom, the values that liberal democracy enshrines. All else, at least in the modern world, is totalitarianism, whether of the right or left. For James, totalitarianism's characteristic intellectual form is ideology: the belief that you possess an idea that explains everything (in academia, they call that "theory"). With such a key in hand, you can give yourself permission to stop learning, stop doubting yourself, stop listening to other people—all the activities that humanism most requires. If your ideology is messianic (and which of them is not?), you will even feel justified in shutting other people up—if necessary, by killing them.

Nazism and Communism were the twentieth century's two great totalitarian ideologies, and James devotes a large number of his entries to figures involved with one or the other—as perpetrators, apologists, resisters, or victims. If James's cultural imagination is rooted in Vienna, his political imagination is rooted in the decades when Hitler and Stalin forced European intellectuals to make the direst of moral choices. The cumulative message of these entries is that history has a way of finding you out. And so the reason to read history, James quotes Zweig as saying, is "to see how other men had acted" when tested by events, and to measure oneself against them. Faced with Hitler or Stalin, some, like the saintly Sophie Scholl, made themselves a martyr in the cause of righteousness; some, like Nadezhda Mandelstam, survived to bear witness; some, like Ernst Robert Curtius, the great romance philologist, withdrew from public life; and some, like Jean Cocteau, collaborated.

And then there was Jean-Paul Sartre. Sartre is the book's antihero, "looming in the corner like a genius with the evil eye." For James, Sartre's response to both Nazism and Stalinism was just about the worst an intellectual can do. After largely acquiescing in the occupation, he retroactively co-opted the Resistance by placing himself at the head of the "post-Liberation witch-hunt" that "called down vengeance on people whose behavior had not really been all that much more reprehensible than his own." After the war, he became the pope of the Stalinist left not only in France but around the world, an apologist for the Gulag even after his break with the Communist Party. Sartre was the paragon of the ideologically committed leftist intellectual, James's bête noire, and it is a major project of *Cultural Amnesia* to destroy the credibility, intellectual as well as moral, of him and everybody like him. James's own political heroes are liberal intellectuals like Sartre's great opponent Raymond Aron, thinkers who exposed Communism and defended the sanity, strength, and value of liberal society.

But Sartre's sins were stylistic as well as political, and they bring us to James's humanist aesthetics and its connection to his humanist politics. For James, Sartre's abstruse, impacted rhetorical style was designed to conceal more than just the vacuity of his thought: "If Sartre wanted to avoid examining his own behavior—and clearly he did—he would need to develop a manner of writing philosophy in which he could sound as if he was talking about everything while saying nothing." And it isn't just Sartre; it's also Heidegger, Derrida, Lacan, and the rest of the obscurantist International. Clarity is the enemy of self-deception, and of the mass deception known as ideology. Style is not an ornament of thought; it is its very substance. And thinking itself is an ethical act. Humanism, which seeks a complex integration of experience, demands the most difficult style: a simple one. "Great writing," James insists, "is not just writing," because it must respond to, and thus forces us into awareness of, the whole of reality. The crabbed, pedantic cant that's now required of academics responds to but a fraction of reality; the abstract bombast of ideologues responds to no reality at all.

Great writing takes largeness of soul. Good writing merely takes a reader who has the option of turning the page. The Viennese writers who were denied the chance to produce dissertations for an audience of one, James says, "were driven instead to journalism, plain speech, direct observation—and the necessity to entertain." They wrote essays, reviews, sketches, and squibs; they also wrote in longer and more conventionally prestigious forms, but always in styles that had been honed by the whetstone of conversation. *Cultural Amnesia* is an extended defense of literary journalism as occupying not only an honorable place within the hierarchy of cultural discourse, but the topmost one. For journalism demands both simplicity and compression, and compression makes language glow. James's stylistic models are writers like Peter Altenberg, who could "pour a whole view of life, a few cupfuls at a time, into the briefest of paragraphs." His highest hero, "the voice behind the voices," is Tacitus. It was Tacitus who wrote the sentence out of which, James tells us, the entire volume grew: "They make a desert and they call it peace." Having heard the line as a young man, James "saw straight away that a written sentence could sound like a spoken one, but have much more in it."

Indeed, *Cultural Amnesia* is a collection less of great figures than of great sentences. Each entry focuses on one or more quotations, providing commentary that, no matter what it deals with—pornography, movie dialogue, the politics of literary exile, the problem of high seriousness in modern art—is invariably absorbing. Reading the book feels like having a conversation with the most interesting person in the world: you're not saying much, but you really just want to keep listening anyway. James is such a good talker, though, because he is himself a virtuosic listener. When he says the book took forty years to write, he means it, for its quotations are the harvest of the notebooks that he's kept for all that time, and the notebooks are the harvest of his insatiable reading.

Ever since running into Tacitus, James has been a connoisseur of aphorisms and aphorists, of writing that is both conversational and compressed, and of the kinds of minds that produce it. He is also, no coincidence, a connoisseur of music. "Echoes of a predecessor's rhythm, pace, and melody are rarely accidental," he writes, a sentence that contains four terms that might refer to music, but that refers to writing. Rhythm is central to James's conception of style, and so are "echoes"—that is, memory. He is himself an incandescent and virtually habitual aphorist—I wanted to heed his advice and copy out his choicest sentences into a notebook of my own, but I would have had to transcribe the entire book—and his love of the beautiful phrase goes deeper than mere appreciation. "Few writers have ever had a more identifiable tone of voice than Egon Friedell," he writes, "but the tone was a synthesis of all the voices he had ever heard, and so is ours." In gathering the voices that inhabit his own, the echoes he hears in his head, James has indeed produced an epic on the growth of his mind, a song of himself.

Still, for all his talent for aphoristic utterance, and his sensitivity to other people's, James has some questionable ideas about style. For one thing, he thinks that the closer that good writers get to the truth, the more they tend to sound the same, as if wit obeyed a single set of principles that all its practitioners follow. For another, he believes in the existence of an ideal English prose style, and that that style was achieved by a couple of writers, and a couple of writers only, in the years between the world wars. The two positions are related. If you believe that there is a single template for good writing, you must also believe that some writers approach it more closely than others, and you may also believe that a few writers even achieve it. For James, the writer who achieves it, at least in English, is Evelyn Waugh. "Nobody ever wrote a more unaffectedly elegant English; he stands at the height of English prose; its hundreds of years of steady development culminate in him." Yet despite the absoluteness of the judgment, Waugh shares the summit, James seems to believe, with F. Scott Fitzgerald, practitioner of what he calls "the ideal natural, neutral style."

There are several problems here. Languages don't develop, much less steadily; they only change. Sir Thomas Browne wrote one kind of English prose in the seventeenth century, Samuel Johnson in the eighteenth, John Ruskin in the nineteenth, Joan Didion in the twentieth. Each may represent a kind of local summit, but none is higher than another, only more or less pleasing to particular ears, which are inevitably formed by the linguistic climate of their time. It is probably no accident that Waugh and Fitzgerald flourished in the years before James was born. A neutral style, moreover, isn't necessarily better than a highly accented one. I love Waugh's elegance, and I also love the virtuosic kvetching of *Portnoy's Complaint*, and I don't see why I should have to choose between the two. Art is not *American Idol*; there doesn't have to be a winner. In any case, there is actually no such thing as a neutral style, only styles that try to sound that way. In Waugh and Fitzgerald, we have two outsiders who were trying to assimilate within—to come across as "neutral" to—intensely guarded aristocracies that prized the appearance of naturalness and elegance. Finally, it isn't clear that James believes in neutral styles himself. As he says about Egon Friedell, and implies in all the volume's many stylistic appreciations, every good voice is an idiosyncratic one. There's no mistaking Wilde for Shaw, or Pascal for Rochefoucauld, or Martin Amis for Clive James.

There are also problems with James's political ideas. After a lifetime of fighting with doctrinaire leftists, he's become a little doctrinaire himself in his dismissal of progressive thinking. There's scarcely any sense in *Cultural Amnesia* that liberal democracies ever do anything wrong. He makes excuses for the Red Scare, soft-pedals colonialism, and fails to distinguish between political and economic freedom. He does remark that the two components of "liberal democracy" must remain in balance, but he ignores the fact that capitalism, and capitalist governments, have often been inimical to freedom and democracy alike, especially within the developing world. As for the latter, James remarks that "most of the poverty on earth is caused by the number of people being born who would ordinarily never have been conceived." Even if we amend "been conceived" to "survived," the statement is incredibly simplistic and ill-informed. However broad the reach of James's erudition, it apparently does not extend to economics.

But there is a larger issue, too. For all of his acuity about the moral quandaries that totalitarian regimes present to intellectuals and others, James seems not to entertain the possibility that liberal democracies can pose such dilemmas, as well, even if less tragically or urgently. To say that we're better than Stalinist Russia sets a pretty low bar. Granted that *Cultural Amnesia* is intended to convey the experience of earlier generations to the latest one, I see no purpose in reminding us that history has a tendency to find you out without pointing out, at least in passing, how it is doing so right now. Fascism may essentially be finished, as James insists, but history is not, and one would think that he, of everybody, knows that. Instead, astoundingly, he concludes the book by declaring precisely the opposite. "The young might do well to tie a handkerchief over the rear-view mirror and just get on with it. The world is turning into one big liberal democracy anyway." This is a statement in which Francis Fukuyama and Dr. Pangloss hold hands and jump off a cliff. It also sounds exactly like the kind of thing that people were saying just before the start of that era of peace and justice known as the twentieth century.

These last-minute reversals are rather stunning, but they do little to diminish this splendidly valuable book, and indeed may be inseparable from its many strengths. Does he contradict himself? Very well then, he contradicts himself. He is large, he contains multitudes.

[2007]

As for the founders, all have moved on from day-to-day operations (though most remain affiliated with the magazine). Three have won recognition as novelists: Benjamin Kunkel (*Indecision*), Keith Gessen (*All the Sad Young Literary Men*), and Chad Harbach (*The Art of Fielding*). Marco Roth has published a memoir, *The Scientists*. Allison Lorentzen is an editor at Viking.

Then there is Mark Greif. From the very first issue, almost the first word, Greif was unmistakably the journal's cleanup hitter, the biggest slugger in its lineup. Of eleven essays in the inaugural number, Greif accounted for five. One, "Against Exercise," is a modern classic. ("Were 'In the Penal Colony' to be written today," it begins, "Kafka could only be speaking of an exercise machine.") All were immensely assured, minutely observed, imperiously eloquent, pitilessly frank. Mainly, they were really fucking smart. The tone, the wit were something to behold.

> We leave the office, and put the conveyor belt under our feet, and run as if chased by devils.

> At last the doctor takes his seat, a mechanic who wears the white robe of an angel and is as arrogant as a boss.

> His reign speaks of a time of perfection [this was George W. Bush], when even an idiot might rule. His ascension to the throne is the gesture of a completed democracy.

It was one of the most impressive debuts for a young American thinker since Susan Sontag forty years before. Greif wrote like a master. He was all of twenty-nine.

Other pieces followed in the years to come: "Afternoon of the Sex Children," "Radiohead, Or the Philosophy of Pop," "Octomom, One Year Later"; pieces on Palin, punk, tattoos; a brace of essays on the contemporary fetishization of experience—or rather, of "experiences." I won't insult him by calling him a public intellectual. He is an intellectual, full stop. The problem with the term "public intellectual" is that it is, or ought to be, redundant. An intellectual is not an academic who can write plain or a journalist who can write smart, but something else altogether. The self-consciously anachronistic element implicit in the launch of *n+1*, the effort to revive a moribund tradition, is most conspicuous in Greif. He speaks of "the obligations of intellect," sounding like no one so much as Lionel Trilling, standard-bearer of the postwar cohort. There

MARK GREIF: FACING REALITY

The journal *n+1* began publication in 2004. Its intentions were immediately clear: to revive the little magazine as an intellectual presence in American culture. The midcentury stalwarts were long since moribund. *Commentary* was a right-wing rag. *Dissent* staggered on in obscurity. When *Partisan Review* had folded the year before, people were surprised to learn it still existed. More recent pretenders, like *Lingua Franca*, had come and gone. The *New York Review of Books*, true heir to the literary energies of postwar progressivism, having followed the intelligentsia into the academy, was still immensely worthy but increasingly sclerotic.

N+1 was a blast of new blood, smart and clever in every direction. Its editors were young and hungry. Its writing was cheeky and wise. Its thinking came at you from unexpected angles, agile and brilliant and deeply informed. If the magazine was also sometimes coyly self-regarding—a little insular, a little pompous, a little too pleased with itself—then these were forgivable vices of youth. It largely cashed the promise tendered by its title. The editors declined to gloss the journal's name, but the reference seemed to be to mathematical induction (think back to eleventh grade), where for any number n, n+1 represents the following term in the sequence of integers. The project was to go a step beyond—beyond, as the journal put it in the title of its editorial column, the intellectual situation. The ambition was to think the next thought: to think a novel thought.

Eleven years on, *n+1* has established itself as the bellwether of the new generation of literary intellectuals. Its enterprises now include a website, a line of books, a sister journal of the visual arts (*Paper Monument*), frequent panels and readings, and, as of last September, a tenth-anniversary anthology, *Happiness*. The journal was among the first to publish Elif Batuman, Wesley Yang, Nikil Saval, and Emily Witt, among others. It's safe to say that many bright young aspirants, in Brooklyn and beyond, now daydream of joining their ranks.

is much of Trilling in Greif (a talent for surprising conjunctions, an eye for the moral pretensions of the liberal class), much also of Sontag (a certain dry disdain, a taste for low forms). But what he shares with both, and with the line they represent, is precisely a sense of intellect—of thought, of mind—as a conscious actor in the world: something that places obligations on itself, that understands itself to have a public role and public mission.

The nature of that mission is defined in negative in Greif's brief essay on George W. Bush, his opening salvo in the first issue (and, at thirteen hundred words, a miniature masterpiece).

> He makes up orders that are assembled from the bric-a-brac of instruction, correction, remembered adage, childhood experience, assumed law, scripture, in a collection of string, paper trash, and bits of bright foil. . . . He is not facing reality and trying to think; he is squinting and trying to remember his lessons.

Facing reality and trying to think: the matter in a nutshell. But the most important word is not "reality" or "think"; it's "trying." Thinking is hard enough. *Trying* to think—overcoming the comfort of not thinking, which tempts us everywhere at every moment—is even more difficult. To be an intellectual is not an intellectual activity alone; it is a moral one, as well.

The essay on Octomom begins to give a sense of what this means, and also of the way Greif's pieces tend to work. We start with a cultural artifact: Nadya Suleman, the mother of octuplets as well as of six previous children, all conceived through in vitro fertilization, unemployed and on public assistance, obsessed with emulating (or becoming) Angelina Jolie, an object of horrified public fascination throughout the early months of 2009. But the artifact is glimpsed especially through its filters in the media. We watch Suleman, but more, we watch the way she's being watched—on Fox or NBC, by Ann Curry or Judge Judy—the meanings that accrete around her, the beliefs that these reflect.

Connections begin to be made. Octomom enjoyed her fifteen minutes in the midst of the financial crisis; it was she who was shamed and blamed for abusing public resources, not the bankers.

> [I]n the language we were all then coming to learn: Nadya had leveraged her disability payments into six babies, collateralized them (as a state liability likely to pay revenues for years to come), and then quite brilliantly leveraged those six babies into eight more.

The piece extends its reach, sweeping in an ever-greater range of relevancies. Through Jolie, "America's most famous baby-getter," through the politics of abortion, with its rhetoric, on the right, of "the saved (and salvational) baby," through a pair of reality shows, the upper-class *My Super Sweet 16* and the working-class *16 and Pregnant*, through "the overdiscussed *Juno*," with its twinning of teen mother and infertile professional woman, the essay arrives at its ultimate target: the emergence, in recent years, of "a class-stratified baby economy." Reproductive technology has come to mean that having children now, at least at the kind of advanced age that has become the norm among the educated upper middle class (the result of delays that are intended to secure one's membership in that class), is a "right," yes, but also capital-intensive. In other words, like sending your kids to a fancy college, it is a right as long as you can pay for it. In other words, it is a privilege. Suleman's sin was to obtain at public expense what the affluent of all political persuasions feel belongs to them alone.

Greif is showing us what economic status means, in its rawest and most basic form: the power to spend more money on your children, including on having them in the first place, than other people can on theirs. Liberals are only liberal until it counts, until it hits their kids. The piece—and this is typical of him—is stunningly self-implicating. It finally points its finger not at the bankers or the journalistic hacks, not at Suleman or Jolie, but at the writer himself and, by extension, at his readers.

Look across the multiplicity of Greif's concerns, and a pattern begins to emerge: a piece on exercise, a piece on sex, a piece on food, a piece on reproduction, the pieces on experience, which largely deal with the desire to seek out or, conversely, protect oneself from stimulation. Greif's work, at its most characteristic, is an attempt to convey what it means to have a body at the present moment in the development of technological capitalism.

What it means, to put it simply, is that you're never left alone. "A description of the condition of the late 1990s," he says at one point, "could go like this: At the turn of the millennium, each individual sat at a meeting point of shouted orders and appeals, the TV, the radio, the phone and cell, the billboard, the airport screen, the inbox, the paper junk mail." And that was fifteen years ago. But what those orders principally superintend is our physical self. From liberation, as he puts it, we have come to liberalization, the investment of the body by the market. Sex is the least of it. In our "medicalized culture," "a hedonistic order divided against its own soft luxuries," pleasure comes second or worse. Hence the gym, the organic grocery, the vitamin pill, the clinic. You're never left alone, and you never leave yourself alone. "We have no language but health," he says, but health "means having health produced for us, by prevention and treatment." It means producing it ourselves, by discipline and vigilance.

The pathos of his writing lies in this: that within his mighty prose, as if protected by its bold sophistications, lies the vulnerable, breathing human body, seeking shelter from the technics that beset it. Greif's approach is first of all phenomenological. He starts from where he is, one person alone in a room trying to make sense of what he sees around him and of what it makes him feel within him:

> "The Sexual Revolution Hits Junior High," says my newspaper, reporting as news what is not new. Twice a year *Newsweek* and *Time* vaunt the New Virginity. No one believes in the New Virginity. . . . My newspaper tells me that menstruation starts for girls today at 11, or as early as 9. No one knows why.

Greif's goal is to reclaim that very sense of privacy his essays give, the ability to be alone with oneself and one's thoughts, one's body and its needs. This is not a retreat from politics; for Greif, it is the beginning of their possibility. Citing Hannah Arendt on the Greeks, he puts it like this: "A hidden sphere, free from scrutiny, provides the foundation for a public person— someone sure enough in his privacy to take the drastic risks of public life, to think, to speak against others' wills, to choose." But he knows that we are very far from the conditions of the polis. In the essay on Radiohead, he stakes out a fallback position. Not participation but defiance. Not privacy but self-enclosure, if only as in a glass house. "You live continuously in the glare of inspection . . . [s]o you settle for the protection of this house, with watchers on the outside, as a place you can still live." Live, we might add, and also look out, look back. Face the watchers and attempt to think.

Radiohead? Yes, Radiohead. To intellectualize about pop music, as he does in the piece, is neither novel nor courageous. What is both is that he's willing to emotionalize about it: to confess the feelings that it makes him feel and stand by them. To keep faith with the teenage belief, even while he scrutinizes it, that pop can make a difference, if only to you. Greif is willing to be vulnerable: like David Foster Wallace, albeit in a very different key, to forgo the protections of irony and nihilism. He is willing to be earnest, because—it's perhaps his most privileged word—he insists on being "serious." He insists, that is, that art and thought should bear on life. That art is not for art's sake, nor thinking a perpetual deferral of commitment. That they should change the way you act, the way you are.

"We know the real target of philosophy is life," he writes. "Everyone feels it who has not been irreparably debauched by learning." The statement appears in his essay on Stanley Cavell, the Harvard philosopher, who was, the piece explains, his great pedagogical encounter. Following Cavell following Thoreau, Greif expounds the concept of "perfectionism," by which he means something very different than a neurotic relationship to external expectations. Perfectionism, for Cavell, means "[t]he call to a next self," a "different, new, and better" self. The doctrine, Greif acknowledges with some chagrin, "resemble[s] the enterprise called self-improvement." But, he adds, "[w]hat matters in a book is that it is the book you need, not where in the library it may be found." The only difference between perfectionism and self-improvement, though it's not a little one, is that the latter aims at "fixity," the attainment of a completed or successful self, whereas perfectionism understands that the next self is never the final one. Around every circle another can be drawn. For every n there is an n+1.

The process sounds a lot like growing up. Greif's work is as an attempt to reassert the values of adulthood—dignity, restraint, civilization—in an age of perpetual immaturity. He believes in authority, if only the critical authority that is earned through learning and insight. He recognizes, as Sontag did despite her reputation, the distinction between high and low. He asks that we challenge ourselves: not physically, as the culture expects us to do (in the gym, the yoga studio, the road race), but morally and intellectually. He wants us to put away childish things.

He wants, that is to say, a different, new, and better world. "Let the future, at least, know that we were fools," he writes. "Make our era distinct and closed so that the future can see something to move beyond." Yet he confesses not to know entirely what such a future might resemble. What would remain, he ends his essays on "experience" by asking (and this was in 2007, still the early days of social media), if we stopped aestheticizing our existence, stopped turning it into a series of frameable moments? "Circling life from the cluttered outside, one asks its meaning again and again," he remarks, but "[m]eaning starts to seem a perverse thing to ask for, when what we are really asking is what life is when it is not already made over in forms of quest or deferral. Could *this* life be reached—unmediated? Would there be anything there when we found it?"

Getting to the next thought is one thing; getting to the next world, even in thought, is something incomparably harder. But that the two are intimately linked—that ideas can be time machines—is the intellectual's essential premise. If there is at times an antiquated cast to Greif's prose, the notion seems to be to make a style that carries in itself a knowledge of the necessary past. In his essay on Cavell, he has this to say about the undergraduate experience: "The challenge is to be curricular"—as opposed, that is, to extracurricular— "to run through the course set by civilization up to one's own time, and then exceed it." To learn the past so as to make the future.

Such is the point of *The Age of the Crisis of Man*, though it takes us the entire volume to discover it.* The book's ostensible ambition is to excavate a buried chapter in the recent history of American thought, though before too long it seems that what we are rereading isn't so much *a* chapter as the central one. Starting in the 1930s and moving through and past the war and into the 1960s, Greif describes the emergence, growth, transformation, and decline of what he calls the discourse of man, or of the crisis of man.

For about a quarter century, beginning roughly with the rise of Hitler, "man" and the threats to "man"—from fascism right and left, from technology and organizational bureaucracy—were everywhere in American thought, highbrow and middlebrow, philosophical, literary, and journalistic. In the factories and concentration camps, in the face of industrial violence and totalistic social control, was man now disappearing, effaced or reengineered beyond recognition? Without him, what would become of Enlightenment values—freedom, humanism, democracy—to which man, and the rights of man, had been foundational? What is man, to start with? Suddenly it seemed that everybody had to try to say. "Man became at midcentury the figure everyone insisted must be addressed, recognized, helped, rescued, made the center, the measure, the 'root.'"

Greif reminds us of the term's ubiquity: *The Condition of Man*, "The Root Is Man," *One-Dimensional Man*, *God in Search of Man*, *The Human Condition*—Lewis Mumford, Dwight Macdonald, Herbert Marcuse, A. J. Heschel, Hannah Arendt—and yes, *The Family of Man*, Edward Steichen and Carl Sandburg's traveling photographic extravaganza. Greif would also have

---

* *The Age of the Crisis of Man: Thought and Fiction in America, 1933–1973* (Princeton: Princeton University Press, 2015).

us add, in fiction, *Dangling Man*, *Invisible Man*, *A Good Man Is Hard to Find*, and even *The Old Man and the Sea*. He reminds us that man, specifically man in crisis, was central to the reception by American intellectuals of Sartre and Kafka, the major philosophical and literary influences of the postwar years.

But beneath these points of reference Greif uncovers—well, he uncovers, it seems, the bulk of midcentury thought, magnetized by his perception into new configurations and relationships. Mumford lines up with the Frankfurt School. Pearl Buck, the middlebrow novelist, keeps company with Karl Polanyi, the economic historian. Boasian cultural relativism talks back to UNESCO and its universalizing rhetoric. William Faulkner's "vaporous" Nobel Prize speech, with its "hortatory boilerplate," turns out to be a central document in the recruitment of the novel to the cause of man. Moving into the '60s, we see how the discourse of man, by now a tired cliché, was dismantled by the new critiques, so that Malcolm X makes humanism into "whiteism," Betty Freidan wonders whether "man" includes her, and radicals take aim at someone whom they now refer to as the Man.

Greif observes the postwar decades with a lofty, mapmaker's eye. Difference "was a matter for social identity in America," but "the concept controlled deeper and more multiple locations in French theory." "Committed as Sontag was from an early age to the glamour of thought, pieces of the crisis of man appear throughout her intellectual formation in broken, uprooted form." As the latter passage indicates, the pleasures here are sociological as well as intellectual. Nowhere in the book does Greif advert to his experience as student, writer, editor, and now professor (at the New School, no less, one of the postwar period's key institutional scenes), but they everywhere inform his account. Lévi-Strauss "return[ed] to France to resume a metropolitan career." Wittgenstein "forged a communicating link between Vienna and Cambridge." Camus "was not a systematic thinker, but then he was not a mandarin as Sartre was, and he came to be beloved by the New York Intellectuals in a way that more philosophically demanding rivals were not."

This is a writer who knows what it means to operate within the world of thought, who understands ambitions and connections, rivalry and mentorship, the role of magazines both little and big—how all this bears not only on careers but on ideas. With his patient sifting of the archives—the book was more than ten years in the making—he is able to create a densely woven genealogy. Add to this his talents as a reader. The volume's middle half takes up the literary side of the discourse of man, the ways that fiction writers tested that grand abstraction against the concrete particulars of social experience.

His sections on O'Connor and Pynchon are incisive; the ones on Bellow and Ellison—close associates he treats in interdigitated chapters—are nothing short of brilliant.

Still, I kept thinking, what exactly is the point? Who, beyond the specialist, should care? Was there a linkage here to Greif's investigations as an essayist, or were his intellectual and academic projects simply separate things? Was there a linkage here, in other words, to the present, and to the questions he puts to the present? The study's very name suggested otherwise, restricting its horizons to an age that ended more than forty years ago.

Only in the final chapter do we start to see the bigger game. As the inquiry moves forward to its final years, a large, familiar structure comes in view: the split, so central to the intellectual life of the last four decades, between Anglo-American analytic philosophy and continental theory. "The duality belonged to the university, but it also rules in political and moral life, in spheres of policy, activism, charity, and law. Universalism or difference, human rights or political liberation, law or critique, normativity or the struggle for power and representation." Greif's achievement is to trace the opposition—"two separate and purportedly incompatible philosophical projects of justice and liberation"—to a common root: the discourse of man, in the age of the crisis of man.

But he also does more. In a bravura conclusion, he demonstrates the continuities between that age and our own: between modernism and the period that in its very name proclaims that it has moved beyond it. Greif's history turns out to be a prehistory—our prehistory. The discourse of man may be dead, but its ghost, he shows, continues to possess us. All of its concerns, which seem so dated now, are ours as well—are ours as yet. Only our language is new, our panoply of proud and precious "posts," which seek to set us against, set us above, our intellectual parents. The age of man brooded about technology, about the shape of history, about the future of faith, and about the meaning of man as such: questions we have not transcended but only translated, respectively, as the postmodern, the posthistoric, the postsecular, and the posthuman—terms that speak as if we'd just discovered them, intrepid spirits that we are, on the far side of some continental divide of consciousness.

Contemporary thought, Greif says, "is a Frankenstein put together of spare parts cast off by modernity or the Enlightenment." It represents not novelty but "compulsive repetition and illusory escape in the disguise of critical thinking." We are still asking the same questions. We are still giving the same answers. We think we've gotten somewhere new, but so did those who came before, in the age of the crisis of man. The situation, Greif writes, "scripts our novelties for us." Postmodernism's not an n+1 to modernism's n. Its name, in fact, bespeaks perseveration, the same thing again and again, in whatever different forms: n, N, *n*, ñ, n!

The challenge, once again, is to be curricular: "to read through the last century"—in particular, to provide "an alternative construction of mid-twentieth-century thought"—in order to establish a "starting point for twenty-first-century thought." Modernity, Greif says, is "a bit like the weather—everyone complains, but no one will do anything about it." In other words, we're stuck, and everybody knows we're stuck: politically, ideologically, intellectually. The challenge is to do something about it: to face reality, and desperately, for all we're worth, to try to think.

I'm not completely satisfied with Greif's conclusion. For one thing, he moves pretty swiftly from the early 1970s to now. I'd have liked a fuller account, though granted that would probably have meant (and might mean still, one hopes) a second book. For another, his insistence that we've come around again to man—this time in the talk among environmentalists of "the Anthropocene," a new geological age defined by human activity and therefore calling for a grand new round of intellection on the history and meaning of the human, one that's sure to be "preprogrammed" by the last one—requires, at the least, a bit more flesh. Are we really headed quite so quickly off that mental cliff?

But I love his insistence, in this connection and throughout the book, on the conditions and motives of thought. What really interests him about the question of man at midcentury was not what people said—everybody seemed to recognize that nobody was going to produce a satisfying answer—but that they felt compelled to say it. What are we expected now to think about, and why? What "rule[s] and regulate[s] what is thinkable, what must be spoken of and genuflected to"? And how much are these expectations and the thoughts they generate, as he puts it in a fabulously useful term, "autotherapeutic": "work done by thinkers" not upon the world, but "upon themselves"—to help them feel superior to the past, or to make them feel as if they're doing something about the future? Before we can start to think better, we need to stop and think about the way we're thinking in the first place.

Greif, it must be said, has managed only to provide a starting point: not the first step, even, but the zeroth. Still, it is a step. One eagerly awaits his next.

[2015]

HUNTING THE WHALE

Martin Amis once remarked, apropos of the idea of writing a book about America, that you might as well try to write one about people, or life. He might have added, or the English novel. Yet here we have the fruits of such an enterprise in all their cyclopedic, cyclopean glory: Michael Schmidt's *The Novel: A Biography*—eleven hundred pages spanning nearly thirty dozen authors, starting with the pseudonymous Sir John Mandeville (he of the fourteenth-century *Travels*) and ending forty-five brisk, brilliant, intimate, assured, and almost unflaggingly interesting chapters later with Amis himself.*

Surely such an effort represents the labor of a lifetime, one would think. In fact, it is a kind of sequel to *Lives of the Poets*, a comparably commodious compendium. Schmidt, who was born in Mexico, went to school in part in the United States, and has made his career in Britain, is himself a poet and novelist as well as an editor, publisher, anthologist, translator, and teacher. Given the fluidity with which he ranges across the canon (as well as quite a bit beyond it), one is tempted to say that he carries English literature inside his head as if it were a single poem, except that there are sections in *The Novel* on the major continental influences, too—the French, the Russians, Kafka, Cervantes—so it isn't only English. If anyone's up for the job, it would seem to be him.

Still, eleven hundred pages (and rather big ones, at that). I wasn't sure I had the patience for it. Then I read this, in the second paragraph. Schmidt is telling us about the figures whom he has enlisted as our guides along the way, novelist-critics like Henry James, Virginia Woolf, V. S. Pritchett, Gore Vidal, and many others:

---

* *The Novel: A Biography* (Cambridge: Harvard University Press, 2014).

They are like members of an eccentric family in an ancestral mansion. . . . Some are full of respect, some reserved, others bend double with laughter; the rebellious and impatient slash the canvases, twist the cutlery, raise a toast, and throw the crystal in the grate. Their damage is another chapter in the story.

It wasn't the notion that Schmidt was going to orchestrate the volume as a dialogue with and among these practitioners, though that was promising. It wasn't the metaphor of the eccentric family per se, though that was interesting. It was the writing itself. The language was alive; the book would be alive, as well. Take a breath, clear the week, turn off the Wi-Fi, and throw yourself in.

Schmidt's account is chronological, but loosely so. Early chapters flash forward to the present or near present, so that Aphra Behn shares quarters with Zora Neale Hurston, Daniel Defoe with Capote and Coetzee. Schmidt is weaving threads, picking out lines of descent: the Gothic, the exotic, the vernacular, the journalistic; manners, genres, voices, verisimilitude. Through Mandeville and *Foxe's Book of Martyrs* and *The Pilgrim's Progress*, we see the novel (or rather its precursors) find a sense of form, coalesce from a sequence of incidents into a coherent structure. Through Defoe and Richardson and Fielding, the eighteenth-century emergence, we see it becoming the novel. The word "novelist" appears in 1728, in the wake of Defoe's great run from *Robinson Crusoe* to *Roxana*, as good a starting point as any for the genre's existence as a self-conscious entity.

"A Biography": Schmidt's subtitle is cunningly chosen. The novel begins as a big-headed infant, takes its first uncertain steps, then slowly gathers its capacities. Once they've been invented, they're available to all. "Earlier novelists address the reader directly," Schmidt remarks in reference to Laurence Sterne in *Tristram Shandy*, "but not personally." Later, in Austen, "something new and remarkable begins to happen": by perfecting the technique of free indirect discourse, in which the minds of narrator and character merge, she creates protagonists who feel so real "that they can step outside the frame of their particular novel and companion us." By the time of the Brontës in the middle of the nineteenth century (we're a fourth of the way through the book), "the form had become versatile and capacious: Scott filled it with history, the Gothic writers with dream." Chronology is change but also enrichment; fashions and phases will get our understanding only so far. Every novelist is free to reach back into history, pull out an earlier trick, and make it new.

In *Aspects of the Novel*, E. M. Forster famously requests us to imagine the English novelists not as floating down the stream of time, "but as seated together in a room, a circular room," all writing at once. In Schmidt, they get up and mingle. The book, at its heart, is a long conversation about craft. The terms of discourse aren't the classroom shibboleths of plot, character, and theme, but language, form, and address, the real studs and sheetrock. Here is where we feel the force of Schmidt's experience as an editor and publisher as well as a novelist. He knows how books get written, and not just in technical terms. He tells us that Fielding got £800 for *Amelia*, guides us through the office politics of literary London circa 1900, lets us in on who became a drunk, got divorced, had an outsider's chip on their shoulder. The book is a biography in that sense, too—the lives of the novelists.

Schmidt understands that novels are written for readers—not "ideal" readers, not readers in the abstract, but actual people out there in the market—and he explains how books and buyers shape each other. Arnold Bennett, who made himself rich in the years before World War I, played to the audience created by mass literacy. "He knew what the new reader wanted: authority, instruction, a way of feeling safe in the world of books, of not being wrong-footed by a natural liking or an exposed ignorance." The literary novel—the modernist novel in the wake of Flaubert—arose against the same phenomenon. Its way, Schmidt suggests, had been prepared by Poe, who not only invented a genre, the detective story, "he invented, by extension, the reader of that genre," who then "impacts upon the future writer with . . . techniques of suspicious reading, where every detail is interrogated and weighted."

Around the insights of his artist-docents, of Graham Greene and Anthony Burgess and Joyce Carol Oates, Schmidt weaves his own dense tapestry of aperçus. "[Jack] London and Hemingway share a direct style, but London pulls the whole melting mess of the iceberg up on shore for us to see." Poe's ability to frighten a reader, "especially late at night," has in part to do with "the spaces that vowels carve out of the darkness." Like Jonathan Franzen, Jeffrey Eugenides and other young writers "practice a detachable moralizing and deliver civic sides." There are pleasures such as this on almost every page. For Jewish writers after World War II, central Europe "provides a living, alternative, polyglot modernism to the cultural hunger Pound and Eliot fed with a deliberated amalgam constructed out of safely dead cultures." Salman Rushdie, unlike his Indian predecessors, "does not busk to British or American readers but addresses his subject directly, as if to create Indian and Pakistani readers."

Note the breadth of Schmidt's attention, the variety of angles from which he's able to approach a book. He has his favorites (Fielding, Conrad, Naipaul, Amis), as well as those he thinks are overrated (Thomas Pynchon, Ian McEwan, Paul Auster), but he takes each writer on their own terms, and in their own times. He doesn't expect Dos Passos, with his political engagement and documentary style, to look like Nabokov, the avatar of aestheticism. He doesn't ask the writers of the past (or present) to affirm his social views. Some get a couple of paragraphs, a few get ten pages or more, but each is seen as if intensely spotlit, their own story as well as part of a greater one.

There's a reason that we call them novels. The genre, Schmidt remarks, "takes in and takes on invention like no other literary form." Modernity's preeminent artistic innovation, the novel is perpetually striving to achieve the new. Its very looseness, its lack of rules and notorious difficulty of definition, is the secret of its strength. What is a novel? Almost anything that writers have attempted to persuade us that it might be. Fiction has always been conspicuously porous to other forms, especially those that we designate with a term that would seem to negate it, "nonfiction": travel, history, journalism, biography, true crime—in our own day, most obviously, memoir. "Reality hunger," to borrow the title of David Shields's recent anti-novel manifesto, is hardly something new. The novel has always been a glutton for the real.

For one thing, it simply has more room than other forms (though serial television has emerged as a rival). Unconstrained by conditions of performance, it makes the most rotund Wagnerian opera, let alone the longest movie, play, or symphony, look anorexic by comparison. Schmidt remarks that the novel arose from medieval genres, with little relation to the classical tradition, but as it grew it claimed the epic goal of plenitude, the ambition to incorporate the whole of life. So many landmark novels are not only huge; they seem to seek to swallow the entire the world: *Don Quixote, Moby-Dick, Middlemarch, Ulysses, War and Peace* (whose title might be glossed as *Iliad plus Odyssey*, an epic times two), Proust's *Recherche*, the titanic sociographic cycles of Balzac and Zola, the whole Joycean line of Gaddis, Pynchon, DeLillo, and David Foster Wallace, who wrote a book whose title dares the adjective "infinite."

The novel is novel, but it is also, typically, news—the tidings of the world around us. It is no coincidence that a number of the genre's greatest exponents, starting with Defoe himself, were journalists as well. The novel reaches in and out at once. Like no other art, not poetry or music on the one hand, photography or movies on the other, it joins the self to the world, puts the self *in* the world, does the deep dive of interiority and surveils the social scope. That polarity, that tension—call it Richardson versus Fielding, the novels of the soul and of the road—has proven endlessly generative. You can put your-self at any moment, as a writer, anywhere you want to on the spectrum, from the most introspective to the most documentary, invent whatever methods you can think of to bring both self and world into focus.

The self in society: the modern question. The novel is coeval with other phe-nomena that first appear in full-fledged form in the eighteenth century—like privacy and sympathy and sensibility and boredom, all of which are closely linked to its development. Novel reading is indeed unusually private, unusu-ally personal, unusually intimate. It doesn't happen out there, in front of our eyes; it happens in here, in our heads. The form's relationship to time is also unique. The novel isn't static, like painting and sculpture, but though it tells a story, it does not unfold within a specific interval, like music, dance, theater, or film. The reader, not the clock, controls the pace. The novel allows you the freedom to pause: to savor a phrase, contemplate a meaning, daydream over an image, absorb the impact of a revelation—make the experience uniquely your own.

More than with any other work of art, the relationships we have with nov-els are apt to approach the kind we have with people. For a long time, novels were often named after people (*Tom Jones, Emma, Jane Eyre*), but that is not the crux of it. What makes our experience of novels so personal is not that they have protagonists, but that they have narrators. Paintings and photo-graphs don't, and neither, with rare (and usually unfortunate) exception, do movies or plays. Novels bring another subjectivity before us; they give us the illusion of being addressed by a human being.

They are also exceptionally good at *representing* subjectivity, at mak-ing us feel what it's like to inhabit a character's consciousness. Film and television, for all their glories as narrative and visual media, have still not gotten very far in that respect, nor is it easy to see how they might. The camera proposes, by its nature, an objectivist aesthetics; its techniques are very crude for representing that which can't be seen, the inner life. ("I hate cameras," Schmidt quotes Steinbeck as having remarked. "They are so much more sure than I am about everything.") You sometimes hear that this or that new show is like a Dickens novel. There's a reason that you never hear one likened to a novel by Virginia Woolf or Henry James.

 ovels call us out. "In the intensity of our engagement," Schmidt remarks, "we ourselves are judged." The statement is made in connection with Richardson, but it applies to his progeny, too—the whole tradition, central to the English novel, of strenuous moral struggle. As the characters are tested, so are we. *What* you read becomes a mark of election, and even more, *how*. ("Books—oh! no," says Elizabeth Bennet to Mr. Darcy. "I am sure we never read the same, or not with the same feelings.") The novel was a smithy, perhaps *the* smithy, in which the modern consciousness was forged.

The modern consciousness, but not the postmodern one. The novel's days of cultural preeminence are long since gone. The form arose to primacy across the nineteenth century, achieved a zenith of prestige in modernism, then yielded pride of place to the new visual media. It is no accident, perhaps, that the modernist anni mirabiles after World War I (the years of *Ulysses*, Proust, *Mrs. Dalloway*, *The Magic Mountain*, *The Great Gatsby*, and more) happened just before the invention of the talkies—a last, astounding efflorescence.

This is not to say that great novels haven't continued and won't continue to be written. It is to start to understand why people have been mooting the "death of the novel" ever since that shift in cultural attention, as well as why the possibility is met, by some, as such a calamity. Privacy, solitude, the slow accumulation of the soul, the extended encounter with others—the modern self may be passing away, but for those who still have one, its loss is not a little thing. Schmidt reminds us what's at stake, for novels and their intercourse with selves. *The Novel* isn't just a marvelous account of what the form can do; it is also a record, in the figure who appears within its pages, of what it can do to *us*. The book is a biography in that sense, too. Its protagonist is Schmidt himself, a single reader singularly reading.

All of which brings us to another, only slightly less ambitious book, Lawrence Buell's *The Dream of the Great American Novel*.* Buell, professor emeritus at Harvard, is a distinguished figure in the field of American literature. His book, the harvest of a long career, is both less and more than its title suggests. Buell begins by tracing the history of his titular subject: the birth, after the Civil War, of the notion of what Henry James would soon refer to as the GAN, that one grand fiction that encapsulates the national experience; the concept's fall from critical favor in the middle decades of the twentieth cen-

---

* *The Dream of the Great American Novel* (Cambridge: Harvard University Press, 2014).

tury; and its persistence, to this day, as a popular and journalistic aspiration, talking point, and parlor game.

But Buell is less interested in the "dream," the concept as a cultural phenomenon, then in constructing a taxonomy of GAN contenders—and thus, in large measure, of American fiction as a whole. This is where the ambition comes in, as well as Buell's enormous erudition. He's read everything, it seems, that bears upon the question: all the novels, all the criticism, all the history, all the literary theory. Buell identifies three principal GAN "scripts": the "up-from" story of the self-made man (*An American Tragedy, The Great Gatsby, The Adventures of Augie March, Invisible Man, American Pastoral*); the "romance of the divide," meaning primarily the racial divide (*Uncle Tom's Cabin, Huckleberry Finn, Absalom, Absalom!, Gone with the Wind, Beloved*); and the "meganovel" of democratic community (*Moby-Dick, U.S.A., Gravity's Rainbow*). A fourth paradigm, which sits uneasily athwart the rest, is represented by a single book, *The Scarlet Letter*, a novel "made classic by retelling"—a GAN contender, in other words, by virtue of sheer iconicity.

Buell's book—which keeps half an eye on the commercial market, and hopes for a general reader—tells us a great deal about American fiction. What it also tells us, in its every line, is much of what is wrong with academic criticism. We can start with the language, as we did with Schmidt. Here is a fair sample of Buell's prose:

> Admittedly any such dyadic comparison risks oversimplifying the menu of eligible strategies, but the risk is lessened when one bears in mind that to envisage novels as potential GANs is necessarily to conceive them as belonging to more extensive domains of narrative practice that draw on repertoires of tropes and recipes for encapsulating nationness of the kinds sketched briefly in the Introduction—such that you can't fully grasp what's at stake in any one possible GAN without imagining the individual work in multiple conversations with many others, and not just U.S. literature either.

That's one sentence. There is an idea in there somewhere, but it can't escape the prose—the Byzantine syntax and Latinate diction, the rhetorical falls and grammatical stumbles. Schmidt's smooth sentences urge us ever onward. Buell's, like boulders, say stop, go back.

The truth is that by academic standards, Buell's writing isn't especially bad—which makes him, as an instance, even worse. By the same token, he isn't noxiously ideological in the current style, isn't an "-ist" with an ax to grind or swing—all the more reason to deplore how thoroughly (it seems, reflexively) his book bespeaks the reigning ideologies. Buell, whose careful terror seems to be the possibility of saying something politically incorrect— the book does so much posturing you think it's going to throw its back out— appears to have absorbed every piety in the contemporary critical hymnal. You can see him fairly bowing to them in his introduction, as if by way of ritual preparation. There they are, propitiated one by one—Ethnicity, Globalism, Anti-canonicity, Anti-essentialism—like idols in the corners of a temple.

The frame of mind controls the readings. Novels aren't stories, for Buell, works of invention with their own disparate purposes and idiosyncratic ends. They're "interventions" into this or that political debate—usually, of course, concerning gender, race, or class, as if everyone in history had had the same priorities as the English professors of 2014. Every book is scored against today's approved enlightened norms. *Gone with the Wind* loses points for "containing" Scarlett and embodying an "atavistic conception of human rights" but wins a few back for being "even more transnationally attuned than *Absalom*," exhibiting "maverick tendencies in some respects as pronounced as Faulkner's," and engaging in "an act of feminist exorcism that *Absalom* can't imagine." Go team!

With *Uncle Tom's Cabin*—a book that makes this kind of reading sweat, being heroically progressive by the standards of its day but embarrassing by ours—pages are spent in parsing its exact degree of virtue. Witnesses are called:

> Here, as critic Laurie Merish delicately puts it, Stowe "fails to imagine African Americans as full participant citizens in an American democracy." George Harrison's grand design to Christianize Africa looks suspiciously imperialistic to boot, veering Stowe's antislavery critique in the direction of what Amy Kaplan trenchantly calls "manifest domesticity."

I feel as if we're back in Salem. Maybe he should just have thrown the book into the water, to see if it would float. Buell is a writer, one should say, who uses terms like "cracker," "redneck," and "white trash" without self-consciousness or irony, a fact that makes his moral teleology all the more repulsive—his assumption (and it's hardly his alone) that all of history has been leading up to the exalted ethical state of the contemporary liberal class.

The one kind of standard that Buell will not permit himself is an aesthetic one. Like many academics now, he'd rather cut his tongue out than admit in public that he thinks a book is good or bad. He fidgets for a page before screwing up the courage to suggest that Stowe's *Dred*, a sort of thematic sequel to *Uncle Tom's Cabin*, "seems destined for less success as an act of fictional outreach." A long paragraph ponders why *The Marrow of Tradition*, by the African American writer Charles Chesnutt, never achieved the popularity of *Huckleberry Finn*—before the next one tells us even multiculti critics think it's pretty lousy.

This is not about applying some timeless measure of artistic value. It is simply about owning up to one's own preferences—to one's own pleasures. Just as Buell's prose conveys the impression of having been produced by a machine, so does his book as a whole. He never tells us why you'd actually want to read these works. The omission points to an unresolved ambiguity: is he talking about Great American Novels or just great American novels, and is there a difference? He can't address the question, because he can't acknowledge the existence of the second category. Never mind his "scripts," which dwell upon the kinds of thematic considerations that get novels onto curricula now and turn them, as Schmidt puts it, into "'text[s]' to talk about and around." What sorts of qualities have made people champion certain books but not others, and do so decade after decade? Buell likes to cite the various blogs and forums where ordinary readers debate their favorite "greats" (among other things, it gives him the chance to make populist noises), but he isn't actually interested in the experience of individual readers, including his own.

And that explains another omission—or rather, a large set of them. There are a lot of great American novels, and great American authors, that he hardly deals with at all. Many pages, in the aggregate, are spent on mediocre or forgotten works that fit his paradigms. Hemingway, meanwhile, believe it or not, is mentioned only incidentally. Henry James is represented, in a brief consideration, by a second-level work, *The Bostonians*. *Lolita* gets a little more than a page, as does *Blood Meridian*. A whole related run of work is essentially absent: *The Naked and the Dead*, *The Catcher in the Rye*, *On the Road*, *In Cold Blood*, *Catch-22*, *Slaughterhouse-Five*. If your first reaction to that list is that all of those books were written by white men—if you think that literary criticism is best conducted as a demographic census—then you might just be part of the problem.

But that is not the point. The point is that a lot of readers, of whatever race or gender, have loved those books and thought them great. Instead of starting with his scripts and themes, Buell should have started there: with the passions that make people want to read, and write, in the first place. That is finally what's at issue, when we speak about the state of academic criticism: the kind of reading it promotes, the kind of readers it creates—who shape, in turn, as Schmidt explains, the kinds of novels that get written.

The notion of the Great American Novel, Buell tells us, is largely without parallel in other countries. Essential to its constitution, it would seem, is precisely that dimension of "dream": of tantalizing elusiveness, as if its fulfillment lay forever in the future, like America's itself. The quintessentially modern form, for the quintessentially modern country. The novel rose with modern selves because the novel, classically, relates the story of an individual attempting to create herself against existing definitions. That possibility is also under threat, as the bureaucrats of identity, within and without the academy, attempt to keep us in the grids to which they have assigned us. The question of the novel's future is important, but equally important, as Schmidt and Buell so differently reveal, is the question of its past: of how we receive it, of how we will consent to let it make us.

[2014]

HOW'S THAT AGAIN?

Like any language pedant, I take a grim pleasure in observing the decline of the English tongue. All the old, interesting meanings seem to be dying off one at a time. "Vagaries" now means, vaguely, "vague bits." "Penultimate," of course, means "really ultimate" (to go along with "very unique"). "Hoi polloi" is now the upper crust, rather than its opposite, presumably by assimilation of *hoi* (Greek for "the"—*polloi* means "many") to "high." "Beg the question" is a lost cause; the universal definition now is "raises the question," not "takes the answer for granted." As for "disinterested," that lovely not-quite-synonym for "impartial," forget it.

But I especially relish the errors of experts—the blunders committed by well-known writers and/or authoritative cultural outlets. Writing in the *New Yorker*, Nicholas Lemann, then the dean of the Columbia School of Journalism, used "locus classicus" to refer to a person (though one would think that "locus" would be clear enough). The *New York Times* has given us "probative" to mean "representative," "full boar" in a column by Maureen Dowd that was not about pigs, and "apologist" to signify "one who apologizes" (in an editorial, no less). Like everybody else, the *New York Review of Books* believes that "bemused" means "amused" (not "confused") and "willy-nilly," "higgledy-piggledy" (not "by compulsion"). NPR has perpetrated "notoriety" for "fame," "misnomer" for "misconception," and "per se" for "so to speak"—all of them now apparently ubiquitous. The *Nation* has offered "bugaboo" for "taboo"; Sandra Tsing Loh, in the *Atlantic*, has equated "wax" with "talk" (an increasingly common howler that derives from "wax eloquent"); and Ann Beattie has contributed "reticent" for "hesitant" or "diffident," which is well on its way to becoming the standard meaning. I told you I'm a pedant.

There is a lesson here. Idiomatic mistakes, at least the ones that stick, are not produced by the hoi polloi. They happen when people try to sound educated—or, to be precise, when educated people try to sound more educated than they actually are. A little learning is a dangerous thing. You hear a word like "vagaries" or "misnomer," you think it sounds impressive, you think you know what it means, and you deploy it the next chance you get. And then somebody who has less cultural capital than you, and who looks to you as an authority, picks it up and uses it in turn.

On the other hand, we all do it. I used to think "noblesse oblige" just meant "nobility," for some reason, until I saw the wince on a colleague's face when I used the phrase that way. Now I look things up if I'm not sure, but the problem is precisely when you *are* sure, and if I'm sure of anything, it's that I'm sure more often than I have any right to be. Besides, this is one of the ways that the language evolves. There are many words and phrases that I use without a thought that once meant something else, sometimes not so long ago. (Look up "nice" in the OED, if you want to see the process in especially vigorous action.) Semantic drift is partly the record of educated stupidity, and at a certain point you simply must surrender to it. "The hoi polloi," for instance. A truer pedant would have blanched at that, since the "the" is redundant. But I'm speaking English, not Greek, and "the" has long been standard. I'll keep on using it, even if it makes me part of hoi polloi.

[2013]

My People

BIRTHRIGHTS

One morning in tenth grade, my Bible teacher started class by holding up a copy of the *New York Times*. He was the one that we called Little Adler, to distinguish him from his older, taller brother, Big Adler, who also taught at the school. Little Adler was a good guy, at a place that was notably short on them. A modest, bearded man, slightly stooped, he was compassionate, he had a dry sense of humor, and he was the only teacher that I came across, in my ten years of yeshiva day school education, who told us that it was okay to ask questions—meaning fundamental questions, questions of belief.

"Every story on the front page today," he announced that morning, "is about the Jews." Then he proceeded to point at them one by one, explaining why. Some were obvious. This was the year of the Camp David Accords, and there were one or two articles about that. But the front page of the *Times*, back then, had eight or nine stories, and as he worked his way around the page, his reasoning became increasingly Talmudic. Nonetheless, in every case, he managed to find a way to connect the events in question to the fortunes of the Jewish people. "And," he concluded, "you can do this every day." Every day, in other words, one way or another, every story on the front page of the *New York Times* was ultimately about us.

I grew up in a world that had a thick black line down the middle of it. On one side were us, the Chosen People, the "holy nation." On the other side were them, the goyim. Each day in morning prayers we thanked the Lord for not making us Gentiles. On Saturday nights we said the havdalah, the prayer that marks the close of the Sabbath. "Blessed are you O Lord our God king of the universe," we recited before the flickering light of a braided candle, "who distinguishes between sacred and profane, between light and darkness, between Israel and the nations, between the seventh day and the six days of creation." It was an early lesson in grammatical parallelism.

The goyim were inferior to us. They indulged their brutish appetites. They ate pig. They ate horse. They ate shrimp, which was practically like eating insects. They ate "creeping things that crawleth upon the ground." They drank themselves blind. *Oy, oy, oy,* went a Yiddish ditty, *shikker iz a goy,* a drunkard is a Gentile. The maid was the *goya;* foolish pleasures were *goyishe naches,* Gentile delights; a dummy had a *goyishe kopf,* Gentile head. One night my father and I were watching a cop show. The detective's friend had just gotten out of prison. "What can I get you?" the detective asked. "A bottle and a blonde," the friend replied. "Of course," my father said. "Why of course?" I asked. "Because that's how a goy celebrates," he said.

The goyim hated us—every one of them, without exception. The only difference was whether they did so openly or not. Scratch a goy, my father would say, and you find an anti-Semite. Their hatred was eternal: it had existed since our beginning as a people, and it would persist until the coming of the Messiah. History did not progress but turned back on itself in an endless loop: persecution, redemption, persecution, redemption. The antagonists were not merely similar; they were identical, and had a name: Amalek. In the Book of Exodus, after Moses has led the Children of Israel in flight from Egypt— "when you were faint and weary," he later reminds them—they are attacked by a tribe of that name. After the battle, Moses builds an altar and swears an oath: "The Lord shall be at war with Amalek for all generations." It was Amalek whom we saw in history's perseveration: Assyria, Babylon, Haman, Antiochus, Rome, the Crusades, the Inquisition, Chmelnitzki, the pogroms, Hitler, the Soviet Union, the Arabs. "In every generation and generation," we sang at the Passover Seder, "they rise up to destroy us."

History, beyond that, was a blank. Of everything else that had happened to the Jewish people, or had been done by them—medieval Hebrew poetry, the life of the shtetl, Yiddish theater, the German-Jewish bourgeoisie; the ancient Jewish communities of Rome, Salonika, Alexandria; the Jews of Yemen, Morocco, Cochin; Baruch Spinoza, Moses Mendelssohn, Heinrich Heine—we were programmatically ignorant. Between the Exile and the State of Israel, history was one unchanging scene of persecution.

At the same time, as Little Adler reminded us that morning, history was all about us, now as in the past. Wasn't Christianity, after all, a bastard outgrowth of the Jewish faith? Wasn't their Bible primarily stolen from ours, and the very messiah they worshipped a Jew? And Islam grew out of Christianity, and Hitler started World War II to exterminate the Jews, and Israel occupies the crossroads of the world, they couldn't stop talking about it at the United

Nations, and in the end of days the final battle would be fought on Mount Megiddo between Gog and Magog, symbolized by an eagle and a bear, which obviously referred to the United States and the Soviet Union.

Our job was to keep the commandments. There were a lot of commandments (613 delineated in the Bible, plus thousands more elaborated by the rabbis). There were things you couldn't say and things you had to say, things you couldn't do and things you had to do. Prayers morning, afternoon, and evening; blessings before sleep, after using the bathroom, before and after meals; holidays and fasts throughout the year. No mixing meat and dairy, no bread (or rice or beans or corn) on Passover, no using electricity, or playing music, or driving a car, or riding a bicycle, or handling money, or cooking, carrying, writing, tearing (I could go on) on the Sabbath. Boys and men wore yarmulkes and *tzitzis*, a tasseled undergarment. Women dressed modestly and covered their hair. To violate one of these precepts, which carried the force of taboo, was to commit an unthinkable act, an offense against the group as well as God. It was to mark yourself as other, beyond the pale, a kind of pollution. And in our tight-knit world, with scores of families living in close proximity, you felt the eyes of the community eternally upon you.

We were aware that there were other, non-Orthodox Jews—the Reforms and Conservatives—but with them we had nothing to do. They were practically goyim themselves, with mixed-gender seating and prayers in English. Their children forgot who they were. Worse still were the traitors, the self-haters, the Jews who held us up to mockery before the world: Philip Roth, Woody Allen, Mel Brooks, all of whom our rabbi sermonized against. The dirtiest words in our lexicon were "assimilation" and, still worse, "intermarriage." With those you completed the work of Hitler, though they wouldn't save you from the next one. The German Jews had been assimilated, and look what had happened to them. My father had escaped with his parents from Czechoslovakia by the skin of his teeth in 1939, three days ahead of the Nazi invasion. "If you forget that you're a Jew," he liked to say, "the goyim will always remind you."

That was my world, unquestioned, until around the time I turned fifteen, that year that I had Little Adler. Then, browsing in the school library one day, I came across a book by Sigmund Freud. I was curious about psychology, and I had heard enough to be curious about him. The book was *Civilization and Its Discontents*. On the first page, I read this:

I had sent [a friend] my small book that treats religion as an illusion.

A few pages later, I read this:

The derivation of religious needs from the infant's helplessness and the longing for the father aroused by it seems to me incontrovertible.

A few pages later still, I read this:

The whole thing is so patently infantile, so foreign to reality, that to any-one with a friendly attitude to humanity it is painful to think that the great majority of mortals will never be able to rise above this view of life.

And just like that, within the space of twenty minutes, the scales fell from my eyes. *Of course* the whole thing is ridiculous, I thought. Of course there is no God. How could I have ever believed any different?

I kept the revelation to myself, but it must have leaked out of my skull like a kind of radioactivity, because soon my friends, then the teachers, figured out my secret. I had contracted—unspeakable word—atheism. My presence in the school became intolerable. I was permitted to finish the year to avoid the stigma of expulsion, but only with the understanding that I wouldn't be returning in the fall. Leaving meant giving up most of my friends. It meant transferring to public school, which was tantamount to stepping off the edge of the known universe. And it turned out to be the greatest thing that had ever happened to me. In Nabokov's *Invitation to a Beheading*, the hero, in the final scene, is lying on the executioner's platform, about to have his head chopped off, when:

with a clarity he had never experienced before—at first almost painful, so suddenly did it come, but then suffusing him with joy, he reflected: why am I here? Why am I lying like this? And, having asked himself these simple questions, he answered them by getting up.

I had lived inside an iron cage that I'd mistaken for the limits of my world, and all I had to do to walk away was walk away. Before I did it, it was unimag-inable. As soon as I had done it, it was inevitable.

But reading Freud, in truth, was not the only or even the main event that levered me out of the world of my childhood. The previous summer, following in the footsteps of my siblings (who were considerably older and not as dug in to the Orthodox world), I had gone to a progressive Zionist summer camp on the banks of the Delaware River. For the first time, I experienced a way of being Jewish that was joyful and positive rather than scowling and dark. We had morning services, but they were creative and thoughtful, not rote. We celebrated the Sabbath, but as a day of peace and fellowship, not strictures and surveillance. We sang, we danced, we put on plays. There were girls, like at school, but they actually smiled at you. There were Jews of all kinds, but we were Jewish together as equals. My counselor, who was skipping college to move to a desert kibbutz, was a self-professed Maoist. My unit head was an intensely charismatic hippie rabbi. That summer opened many windows in my mind, and by the time I got back to yeshiva that fall, my consciousness was already in motion. Freud just gave me the intellectual push to head in the direction that my feelings were already pulling me.

The camp was part of a Zionist youth movement, and from the day I left yeshiva till the year after college, the movement was the center of my life. I owe it more than I can say, but, in retrospect, it had more in common with my day school world than I would ever have admitted at the time. Instead of Orthodoxy, to structure our worldview, we had our ideology—a word that we used without a trace of irony and often with an edge of adolescent fervor. Under its aegis, we likewise cleaved the world in two, with Jews on one side and everyone else on the other. We talked incessantly about our Jewish identity, as if we had none else. We pronounced the words "assimilation" and "intermarriage" as reproachfully as they had in my synagogue. We didn't stigmatize the Gentiles, but we knew our place was not with them. Our place was in Israel. Life in the diaspora, we told ourselves, was untenable as well as inauthentic. It had happened in Europe (nobody needed to ask what "it" was), and it could happen here. To be truly Jewish, you had to live a fully Jewish life, which meant, for us, not an Orthodox one, but one in an environment where everybody else was Jewish, too (the cop, the grocer, the bus driver), just as everyone in France is French—where the national life was steeped in Jewish history, governed by Jewish rhythms, and conducted in the Jewish tongue. America, however hospitable, was not, we were sure, our true home. Our conduct was ruled, not by the 613 commandments, but by one very big one: that we "make aliyah," move to Israel ("aliyah" means "ascent"), an event that we imagined as a personal transfiguration. Anything less was a failure.

Why, after extricating myself from one belief system, did I throw myself into another? Mainly, the movement was just a wonderful environment in which to be young. It brought me friendships and community, a focus for my intellectual energy and an arena for my idealistic passion. But the movement and its ideology, I see now, also served some deeper psychic needs. As I moved out of Orthodoxy and into the American jumble—as I met Gentiles, for pretty much the first time, in high school and college, as well as Jews who truly didn't give a damn about their Jewishness—Zionism gave me a sense of stability and certainty. It told me who I was, what I should do, and where I belonged and with whom. It gave me a system to structure not only my beliefs, not only my affinities, but also my decisions, my future. It solved the problems, in advance, that are raised by being young.

Zionism also provided me with the righteousness and glamour of an oppositional stance with respect to American society—especially since our goal was not only aliyah but, ideally, aliyah to a kibbutz, a collectivist agricultural settlement, so that the opposition was not only to America per se but also to its shallowness and materialism. More deeply still, it provided me with a defense against otherness—above all, against the otherness within myself, the threat that it posed in the shape of forbidden desires, forbidden possibilities. The possibility, for example, of falling in love with a non-Jewish woman. Zionism enabled me, in other words, to evade the contradictions and complexities that went along with growing up not only Jewish but American. Like Orthodoxy, it simply canceled the second term.

I left Zionism, in my early twenties, as I had left Orthodoxy: for one intellectual reason and lots of psychological and existential ones. If the premise of Orthodoxy is the existence of the Jewish god, the premise of Zionism is that "it" can happen here. And at a certain point I realized that, no, it can't. There was anti-Semitism in America—some of it violent, some of it organized, some of it even both (this was the '80s, the age of the rise of the right-wing militias)—but there wasn't going to be a Holocaust. America was a different kind of society than Germany, than any European country. Which meant that the argument for aliyah could not be exclusively negative. There had to be something drawing me to Israel as well as something pushing me there. Spending a year in the country after college, I discovered that there wasn't—or at least, that there wasn't enough. Israel was beautiful and charismatic, but it was also, ultimately, alien. Its culture was Jewish, but its culture wasn't mine. The place was full of Jews, but not ones that I had a lot in common with. It wasn't, after all, my home. My home, with whatever ambivalence, was America. My home was with other Americans.

The question became, on what terms? The problems of being young were problems once again. Who was I, and what was my place in the world? Solutions began to arrive when I started paying attention to the parts of myself that I'd held in abeyance, the ones that didn't fit the story that I'd learned to tell about myself. Above all, my love of literature, the fact that novels spoke to me more intimately, more stirringly, more persuasively, than anything else in my life—that it was in reading that I knew myself and felt myself most deeply. In high school, the one class that actually felt real, like it was about something that existed as more than a "subject," an academic exercise, was the one where I discovered Dostoyevsky and Camus. In college, as a science major, I'd hold a book beneath my desk in class. During my months on kibbutz, that year after college, I read my way through Nabokov and Kundera. I had been trying to tell myself something and, eventually, I started listening. Instead of treating reading as a private passion while I gave myself to other things, things I didn't ultimately have my heart in, I needed to make it the center. I needed to go where my heart was.

Three years after I got back from Israel, I enrolled in a PhD program in English literature. To embark on the study of Western culture, in any of its aspects, is, as a Jew, to venture onto hostile ground. Anti-Semitism is foundational to Christianity and endemic to Western art and thought. In the English literary canon, it is famously present in Chaucer, Shakespeare, Marlowe, Dickens, T. S. Eliot. Anti-Semitic stereotypes and sentiments surprised me in Conrad, Hawthorne, Woolf, Waugh, Henry Adams, Henry James. They were waiting for me in Voltaire when I took a course on the Enlightenment; in Céline, when I studied for my oral exams. These were people who didn't like me. But they also were not going to stop me. They were not going to stop me from claiming a right to the Western tradition. They were not going to stop me from feeding myself with its fruits. They were not even going to stop me from liking their work—and in some cases, loving it, studying it, and teaching it. That they would have sought to exclude me was not going to bully me into excluding myself. That they would have sought to deprive me was not going to shame me into depriving myself. They wanted—like the rabbis and the Zionists, in different ways—to keep me in the ghetto, but I wasn't going to let them.

Was I "colonizing" myself? No, I was educating myself. I was forming myself, with the freedom that America allowed me and the elements it made available to me. I was rebirthing myself, by choosing a new set of forebears, a new inheritance. I was also choosing how I wished to be American, because there are as many ways as there are Americans. Besides, being colonized is not the worst thing, if you do it voluntarily—a lesson that I learned from literary history itself. Joyce, Faulkner, Rushdie: these and many other writers, by placing themselves under the tutelage of metropolitan cultures, had freed themselves from the parochialism, the mental confinement, the moral and aesthetic backwardness, of their places of origin. Better to be colonized like that than to remain forever captive to the group.

As I moved out, internally, into a wider American space, I also moved out socially. In college, I had formed my first real friendship with a non-Jew, one of my freshman suitemates. He was Italian-Polish, from deepest Brooklyn, and had gone to an all-boys Jesuit high school. When I first met him, he was wearing a large wooden cross. Before long, he had taken it off. Our affinity was obvious: we were each in flight from intensely religious backgrounds and each voyeuristically curious about the other's. But hanging out with him, as well as with a bunch of his high school friends who were also going to college in the city, allowed me to still play the Jew, to still mark my difference. As I moved through my twenties, what was new about my friendships was that I didn't need to do that anymore. At a certain point, I realized that I no longer asked myself, when meeting someone new, whether or not they were Jewish. That, for me, was a happy day.

So what is my Jewish identity now? I don't practice, at all (my observance of Passover consists of calling my sister, who is still Orthodox, and wishing her a happy Passover). I'm not affiliated, at all. On Israel I've given up. But I still feel as Jewish as ever. I still am as Jewish as ever. I was formed as a Jew—my consciousness, my sensibility—and that isn't ever going to change. I'm not half-Jewish and half-American; I am entirely both. I am also entirely a writer, a husband, a teacher (this last despite the fact that I no longer teach). I'm not Jewish in a way that any organized Jewish entity, of whatever kind, would approve of. And I couldn't care less.

This is not an essay about being Jewish—or rather, it is not only about being Jewish. It is about identity groups, and what it means to live inside one. For everything I saw growing up as an Orthodox Jew and, to a lesser extent, as a Zionist, I see in the formations—highly mobilized, politicized, and ideologized—that dominate our social space today. Just as Little Adler reminded me that it's all about us, so have the ideologues of African American identity—to take the most conspicuous example—instructed us that it's all about black people. We are told that the American founders undertook the Revolution out of fear of the abolitionist movement that was gathering strength in Great Britain (they didn't, and it wasn't); that the slaves built America's wealth (all of it, not some of it); that blacks were exclusively responsible for abolition (never mind the Union Army, the Radical Republicans, and Abraham Lincoln); that the blacks who came north during the Great Migration created the industrial boom in the Northeast and Midwest (of course, they were drawn by it); that blacks were exclusively responsible for the successes of the civil rights movement (never mind the whites who marched with them, the liberal Democrats, or LBJ); that modern urban policing grew out of Southern slave patrols (when the first metropolitan police department was established in London); that black women are the "backbone" of the Democratic Party (even though they make up only about 10 percent of its voters) and "saved" Joe Biden in the general election (even though the decisive swing, from 2016, was in moderate whites); that Republican efforts at voter suppression, "a new Jim Crow," are directed exclusively at black people (not Democrats as such—blacks, like the college students who are also targeted, being simply an efficient group to aim at); that the insurrection at the Capitol was driven by racism (rather than a stew of right-wing hatreds), and that the police response, so different from what greeted Black Lives Matter, was, as well (even though the crucial difference, as any student of left-wing movements can tell you—Kent State, anyone?—was not black versus white but left versus right); and, in sum—to sweep away all inconvenient particulars—that racism is the single ruling factor in American history, the hidden hand in every institution and development.

We are also told that the history of race relations in America is one unchanging scene of oppression. Nothing alters or alleviates it: not emancipation, not civil rights, not affirmative action. As in 2021, so in 1950, 1890, 1619. Like Amalek, the demon known as white supremacy appears to be immortal, returning under different guises but eternally the same. Progress is unattainable, because the enmity between the races is immutable, not a historical struggle so much as a metaphysical one: black versus white or, when things get really Manichaean, "blackness" versus "whiteness."

We do not find these mental structures only in the area of race, of course. For contemporary feminist orthodoxy—at a time when women earn 58 percent of bachelor's degrees, 64 percent of master's degrees, and 56 percent of doctorates—today is one of the worst times ever to be a woman in America, and America is one of the worst places in the world to be a woman. According to the Human Rights Campaign, the nation's leading gay and lesbian advocacy organization, the rights of LGBTQ Americans are under unprecedented assault—this in the wake of *Obergefell* and *Bostock*, decisions that removed the last significant legal disabilities from those groups. In the world of identity now, what is more, just as in my early milieu, it is everywhere us versus them—with extreme prejudice toward them. All whites are racists. Masculinity is toxic. Working hard and showing up on time are white things (yes, that's a leftist position today). Independence and competitiveness are male things. We loathed and scorned the goyim in my Orthodox community, but at least we kept it to ourselves. Now, public expressions of hatred for the other are not only acceptable but applauded. "I'm so done with white people," a member of the Twitterati will announce, to a chorus of likes, or, "Is there anything that women can't do better than men?" "White," "male," and "cis" (not to mention "Karen") are terms of ridicule and abuse, and speak for themselves.

And just as in my Jewish world, the group demands an unswerving adherence to norms. Deviate, and you're no longer part of the us. Barack Obama isn't "really black" (because he "talks white"). Pete Buttigieg isn't "really gay" (because he "acts straight"). Where integration was once the goal, now assimilation is the bugaboo. Even worse are the apostates: black intellectuals who question critical race theory, feminists who point out feminism's gains, trans writers who challenge the official line on youth transition or the social construction of biological sex. But who is harmed by assimilation? Who is challenged by dissent? The self-appointed leaders—the demagogues, the "spokespeople," the professional Jews, blacks, feminists, gays—who need to keep the walls up to protect their status and their gigs. Even more, the group itself: not the members of the group—the group. "The we closes its ranks to protect the space inside it, where the air is different," Patricia Lockwood writes. "It does not protect people. It protects its own shape."

I grew up in a community that was still deeply scarred by the Holocaust. My father was far from the only former refugee in our synagogue, and my second-grade teacher was a survivor. Many people had lost family, including us. Even today, when I read about the Holocaust, I think, we should have plowed Germany under, after the war, and scattered its inhabitants to the four corners of the earth. So I understand why historically oppressed communities develop the mentality they do. And I also understand the appeal of that mentality, of group identity, to the individual, especially the young individual and especially in America. I don't mean the America of the woke imagination, of oppression and restriction, but its opposite: the America of freedom and possibility, of mobility and flux. The America that says: you can be whoever you want, but you won't get any help in figuring it out. Because freedom is disorienting, and ready-made identities are reassuring. All the more so now. Everywhere the word today—as the images fly by—is "authenticity," "authenticity." We speak of it because we feel the lack of it. But in this age of relativism, of radical skepticism, of anti-institutionalism, when the self is always up for grabs—my situation, as I stumbled out of Orthodoxy, but a thousand times worse—the identity group can claim an ontological solidity, an iron-girder foundationality, that nothing else can. It alone, of all formations, is legitimate. It alone possesses the power to tell you who you are. And that's tremendously seductive, even if it's who you're not, or not completely, or not anymore.

It is especially seductive for those in the process, in the concrete circumstances of their actual lives, of leaving the exclusive environment of the group. That is, for members of underprivileged communities who are rising to join the elite: students of color at fancy private high schools and colleges; their elders in academia, at the *New York Times* or NPR, in Silicon Valley, at the major foundations and think tanks, climbing up the ranks in Washington, DC, in Hollywood, and so forth. *They* are the ones who need to constantly insist on their identity, to reaffirm their separateness against the fact of their participation. Which is why they are the ones who have been preaching the identitarian crusade. It is elites within the Hispanic community who say "Latinx"; the vast majority of Latinos hate the word, when they have even heard of it. It is elites within the black community who propagate the dogma of critical race theory; blacks on average are actually more moderate than the typical white Democrat. It is elites within the Asian American community who inveigh against assimilation; most Asian Americans are busily assimilating. But then, so are the elites, of all groups—so especially are the elites—and it is only their bad conscience, or, more charitably, their understandable ambivalence, that leads them to imagine otherwise. I was at Columbia for one of the uprisings of African American students. "Columbia is a plantation!" the protesters shouted. Columbia was not a plantation. It was an institution that was ushering them, often with generous financial aid packages, into the upper middle class. But that is a destabilizing thought.

I am not suggesting that individuals from marginalized groups who find themselves in elite settings should just be grateful and keep their mouths shut. Nor am I suggesting that they all should do as I did, or that the process of finding your place in the wider world, for such an individual—call it integration, assimilation, or what you will—is ever less than highly fraught. What I am suggesting is that it's a process that you go through *as* an individual— that you must go through, in some fashion—and that to cling to a collective identity, particularly in the artificially exacerbated forms in which they come to us today, is to evade your own reality. "The question of color," James Baldwin wrote, "operates to hide the graver questions of the self." America had told him *what* he was, he once remarked; he went to France, leaving blacks and whites alike behind, to find out *who* he was.

To insist on cultural self-segregation is to limit one's own possibilities. Who would I be if I had only studied Jewish sources, or only read Jewish writers? What is a young woman missing if, as many of them say they do today, she reads only female authors? You won't read Shakespeare? Virginia Woolf did not share that prejudice and would not have become Virginia Woolf if she had. Children should read books, we are told, about people who "look like them." But as Glenn Loury, the black intellectual, recently remarked, everybody "looks like them"—that is, human. No, not everyone is fully free, not yet, but everybody's *mind* is free. The only limits, there, are the ones that you place on yourself. And culture, too, is free. People may discriminate, but books do not. They make themselves available to anyone who cares to read them. Ruth Simmons, the former president of Brown University and the first African American to lead an Ivy League institution, was asked why a sharecropper's daughter would decide to study French literature. "Because," she said, "everything belongs to me." You can't choose where you're from, but you can choose where you want to go. "So, in Macon County, Alabama," Ralph Ellison wrote, "I read Marx, Freud, T. S. Eliot, Pound, Gertrude Stein and Hemingway. Books which seldom, if ever, mentioned Negroes were to release me from whatever 'segregated' idea I might have had of my human possibilities."

The author of *Invisible Man* did not stop being black, of course, any more than I stopped being Jewish. But he worked through to a way of being black in his own individual fashion. And in so doing, he enlarged the possibilities for every African American who followed. A healthy identity, for the group as for the individual, is not rigid and immutable, but creative and ever-evolving. That is progress. That is liberation.

[2022]

A JEW IN THE NORTHWEST

I was standing, like a good Northwesterner, in the produce section of my locally owned organic-food supermarket—this was a couple of years ago, not long after I had moved to Portland from the New York metropolitan area—when I heard a voice in my ear.

"Excuse me," it said. "You're a *Jew*, aren't you?"

My sphincter clenched. There were two ways this could go, and neither one was good. Either the guy I could now sense hovering at my elbow was a Lubavitcher Chasid, engaging in outreach among his fallen brethren ("drawing them near," in the term of art), or he was a Jew for Jesus, eager to tell me about the Lord. If the former, I would sling the brushback pitch that I had learned to keep at hand for such occasions, amply familiar from life in New York. *Ma ha'avodah hazose lachem?* I would say, *What is this worship to you?*—the words of the Wicked Son from the Passover Seder. ("*To you*" the Haggadah explains, "and not *to him*. By excluding himself from the community, he has negated the essential.") If he was a Jew for Jesus, I would probably just start screaming and ripping up his pamphlets, as I did to a guy in the subway once. Christian missionaries tend to transform me into a kind of Semitic Incredible Hulk, a ball of ethnohistorical rage. (A third possibility, that I'd been teleported back to Poland circa 1941 and was about to be invited into a cattle car, I discounted as unlikely.)

When I turned reluctantly to face him, though, I discovered that the guy was neither Jesus freak nor Chasid. He was a typical fortyish Portlander: full beard, big sweater, innocent face. But his eyes were shining beatifically, and that's what tipped me off to what was going on. I had come across this sort of thing before, back in my Israeli folk dance days. There had been a certain kind of Gentile, a sort of earnest, clueless Jew-groupie, who would show up at the workshops just to soak up all the exotic yid energy. That's what this guy clearly was, because he was gazing at me as if he'd finally seen a

unicorn. *Really*, I thought, *you've never met a Jew before?* Well, this was Portland. Maybe he hadn't, at least not as far as he knew. Just being out as a Jew
in this town, as somebody once remarked, amounts to a political statement.
But me—big nose, Levantine complexion, a certain sardonic set to the lips—I
was out whether I liked it or not. So here we were, playing through a version
of the scene that's up there in the tribal mind with Lot's wife and the burning
bush, the one where the camera pans around the table at Annie Hall's family
Easter to reveal Woody Allen in full Chasidic regalia.

"Uh, yeah," I said.

"Hi!" he stuck out his hand. "I'm Kevin!" Pause. "Did you know that it's
Purim today?" I turned back to the chard, too stunned to reply. *Purim?* What
did this *shaygetz* know from Purim?

"No?" he said. "I guess you're not that in touch with your heritage."

Not that in touch with my heritage? Wasn't aware it was Purim? I have
neither believed nor have I practiced since being thrown out of yeshiva high
school at age fifteen (the charge sheet reading, as I would later imagine it, *gross
insubordination and incipient atheism*). But still, thirty years later, I can't catch
sight of a full moon without reflexively calculating the Hebrew date and
reminding myself which holiday must be upon us. (April: Passover; Septem-
ber/October: Sukkos; January/February: Tu B'Shvat, the Jewish Arbor Day;
August: Tu B'Av, very obscure, the Jewish Valentine's Day.) It was March, and
the moon had been a day from full the night before. Of course I knew that
it was Purim.

"It shines out of your face," my persecutor went on. "It's a great tradition.
You should be proud of it!"

My face! My tradition! My God! If you forget that you're a Jew, my father
used to say, the goyim will always remind you. But he was a Holocaust refugee, and I doubt that this is what he had in mind.

I was not the first Jew, I later discovered, to find myself feeling a little conspicuous upon arriving in the Northwest. As with everything Jewish, there was
already a tradition. Not one but two of the leading Jewish postwar literary
figures found themselves marooned in the region at the start in their careers,
both of them victims of academic exile. Leslie Fiedler, the critic, was hired
by the University of Montana in 1941. Bernard Malamud, the fiction writer,
took a teaching job at Oregon State College (now Oregon State University)
in the little town of Corvallis in 1949. Both were city boys from immigrant

communities. Both felt like aliens in the region. Both stayed for years. And both lived to tell the tale of being Jewish in the Northwest: Malamud in the novel *A New Life*, Fiedler in the story "The Last Jew in America"—titles that jointly reflect the complexity of their situations.

When Malamud came to Oregon, he was thirty-five, depressive, lightly published, stubborn, with a scuttled novel and a decade teaching high school, a wife and young son, and nothing but an MA for credential. Having few options or resources, he applied for work at two hundred schools, got offers from two, and chose Oregon State over a college in New Mexico. Other than some summers working in the Catskills and a few months as a census clerk in Washington, DC, he had never lived outside New York. His had been a world of immigrant poverty, Jews and Catholics, City College, Yiddish, his father's dingy grocery store on Gravesend Avenue slowly asphyxiating in the shadow of the El, and the desperate pursuit of intellectual and cultural aspirations—ideals as oxygen.

Corvallis must have seemed like the other side of the moon. Set amidst a bowl of farmland and forest between the Cascades and the Coast Range, the town, population sixteen thousand, had lots of unpaved streets and not a single traffic light. There was no theater, no art gallery, little music, and only two or three decaying movie houses. Oregon State was a cow college, strictly practical: agriculture, engineering, and not much else that anyone took seriously. The English department, housed in a Quonset hut left over from the war, was treated as a service unit, drilling future farmers in grammar and composition. If you wanted to study the liberal arts, you had to go to the University of Oregon, down the highway in Eugene. If you wanted to teach them, you could go and whistle—especially if you didn't have a PhD.

The atmosphere was sleepy and relaxed—also philistine, conservative, provincial, and puritanical. Malamud's departmental colleagues were afraid to drink at parties, lest word get back to their hawkeyed chairman. The new instructor's initial meeting with his immediate boss, the director of composition, was curtailed after a few minutes when the latter announced that he was late for a golf game and took off practicing his swing. The culture, even at the college, was physical, not mental. Football was big, and ROTC. Jews, not so much. When Malamud, looking for a place to live, turned down a particular house as too much for his family's needs, one of the landladies suggested that he "ask some of your people to help you." "Your people" as in "you people," though Corvallis only had about a hundred of them.

A continent from home, and with no foreseeable end to his exile, Malamud was miserable. But he didn't suffer in silence. Turning himself into a one-man arts council, he established creative writing classes for local adults and gathered friends to form a foreign-film society, a Great Books reading group, a lecture series, a chamber-music society, and a theater troupe. His students, whom he disdained, he tried to scandalize out of their narrow backgrounds by playing up the sex in what they read. His superiors, whom he infuriated—chairman, dean, even the college president—he went at with full New York effrontery. The worst of it came when Malamud dared to defend a young colleague who had led a protest at an ROTC march during the Korean War, and in front of the governor, no less. When the director of composition fired the man almost on the spot, Malamud told him that he had "a heart of corn flakes."

Oregon did give Malamud one thing: nature, on a scale and of a beauty heretofore unimagined. For the child of pavements and city stink, merely the first sight of the Adirondacks had been enough to make him feel like Wordsworth in the Lakes. But this was the West. Now, just beyond the little town, were dark-green hills, fields of black earth, and mountains steaming with mist; overhead, rolling skies of "gold, black, silver, grey." It was a new world. Still, no amount of fresh air was going to turn Malamud into an outdoorsman. Slight and sallow, he threw like a girl, drank milk for an ulcer, and had been 4-F during the war. With a pair of friends, he formed a "League of Lopsided Men," admission contingent upon the complete incapacity to fix or make things—the Jew as weakling, less than fully male, the antitype of rugged Western masculinity.

"The picture I am left with of Malamud," a student wrote, "is of a very unhappy man . . . a lonely man. I think he felt Oregon was a foreign country." Oregon, for reasons of incomprehension, distaste, or, in the case of his colleagues, sheer envy, returned the antipathy. By the time that he had been at Oregon State for ten years, Malamud had published *The Natural* and *The Assistant* (his most celebrated novel), won fellowships from Yaddo and the Rockefeller Foundation, and received a Rosenthal Award for fiction from the National Institute of Arts and Letters. But it was only after *The Magic Barrel* won the National Book Award (the collection is still regarded as among the finest volumes of short stories ever published in the United States) that he was allowed to teach classes in literature and creative writing. The college also gave him its bronze medal that year for faculty achievement. The gold went to the inventor of an improved breast cup for cows.

If Malamud was a luftmensch, delicately dreaming, then Fiedler was a tummler: brash, noisy, priapic, Dionysian. Three years younger than Malamud but a generation further into America, Fiedler grew up on the south side of Newark in a tough industrial neighborhood of blacks and Jews. Montana was already the second leg of his Western expedition. A radical by sixteen and notorious college troublemaker, he had been blackballed by the elite eastern graduate programs—"Mr. Fiedler will never be a gentleman or a scholar," wrote one professor, getting it half-right—and had done his PhD at the University of Wisconsin.

If Fiedler was no Malamud, then Missoula was no Corvallis. Oregon was cows: settled, agricultural, conservative. Montana was cowboys: wild, raunchy, libertarian. As Mark Royden Winchell puts it in *"Too Good to Be True": The Life and Work of Leslie Fiedler*, "In Montana, the term *professor* was less likely to call to mind a politically engaged intellectual than the piano player in a whorehouse." (Fiedler's students called him "Doc.") The state possessed a strong radical tradition to balance its landed interests, and Fiedler's chairman had a single rule for his instructors, who could teach whatever they wanted: don't sit down in class.

For a contrarian like Fiedler, Montana was a redoubt from which to do battle with the eastern literary establishment. ("Come Back to the Raft Ag'in, Huck Honey!," the essay that revolutionized the study of American literature by pointing to the homosocial motif that lies at the heart of so many canonical works, and that became the seed of his flagship book, *Love and Death in the American Novel*, was published in 1948 when Fiedler was thirty-one.) A regular in *Partisan Review*, he became, in effect, the westernmost of the New York intellectuals. As a connoisseur of American culture, he also savored Missoula's frontier tang—the wooden-faced cowboys and dead-end Indians he'd see in the saloons, the drifters and ranchers and drunks—which incidentally, washed down with a whiskey or two, offered relief from college politics and the PTA.

Montana gave him distance from the East, but the process also worked the other way. Fiedler's Jewish identity remained acute, not to say aggrieved; his sense of being a misfit, also. Like Malamud—a light unto the Gentiles—he sought to civilize his little corner of the West. He lectured to book clubs and women's groups and brought to Missoula the kinds of literary figures, including Faulkner and Auden, he had made a virtue of leaving behind. And when the place became too much for him—or rather, too little—he did what

Malamud could almost never do and left. Between years at Harvard and Princeton, fellowships in Athens and Rome, summers at the Indiana School of Letters, and an initial stint in the navy (he volunteered after Pearl Harbor), Fiedler managed to spend nearly half his time in Montana somewhere else.

Still, the place that he won for himself—Fiedler the insurgent—he wound up feeling trapped by. Malamud's rebellions were as nothing to his own. An early essay, "Montana; or the End of Jean-Jacques Rousseau," ruffled feathers by describing the regional physiognomy as "not developed for sociability or feeling, but for facing into the weather." Later, when the president of the university obstructed his efforts to integrate the English department, Fiedler attempted to have him deposed. In a small place like Montana, with the leadership of the public university at stake, the whole state oligarchy was swept into the fight. Remarkably, Fiedler prevailed, but the controversy fixed him forever in the local imagination as the university's designated gadfly. He had at last become, he said, "the Montanans' Leslie Fiedler rather than my own."

Malamud and Fiedler, they went West because they had to. Me, I came by choice. I'm an immigrant, not an exile. So what am I doing here, a New York Jew in the land of flannel and tattoos?

It's like this: I fell in love with the place. My wife and I spent a sabbatical here a few years ago just for the hell of it, and by the time it was over, I never wanted to leave. Everybody was so nice! They made eye contact! They smiled at you! They asked you how your day was going, and they really wanted to know. (Their day? Well, their stupid roommate had taken their bicycle without permission and ended up wrecking it, so now they needed a new bicycle *and* a new roommate, which totally sucked.) The niceness was political, as well. The Portland planning genius, which had created a city that was neither a playground for the rich nor a decaying postindustrial wasteland, was all about making room for other people, prioritizing public space over private advantage. Here was a city, a real city, that didn't make you feel like garbage.

And the nature, and the alternative spirit, and the youthful optimism, and yes, goddamn it, the food. We had to buy a futon when we got here. As we walked out of the store into a gorgeous big blue summer sky—having been assisted by a young guy in a skirt and a nose ring who was perfectly friendly, perfectly patient, and perfectly well-informed about flame retardants, off-gassing, organic materials, local manufacture, and all the other issues we had been obsessing over, and who didn't try to pressure or upsell us—I thought, "Portland makes me cum." The city worked, and it worked in a completely different way than New York did. The end of the year was like the last day of summer camp; I wanted to chain myself to a parking meter, so they couldn't take me away.

A few years later, after a messy divorce from academia, I got my chance to return, this time for good. It was the last thing that anyone who knew me expected. I was the latest of the would-be New York intellectuals. Spectacles on my nose, autumn in my heart, just like Isaac Babel said. Gloomy, sarcastic, militantly urban in the Woody Allen–Fran Lebowitz mold. Neurotic and here to talk about it. I wasn't from New York; I was from the suburbs, North Jersey—which made me, once I got to the city (and stayed there for the better part of two decades), more New York than the New Yorkers. Anyone who's followed a similar path will understand this. The city wasn't just a place for me; it was a belief system. The subway stops were my rosary (I would finger them on the map); the streets were my church; the hot dogs were my Eucharist. Art, culture, books, the life of the mind: the same ideals that were oxygen to Malamud and Fiedler were oxygen to me. The city was the place I came of age, the object of my longest-standing love affair.

So now, after ten-years' academic exile of my own, why wasn't I returning? Because Portland had shown me a different set of values. Because I had decided to try another kind of life. Because unlike Malamud or Fiedler, I wanted to take lessons in civilization, not give them. Because I hoped to see what else, in altered circumstances, I might become. So like the first Jew, and countless others since, I went forth from my land, and from my birthplace, and from the house of my father.

There's a joke that I heard as a teenager in Zionist youth movement. We were going to be latter-day pioneers, my friends and I, and move to Israel to build a just society. But one of the people who had already been trying to make a go of it there for a while—wrestling with the red tape, enduring the rudeness, reeling from the culture shock—regaled me with the following:

The Devil appears to a man on his deathbed. "I'm going to give you a choice between Heaven and Hell," he says. "And just to make it fair, I'm going to let you see them first."

Heaven is, well, Heaven: halos, harps—pleasant but dull. Hell, however, looks great: drinking, music, dancing girls. "I'll take Hell," the man says.

Once he dies, though, Hell turns out to be exactly what you would have imagined in the first place: flames, screams, demons, pitchforks. "Wait a minute," the man complains. "That's not what it looked like before."

"No," the Devil says. "But then you were a tourist, and now you're a new immigrant."

I'd forgotten all about that joke until I had returned to Portland. Culture shock? Kevin, my groupie from the supermarket, was only the beginning. "Excuse me, you're a *Jew* . . .": that encounter was about, not simply the Jew as other, but otherness itself as other. There aren't a lot of Native Americans in New York, but can you imagine someone going up to one and saying, "Excuse me, you're an *Indian*, aren't you?" I'm used to people having trouble with my name, but only in Portland have I met ones who not only thought it was funny, but who couldn't understand that *I* didn't think it was funny, as well. A year ago last fall, when I went down to the local Democratic Party headquarters to volunteer for the Obama campaign, I was greeted by one of those politigeek college-boy staffers (sport jacket, tennis shoes, acne), who wanted to start by taking down my name. As I finished spelling it out for him, he fixed me with this Alfred E. Newman smirk, as if to say, *Really? That's your name?* "Really?" he said. "That's your name?"

What, is everybody here called "Smith" or "White"? Maybe. The very notion of ethnicity cannot be said to exist in Portland. "Diversity," maybe, around the edges, but diversity can be another way of keeping separate. Ethnicity, here, is a hipster with a food cart selling nouvelle Asian-fusion jerk chicken: a set of sensations uprooted from their context to be mixed, matched, tweaked, twisted, and twirled. In the eastern cities, it is something else entirely. It is engagement; it is confrontation; it is cultures and communities fighting it out in the urban space: loving and hating one another, love-hating one another, seeing themselves in and against one another. Making their own city. Making their own America. And making one another (and the language, and the country) over in the process. You got a problem with that?

I didn't know this till I got here. It was just the air I breathed; how could I have known it? But I started to figure it out when I realized what I am missing in Portland the most. It isn't "culture" in the sense New Yorkers brag about—museums and theater and so forth, the sense in which I'd once embraced it. It isn't the chance to get a decent cannoli or pastrami, or even a holy Sabrett's. It isn't even the spectral presence of the old New York intellectuals, my spirit guides. It's edge. It's energy. It's irony. It's curiosity. It's everything ethnicity and eastern speed impose on you.

The people here, I've found, are like the climate: mild and lacking in extremes. The getups are interesting; the faces, rarely. The city often strikes me not so much as Western as Midwestern, Mayberry with tattoos. A lot of the young people who flock here, and who give the city so much of its look and character, originate in places like Minnesota or Missouri. They leave to escape the Jesus and the hopelessness back home, come because they felt like freaks and wanted to find a place where they can put rings in their eyebrows, but they don't see how much Minnesota or Missouri they bring with them.

I mention the youthful migrants, but they affirm the local norm: friendly, pleasant, placid, passive. People here, you see them standing in the winter cold and drizzle—smoking, talking, even sitting down and reading—with a positively bovine imperturbability. It's just a different nervous system. (Actual Portland bumper sticker: "More Relaxed Than You, Dude.") No one eavesdrops, no one interrupts, no one mixes in or gets a tone. They look at you, yes, but they don't *look* at you. I see it now, when I'm back in New York. You look at someone—in the subway, on the street, you're sizing them up—and they see you and stare back, so now they're looking at you looking at them, and you're looking at them looking at you. You're not being friendly; you're being *aware*.

It took me coming here, in other words, to find out who my people are. It's not the Jews, or not just the Jews, and if it took me so long to figure that out, that's partly because I'd been raised to believe that it is just the Jews. It's Judeo-Italians, let us say, Judeo-Catholics. Ethnic eastern urbanites—skeptical, noisy, alert, with a mordant sense of humor and the kind of critical self-consciousness that bevels everything with wit and doubt. That is the tribe that I'm proud to be part of. And Kevin was right: it is a great tradition. When I'm back in New York, and I see an *alter kocker* in a homburg crossing Riverdale Avenue, or a grandmother in a housedress sitting in a doorway across from the Cornelia Street Cafe (around the corner from the stretch of Bleecker that I think of as Little Little Italy), or a balding academic in a bistro on the Upper West Side—well, that's when I know that I'm home.

Of course, none of that is Portland's problem. I'm the one who wanted to live here. No, this is my problem, because however hard I try to adapt, I always feel too *something*: too loud, too fast, too tense, too rude, too abrupt, too damn self-conscious. I try to smile at people but always mess up the timing. I say, "How's it going?," but no one's convinced. I'll try to crack a joke—to, you know, represent—and people look at me as if I've started speaking Hindustani. I never planned to stop being myself; I just didn't realize quite how myself I was. I came to see what else I might become and, like every traveler, what I've really discovered is who I already am.

It is the same for the protagonist of Malamud's Northwest novel, also looking, as the title proclaims, for a new life. "S. Levin," the first line calls him, the odd initial a sign of suppressed identity, the old self left behind. Levin is Malamud, give or take—the lowly new instructor from New York, arrived to take up his position at a state school in "Cascadia"—but Malamud in extremis: alone, lonely, a former drunk and lifelong failure, his past a black hole. The opening scene is archetypal, almost allegorical. Bearded, uncertain, Levin sets down his valises and looks around "in a strange land." Introducing himself, he adds merely, "From the East." Levin is the immigrant, the greenhorn, fresh off the boat, as it were, and eager to be filled with a new American identity.

It's going to take some doing, though. Like Malamud, Levin is the classic Jewish milksop. His boss, Gilley, the director of composition, is "tall, energetic, with a rich head of red hair," a sportsman. His wife, Pauline, is "tall, flat-chested"—none of your zaftig Jewish girls—"a lily on a long stalk." While Levin's departmental colleagues shingle roofs and pour concrete, he ventures into lawn mowing and leaf raking, then mans up and learns how to drive. Soon he is voyaging into the countryside. As he passes log trucks, farms, and millponds, he is "discovering in person," he thinks, "the face of America"—the real America, in other words, just as his students "represented the America he had so often heard of, the fabulous, friendly West."

Where he's going on that country cruise is to an assignation with one of those students, a weekend on the coast. He barely makes it. Once, twice, three and four times Levin breaks down or gets stuck or lost on his grimly comic nightmare journey through the mountains. The romance fares no better, one in a series of erotic pratfalls. When a colleague's wife accosts him in the woods, the two of them kindle a long-smoldering flirtation right there on the forest floor—but not before he hangs his trousers on a branch. The life of brawn and instinct's not for him, the American life.

There are other problems. Like Malamud, Levin makes waves in the faculty lounge. He doesn't merely want to get along; he wants to lift the place, throw out the punctuation drills and help his students reach the life of the spirit—make them more like himself, in other words. But he states his case in American terms—the humanities as foundation of democracy—quotes Jefferson, not Schiller. It is the great outsider's strategy (King used it, too): leveraging American ideals against American practice, a way also of making yourself more American. But no one in the college wants a lecture from a first-year man on how to do their jobs—still less from Levin, suspect from the first. For one thing, there's that beard. "I respect beards," Gilley says darkly at their first meeting, "but some of your students may think you're an oddball." "Americans have often worn them," Levin counters. "Are you American?" a barmaid asks, "How come you have that big beard?" One local simply says, "You a Mormon or somethin'?"

A New Life is about trying to assimilate, and with beautiful cunning, the novel attempts to assimilate, too. The word "Jew" is absent in all its forms until the very end. Levin, Jewish? Nothing ever tells us so directly. Instead we get that beard, a mask that reveals, a neon light that pulses *Jew, Jew, Jew.* And there's another metonym. "No more New Yorkers, goddammit," says Gilley, as things begin to boil. Then, "Why don't you go back where you came from—to the stinking goddamn New York subways?"

Yet it's not just being Jewish, or from New York. Levin's time in Cascadia is everywhere shadowed by the collective memory of a recent predecessor, a certain Duffy from Chicago, another fledgling instructor who came to grief by opening his mouth too much. Duffy was Irish; Malamud, who married an Italian woman, also knew about Judeo-Catholics. As for Chicago, "That's East out here," Gilley snaps. From beyond the grave, Duffy sounds the novel's single note of urban wit. "The time is out of joint," his suicide note had read. "I'm leaving the joint." Duffy's office becomes Levin's; Levin reminds everyone of Duffy. The longer he stays in Cascadia, the more we sense that Levin's acting out a script that was written by his doppelgänger, or maybe by the situation. Among the novel's working titles was *The Easterner.* Levin, for all his precious sensitivity, is not an individual, at least not as far as the locals are concerned; he is a type.

Nothing makes this clearer than what ought to be the most individuating circumstance in his life. Levin falls into romance at last—with none other than Pauline Gilley, the "lily on a long stalk." Here is assimilation in earnest. *Pauline*: not only is her name as Christian as they come; it actually means *Christian.* So what's in it for her? Sure enough, she had had an affair with Duffy and is looking to repeat. But it gets even worse. It was Pauline, it turns out, who had seen to it that Levin was brought to Cascadia in the first place, urging her husband to give him the job against his better judgment. And the reason? Five pages from the end, the novel plays the card it's been withholding all along. Says Pauline to her paramour, "Your picture reminded me of a Jewish boy I knew in college who was very kind to me."

It is quite a punch line. Trying to escape his Jewishness, Levin finally learns that it has controlled his fate from the first. He's not S. Levin, ready for reinvention; he is The Jew. As for that new life, he may get one with Pauline—the novel's end is painfully ambiguous—but it won't be in Cascadia. As it did with Duffy, the place repels the alien intrusion.

Malamud, who grew up in a Yiddish-speaking house and married a Catholic, wrote a novel about the impossibility of assimilating. Fiedler, whose parents spoke English and who married a Jew, wrote a story about the near impossibility of not doing so. "The Last Jew in America" is about feeling like the odd man out not, as its title would seem to suggest, among the Christians of Missoula (or Lewis and Clark City, as Fiedler renames it) but among the Jews: "those so-called Jews from the Faculty," "with their gentile wives" and "their goyish eyes, bloodshot from last night's cocktail party." In addition to their equally deracinated brethren downtown, a handful of merchants and lawyers, the place contains just three "real Jews," a trio of oldsters who form a triptych not of ethnic loyalty but of tormented ambivalence.

There is Jacob, the protagonist. He's the one who rails against the "so-called Jews." And what kind of Jew is he? The renegade kind, the fourteen-year-old yeshiva boy in Verenskaya who broke his mother's heart by staying home on Yom Kippur to eat bread and read *Daniel Deronda* (gross insubordination, incipient atheism) in Hebrew translation. The Stalinist kind, at least before the inevitable disillusionment, railing against the Zionists as agents of British imperialism. The kind "who fled the *shtetl* and the graves of my ancestors to be a new man in a new world." And finally, the sentimental kind, looking, late in life, for kindred and community, dreaming of becoming, for the blissfully assimilated children of the still-abashedly assimilated adults, "a kind of portable grandfather, a door-to-door link with the past."

There is Louie, dying in a Catholic hospital on this, another Yom Kippur. For Louie, Jacob will pound the streets, scaring up a minyan for a last Kol Nidre. Louie is the professional Jew, raising money for the UJA, organizing "desultory Seders and Purim celebrations," gathering from the four corners of the earth the ritual substances: Mother's Gefilte Fish, rye bread with *kimmel*, and Mogen David wine. But Louie assumed the role of "town Jew"—now passing, Jacob reluctantly feels, to himself—only after being drummed out of the labor union he had loved with all his heart and with all his soul and with all his might. "A crooked Jew," his rival had denounced him as (if you forget that you're a Jew . . .), and so, having no choice, he became a full-time one.

And then there is Max, Jacob's bête noire: rich, contemptuous, apoplectic. Show up for the minyan? Over his dead body. Once, he and Jacob and Louie had reminisced about the old country, chatting in Yiddish and sharing copies of the *Forverts*. But since then Max has turned into the angry Jew, the fuck-you-both Jew, not an un-Jew but an anti-Jew, not abashedly assimilated but proudly so, militantly so, assimilated in the name of the Six Million. "All the good Jews," he bellows, "are dead." For Jacob, Max is "an insult to the Jewish people," a cartoon out of *Der Stürmer*, the greedy kike with a hooked nose and grossly comic accent—who also happens to cut a big check every year to the UJA.

Jacob gets his minyan, but Max attacks him for hastening Louie's death with all the commotion. In a moment of high scorn, Max sells Jacob his share in the World to Come for a nickel. The situation is biblical, not Jacob and Max but Jacob and Esau, fighting over Louie—Louie as Isaac, Louie as the past, Louie as Jewishness itself. Jacob, Max: every Jew thinks that he's the chosen one, the favorite son. Every Jew, conflicted about his Jewishness, is embarrassed by every other Jew, who is never the right kind of Jew, never a "real Jew."

What will the goyim think? Like *A New Life*, the story takes place against the backdrop of the West—here, too, the real America. (And the backdrop of McCarthyism, a crusade, as Jews and Catholics rose to positions of prominence, to extirpate the "un-American.") To put a Jew in the West, both Fiedler and Malamud knew, is to confront, without the insulation of an encircling community, the place of the Jew in America. Fiedler's story shares a volume with two other interlinked narratives. In "The Last WASP in the World," a son of Lewis and Clark City goes to New York and wins renown as a poet, only to find himself submerged in a world of Jews. East is East and West is West, just as they were for Malamud. In "The First Spade in the West," also set in Lewis and Clark City, a putative descendent of the great expedition's lone African American member insists on his right to call the town his own. Who are we, Fiedler wants to know, when we've left the place we're from? Writing of Malamud himself (in a book called *Fiedler on the Roof*), and thinking of Leopold Bloom, he puts the matter thus: "the very notion of the Western Jew is like that of the Irish Jew a joke in itself."

The American West is no longer what it was, and neither is the American Jew. Portland is the most progressive big city in the country, and Corvallis may be even further to the left. As for the Jews—or this one, anyway—I don't regard myself as less American than anyone else, don't require the West to validate my sense of belonging. I don't worry about being manly enough, or handy enough, or the fact that my parents were immigrants. And whom I have to thank for that are Malamud and Fiedler—them, and everyone like them, everyone who blazed a trail into the American mainstream, my patriarchs and matriarchs, the pushy Jews who pushed their way in: who interrupted, who got a tone, who wouldn't take no for an answer. Pioneers! O pioneers!

In fact, I wonder whether Portland isn't less American than me, and just because it's missing me—missing ethnicity, and what goes with ethnicity and makes up its essence, a sense of history. I understand why the baristas always ask you how your day is going: because today is the only day there is here. To put it another way, Portland does not seem to have any grown-ups. Sure, there are people in their forties and fifties and seventies, but there isn't any-one who represents the past, and the weight of the past, like my old-timers and Italian grandmothers. There isn't any*thing* that represents the past. We drove out to Missoula that first year in town, traversing the Northwest from end to end. What struck me most along the way was that everything seems to be named after Lewis and Clark: Lewis & Clark College, Lewis and Clark High School, Lewis & Clark RV Park, Lewiston, Idaho, and Clarkston, Washington, etc., etc. The suspicion arises that nothing much has happened in the region since the two of them came through.

When Barack Obama was inaugurated, in a great national celebration, the year after we returned to live here, my strongest feeling was one of remoteness from the event, a sense that American history was happening, as it almost always has, somewhere else. In the East, you feel as if you're in the midst of things. Portlanders feel as if they're in the midst of things, but not the things I'm talking about. Hence the following colloquy, overheard at the gym:

"People talk shit about Oregon, but we got the greatest fucking forests in the world."

"Yeah, it's an hour and a half to the beach, an hour and a half to snow-boarding, you got great hiking right here, and it's two and a half hours to the desert. We got it all."

"I know, dude, it's fucking crazy."

He's right. It is fucking crazy. I was gardening one morning when a bliss-ful hippie couple happened by. "Hey," they said, "how's your day going?" Then they praised the perennials, savored the look of the mulch, and urged me with a smile to have a peaceful afternoon. As they strolled on down the street, I realized what they had been doing. They had been "sending positive energy into the universe." How very sweet, I thought, and how remarkably naïve. What kind of place—and a city, no less—allows you to remain so innocent of history that you can wander through the world on those terms?

And yet I remain, and just, perhaps, for reasons such as these. Here is a place that embodies my political values but utterly fails to embody my cul-tural ones, and maybe that's no accident. Portland doesn't much remind me of the country that I know, but I came here, after all, to discover a new America. New York may be the city of my past, but Portland—green, self-limiting, communitarian—may be the city of the future. At least, if we're going to have a future. As any student of America can tell you, you achieve the new by releasing the old. And as any student of another place can tell you—I mean a certain strip of land between the Jordan and the sea—too much mem-ory can kill you.

After a dozen years in Corvallis, Malamud departed for Bennington College, long a magnet for artists. After a couple of dozen in Missoula, Fiedler was recruited by SUNY Buffalo, which was building a first-class department of English. Malamud had "no complicated emotions" about leaving the West. *A New Life*, in fact, is an often-mocking roman à clef about his faculty asso-ciates. Written during his final years in Oregon but published only once he was safely back east, the novel is a kind of farewell stink bomb flung over his shoulder at the place that rejected him. But when Fiedler visited Missoula a few years after his departure, he felt, to his surprise, as if he had come home. "[I]t is a Montana landscape I see when I close my eyes," he said around this time, "its people I imagine understanding, or more often misunderstanding me. And in this sense, I have to think of myself as a Western writer."

As for me, my sojourn in Portland has reminded me of something else I used to hear in Zionist youth movement. It is the most famous line in Hebrew poetry, composed by Yehudah Halevi in twelfth-century Spain. "My heart is in the East, and I am at the end of the West." An immigrant, I realize now, is exactly what I am. You flee the old country for the promise of a better life, and then you spend your time regretting what you left behind. How shall we sing the Lord's song in a strange land? You come for the political values, but then you gripe about the cultural ones. These Americans! The Russians in Brighton Beach stare out across the water as if they were gazing at the Black Sea, and I keep a MetroCard in my wallet. If I forget thee, O Manhattan. I understand why people used to go back to be buried in Calabria or County Cork. Put it this way: I want to live here, but I don't want to die here.

[2012]

THE LIMITS OF LIMITS

In a recent column, David Brooks extolled the virtues of life in the Orthodox Jewish world. Communities are strong; existence is ordered; everyday acts are infused with a higher significance; the burdens of modern individualism are lifted in favor of a commitment to collective purpose. It all sounds really great, especially the part about the upscale kosher grocery store.

As a refugee from Orthodoxy, I have almost too much to say about this, and certainly too much to feel. I won't pretend to be objective. But I do have one advantage over Brooks and other secular Jews who idealize Orthodoxy from a safe distance (the sentimental celebration of traditional life on the part of those who'd never touch it in a hundred years is not confined to Jews, of course). I actually know what existence is like within those paragons of harmony.

Brooks quotes a prominent rabbi to the effect that following the thousands of regulations that govern daily life within Orthodoxy is akin to learning the piano. At first it seems like drudgery, "but mastering the technique gives you the freedom to play well and create new songs." I wish that Brooks had pushed a little on the metaphor, because I have no idea what those "new songs" are supposed to be. The point of learning the rules, in Orthodoxy, is not to adapt or improvise upon them, the way it is in art. It is to follow them exactly and unstintingly. You don't "create new songs"; you sing the same ones over and over and over again. And they're not songs.

Brooks remarks that the laws of Orthodoxy "moderate religious zeal" by "making religion an everyday practical reality." The statement is astonishingly thoughtless. Never mind the zeal that's on continuous display, to disastrous effect, in Israel. The Orthodox are no less immune to competitive virtue than other religious (or nonreligious) groups. The laws are the *objects* of the zeal, which means they tend to grow increasingly restrictive. As it has responded to the threat of secular modernity, Orthodox Judaism, like other traditional religions, has drifted inexorably rightward. And as in those other traditions, the ones who bear the greatest brunt are women. Men compete to heap restrictions on their wives and daughters.

But the greatest limitations are those on the mind. Jews are constitutional lawyers, says another rabbi Brooks refers to, endlessly litigating the divine commandments. Lawyers, yes, but not philosophers. Debate revolves around the minutiae of practice; broader questions of meaning and purpose—the ones that naturally arise when people think about the world—are out of bounds. Orthodox Judaism, at least in my experience, is a spiritually under-nourished place (one reason, it has been said, that so many Jews are drawn to Buddhism). I didn't even understand what spirituality is until many years after I had left that world and discovered my own in the arts. "Warmth" is not spirituality. Lighting candles is not spirituality. If you ask an Orthodox Jew what the meaning of Passover is, chances are they won't say freedom, certainly not freedom understood as a general human concept. They'll say the meaning is that God took us out of Egypt. The meaning is we don't eat bread. Orthodox Jews, in my experience, tend to have incisive minds but stunted personalities. What's finally off-limits, in the tradition, are major portions of the self.

Gazing at the families at the grocery store, Brooks tells us, "I notice how incredibly self-confident they are. Once dismissed as relics, they now feel that they are the future." Why? Because while only about a third of Jews in the New York metropolitan area are Orthodox, over 60 percent of Jewish children are. Soon, he says, the Orthodox will predominate. But smugness is not self-confidence, and fertility is not an argument. I have no doubt that Orthodoxy is a source of great joy and comfort for many of its adherents. But modernity happened for good reasons. The kinds of restrictions that Brooks professes so much admiration for are exactly what so many of us sought to leave behind. Let's not delude ourselves about them.

[2013]

PARADE'S END

The famous-Jew parade, the roll call of Semitic pride. If you grew up Jewish, you know what I'm talking about. *Marx was a Jew. Freud was a Jew. Einstein was a Jew.* Sing it, bubby. Kafka? *Jew.* Brandeis? *Jew.* Mendelssohn? *Jew.* Jonas Salk? Paul Newman? Norman Mailer? Henry Kissinger? Barbra Streisand? Bob Dylan? Bobby Fischer? *Jew, Jew, Jew, Jew, Jew, Jew, Jew.* Lauren Bacall? *I didn't know she was Jewish.* Christ, even Jesus was a Jew. Israel, the Holocaust, and the list of famous Jews: the three touchstones of contemporary Jewish identity.

When Jews enter the larger world, they do great things—that was the line that I heard growing up. They kept us out for centuries, but as soon as they let us in, we set the place on fire. And you know, it's true. But it took me years to realize that the idea cuts the other way, as well. Jews do great things . . . when they enter the larger world. When they don't, they don't. Almost none of those famous Jews actually practiced as Jews: not the ones who identified as Jews (like Freud), not the ones who were proud to be Jews (like Einstein), not the ones whose work was about being Jewish (like Philip Roth), not even the ones who personified traditional Judaism (like Isaac Bashevis Singer).

To do great things—to express their genius in a form that is valuable to the world—Jews not only have to be Jews; they have to stop being Jews—at least, in any active way, any way that traditional Judaism would recognize. That only makes sense. In traditional Judaism, you're not supposed to write songs or novels, or think about economics or physics. You're supposed to sit in a yeshiva and study Talmud. You aren't supposed to enter the larger world at all; you're supposed to shun it. Whenever I drive past an ultra-Orthodox neighborhood, I think, what a senseless waste of comedic talent.

On the other hand, where is the next generation of Jewish renegades supposed to come from, if not from Orthodoxy? The shtetls are gone, and so are the immigrant enclaves. Jews do great things when they enter the larger world—that cuts another way, as well. When they *enter*. If they're already there to start with, I am not so sure. The distinctive attributes of the Jewish genius are those of a marginalized and persecuted people sustained by a legalistic and text-based religion: moral seriousness, verbal dexterity, analytic rigor, dark humor, a tragic sense of life, an outsider's gimlet eye and anxious sense of exclusion. It may be early days, but once you remove the marginalization, the persecution, the texts, and the religion, the cultural DNA seems to peter out pretty quickly.

As for Reform and Conservative Judaism—forms of practice that attempt to strike a compromise between tradition and modernity, affiliation and assimilation—well, I'm sure that lots of successful professionals are to be numbered among their lovely children, but it's hard to imagine a Kafka or a Bellow being reared on such thin broth. Besides, you must have something to rebel *against*. That's what propels you into the world, drives you to prove yourself, gives you the needed injection of insecurity and self-doubt, the never-sated sense of inauthenticity. "Every original Jew turns against the Jews," Alfred Kazin wrote; "they are the earth from which his spirit tries to free itself."

At this point, though, the Orthodox are becoming like the Amish, their segregation self-willed and factitious. My money's on the Asians now, all those Chinese and Indian and Korean kids who are straining at the communal leash in suburban Los Angeles and New York and Seattle. I cannot wait to hear the litany of famous names that they're about to write.

[2011]

DAY OF ATONEMENT

I write this on the twentieth anniversary of the signing of the Oslo Accords. A second agreement, known as Oslo II, was concluded two years later. A few weeks after that, a friend of mine attended an enormous rally in Tel Aviv in support of the peace process. It didn't even feel like a rally, he told me; it felt like a celebration. After nearly half a century of war, terror, and intifada, of prayers and songs and wild, impossible hopes, peace for Israel was finally at hand. That evening, Yitzhak Rabin was assassinated by a right-wing extremist on his way from the event. A few months later, Benjamin Netanyahu was elected prime minister by a margin of less than 1 percent.

Last Saturday, the day after Rosh Hashanah, was the Fast of Gedaliah. Gedaliah was a Jew who was appointed governor of Judea by Nebuchadnezzar after the destruction of the First Temple. Four years later, he was assassinated by a conspiracy of fellow Jews, an event that precipitated the Babylonian Exile. The fast was instituted by the rabbis to commemorate this national calamity.

Let us dispel a couple of myths about the State of Israel. It is not the only democracy in the Middle East, and it hasn't been for several decades. Turkey and Lebanon were democratic long before the Arab Spring. Their democracies have been imperfect, to be sure, but what do you call a country that denies the rights of citizenship to a large proportion of the population it controls, that has done so for nearly three-quarters of its existence, and that has no evident intention of altering the status quo? Given that the claim of Israel's uniquely democratic nature is so obviously false, what work does it do? The same as that performed by Netanyahu's American accent, or that of his ambassador to Washington, the smooth, persuasive liar Michael Oren. It says to their audiences here—their willing gulls in Congress and the press, the Christian fundamentalists with whom the Jewish right had made its pact—we're just like you (and not like *them*). And so it feeds another myth:

that Israel's interests coincide, by definition, with those of the United States. Our leaders have apparently been gifted with prophetic powers. Not only have the countries' interests always been aligned; they always will be.

Look at almost any picture of Netanyahu, especially one that catches him at an unguarded moment, and you will see, written in the language of his sneering smirk, the bottomless cynicism that underlies the strategy of the Israeli right. The proponents of a Greater Israel have always believed that they can outsmart the rest of the world, including their patron, America. Promise peace, perpetuate occupation. Keep delaying the future, and maybe it will never come. In the end, they will have only outsmarted themselves. Israel had forty-four years after the Six-Day War and before the Arab Spring to resolve the conflict with the Palestinians, thirty-one years after the Camp David Accords, which removed the major military threat, and seventeen years after Oslo. Now it's almost certainly too late.

Mipnei chata'einu, we said on Rosh Hashanah: *because of our sins* we were exiled from our land. As a boy in yeshiva day school, I was taught that the Second Temple was destroyed as a punishment for gratuitous hatred, and that it could only be rebuilt as a reward for gratuitous love. Today also marks the start of Yom Kippur, the Day of Atonement. As is typically the case in Jewish prayer, the liturgy will speak in terms of the collective. "We have stolen," goes the litany. "We have slandered. We have given evil counsel." All of us, together, as a people. What is my solution to the Israel-Palestinian conflict? Repentance.

[2013]

PUBLICATION NOTES

The essays in this book appeared, in somewhat different form, in the following periodicals:

American Scholar: "Solitude and Leadership," "The Disadvantages of an Elite Education," "On Political Correctness," "Upper Middle Brow," "A Jew in the Northwest," and all essays whose titles appear in italics.

Atlantic: "Hunting the Whale" (as "How the Novel Made the Modern World").

Chronicle of Higher Education: "The End of Solitude" and "Faux Friendship."

DanceView: "Merce Cunningham: Celestial Mechanics" and "Mark Morris: Home Coming."

Harper's Magazine: "The Neoliberal Arts," "The Platinum Age," and "Mark Greif: Facing Reality" (as "What a Piece of Work").

Liberties: "Harold Rosenberg: The Individual Nuisance" and "Birthrights."

Nation: "The Defunding of the American Mind" (as "Faulty Towers") and "Clive James: Letter to the Twenty-First Century" (as "Cafe Society").

New Republic: "Harold Bloom: The Horror, the Horror" (as "The Shaman").

New York Times Sunday Review: "Generation Sell," "Heroes" (as "An Empty Regard"), and "Just Friends" (as "A Man. A Woman. Just Friends?").

Slate: "Alfred Kazin: Fiery Particle of Spirit" (as "An Infinite Walk").

Four essays are published here for the first time (dates provided after the texts are those of composition): "Culture against Culture," "Change Your Mind First: College and the Urge to Save the World," "Why I Left Academia (Since You're Wondering)," and "The Maker's Hand."

ACKNOWLEDGMENTS

I have been fortunate in my editors. For superintending the essays that appear in this book, my great thanks go to Robert Wilson at the *American Scholar*, Leon Wieseltier at the *New Republic* and *Liberties*, John Palattella at the *Nation*, Ann Hulbert at the *Atlantic* and *Slate*, Evan Goldstein at the *Chronicle of Higher Education*, Giles Harvey at *Harper's Magazine*, Alexandra Tomalonis at *DanceView*, and Susan Lehman at the *New York Times Sunday Review*.

A number of these essays originated as talks. Thanks to the students at Yale's St. Anthony Hall ("The Disadvantages of an Elite Education"); Colonel Scott Krawczyk, Karin Roffman, and Elizabeth Samet at the United States Military Academy ("Solitude and Leadership"); David Peterson at the Mockingbird Conference ("Culture against Culture"); Denise Mullen at the Oregon College of Art and Craft ("The Maker's Hand"); and Maria Frawley at George Washington University ("Change Your Mind First: College and the Urge to Save the World").

Heartfelt thanks to Caroline Zancan, Barbara Jones, Lori Kusatzky, and everybody else at Henry Holt, and to Elyse Cheney, Claire Gillespie, and the rest of the staff at the Cheney Agency.

My deepest gratitude extends to those who guided me along the improbable path to becoming a writer—a youthful dream that, like all dreams fulfilled, has been fulfilled in unimaginable ways. To Tobi Tobias, whose class in dance criticism was the gateway to everything else, and who made or rescued my fledgling career at least three times. To Gary Parks at *Dance Magazine*, who taught me, without letting on, to give my pieces focus. To Andrew Delbanco, who enabled me to make the switch to book reviews by recommending me to his editor at the *New York Times*. To Adam Shatz, who recruited me for the *Nation*, where I began to spread my wings. To Joan Acocella, who told me if I didn't make the leap at forty-four—give up on academia for full-time writing—then I never would. To my agent, Elyse, who came along, with perfect serendipity, the very moment that I did.

I still can't believe that it's all really happened.

ABOUT THE AUTHOR

William Deresiewicz's writing has appeared in the *Atlantic*, *Harper's Magazine*, the *New York Times*, the *American Scholar*, and many other publications. He is the recipient of a National Book Critics Circle award for excellence in reviewing and is the *New York Times* bestselling author of *Excellent Sheep*, *The Death of the Artist*, and *A Jane Austen Education*.